Pearson Revise

AQA GCSE

Spanish

Revision Guide

Author: Viv Halksworth

This book includes Pearson Revise Online access with a revision planner, retrospective tracker, plus make your own flashcards!

Quizzes, videos and flashcards to boost your progress – on every page!

Scan the **Digital resources QR codes** for more ways to revise.

Digital resources

- **Quick quizzes**: Quick-fire practice to check your knowledge.
- **Vocabulary quizzes**: Improve your understanding and retention of all the required vocabulary with just a few minutes' practice each day.
- **Videos**: Help with tricky grammar and tips for the exams.
- **Vocab flashcards**: Test your understanding of all the required vocabulary with ready-made flashcards

Audio for Speaking and Listening at your fingertips

Scan the **green audio QR codes** to immediately launch high-quality recordings of native speakers.

Listen to the recording

Transcripts for all audio files can be accessed on the Pearson Revise Online platform.

- **Exam-style tracks** for realistic assessment practice
- **Targeted pronunciation practice** of Spanish sounds helps build your confidence.
- **Answer-section audio** brings Speaking activities to life.

Higher and Foundation tiers

You can use this book no matter which tier you are doing.

Higher tier vocabulary and grammar are highlighted with the purple background or H symbol.

Everything else is relevant for both Foundation and Higher tier.

durar	to last
participar	to participate
pintar	to paint
actuar	to act, perform
asistir a	to attend
la or~~~~~~	~~~~~~~~

Possessive pronouns (H ONLY) Grammar page 96

These are words like 'mine' or 'hers' where they replace the noun. For example: That's my book. Where is **yours**?

Difficulty scale

The icon next to each exam-style question tells you how difficult it is.

Some questions cover a range of difficulties.

Target grade **4**

Target grade **7-8**

Also available:

The Revision Workbook provides additional practice with hundreds more exam-style questions along with hints on writing the most effective responses PLUS a full set of practice papers – one for each of Foundation and Higher tier – at the back of the book.

How can this book help me revise?

On the page...

1 **Topics** make vocabulary easier to revise.

✓ Revise the words, then see and use them again in many topics!

2 Key **vocabulary**, taken from the approved vocabulary list.

✓ Check which words you already know and learn some new words.

✓ Refer to vocabulary pages at the back of the book for a complete list.

Words/grammar which will only appear on the Higher tier papers look like this: la mente . The rest may appear on either paper.

3 Short reminders on **grammar** points help you revise how to form the language correctly and add 'complexity' to aim for higher grades. Grammar points which are only needed on the Higher papers are marked **H**. **Videos** cover key or tricky areas.

✓ If you need more detail, you can look in the longer grammar section on pages 94–117, watch one of the accompanying videos, or ask your teacher.

4 **Flexible phrases** can be used in many contexts.

✓ Learn these to use in your writing and speaking exams to help boost your confidence.

5 Now, look at the **Worked examples** to see how a student might use this language in an exam-style question. Hints tell you how to approach similar questions, things to look out for and how to improve your answer.

✓ Use some of the language you've learned to answer this question.

6 Then put it all into practice. The **Now try this** is an exam-style question to help you bring everything together and have a go yourself.

✓ Check your answer with the model answer in the answer section – this may include an audio file to help with pronunciation.

You'll see a range of question types – **Speaking**, **Listening**, **Reading** and **Writing** – including the new read aloud and dictation tasks, plus audio files for Listening and Speaking questions.

On Pearson Revise Online...

7 Give your knowledge a quick check with the **quick quiz!**

✓ Scan the QR code to access a set of multi-choice questions relating to what you've just revised.

8 Power up your vocabulary with the **vocab test!** Scan the QR code for quick-fire questions to boost your knowledge.

✓ Do this every day to really build your vocabulary – and see your progress grow!

9 **Videos** help you focus in on mastering your grammar, plus provide overall tips from experienced teachers and examiners.

10 Ready made flashcards covering all the required vocabulary help you test your understanding at the touch of a button.

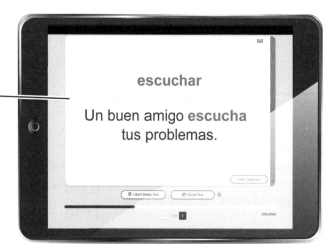

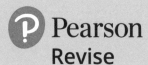

Pearson Revise

Your Pearson Revise Online access also includes a revision planner, progress tracker, plus make your own flashcards!

Contents

1-to-1 page match with the Spanish Revision Workbook ISBN 9781292739762

. . . .

A small bit of small print:
AQA publishes Sample Assessment Material and the Specification on its website. This is the official content and this book should be used in conjunction with it. The questions in Now try this have been written to help you practise every topic in the book. Remember: the real exam questions may not look like this.

Introducing yourself

Digital resources

Todo sobre mí

Hola	Hello
Me llamo …	I am called / my name is …
Tengo … años.	I am … years old.
Mi cumpleaños es el …	My birthday is the …
Vivo en …	I live in …
un pueblo	a village
una ciudad	a town / city
cerca de	near to
Soy del …	I am from the …
norte	north
sur	south
este	east
oeste	west

Los números 1–31

Grammar page 117

1	uno	12	doce		
2	dos	13	trece	23	veintitrés
3	tres	14	catorce	24	veinticuatro
4	cuatro	15	quince	25	veinticinco
5	cinco	16	dieciséis	26	veintiséis
6	seis	17	diecisiete	27	veintisiete
7	siete	18	dieciocho	28	veintiocho
8	ocho	19	diecinueve	29	veintinueve
9	nueve	20	veinte	30	treinta
10	diez	21	veintiuno	31	treinta y uno
11	once	22	veintidós		

✎ Flexible phrases

Mi cumpleaños es el cuatro de junio.
My birthday is the 4th of June.

Note that in Spanish you do not write the months with a capital letter.

Los meses del año

enero	abril	julio	octubre
febrero	mayo	agosto	noviembre
marzo	junio	septiembre	diciembre

Be careful not to confuse June and July; they are very similar in Spanish.

Worked example

 SPEAKING TRACK 1   **Target grade 2**

Listen to this extract from a Speaking task conversation.

Hola David. ¿Cuántos años tienes?
Tengo quince años.

¿Cuándo es tu cumpleaños?
Es el veintidós de enero.

¿Dónde vives?
Vivo en un pueblo cerca de Bristol en el oeste del país.

Listen to the recording

When you get the opportunity, like in this last question, try to develop your answer and give some details.

Soy de Manchester, pero ahora vivo en el sur del país.

I am from Manchester but now I live in the south of the country.

Now try this

 READING   **Target grade 3**

Read Juan's blog about his grandfather. Complete these sentences. Write the correct letter in each box.

Mi abuelo se llama Raúl y tiene setenta y seis años. Su cumpleaños es el doce de marzo. Es argentino, de un pueblo cerca de Buenos Aires, pero ahora vive cerca de nosotros en Valencia, en el este de España.

1 Raúl is …

A	77.
B	76.
C	67.

☐ (1 mark)

2 His birthday is in …

A	March.
B	April.
C	May.

☐ (1 mark)

3 He is from …

A	Argentina.
B	Valencia.
C	Northern Spain.

☐ (1 mark)

4 He now lives …

A	in Buenos Aires.
B	near his grandson.
C	in the west.

☐ (1 mark)

Digital resources

Physical descriptions

¿Cómo eres?

Soy alto/a.	I am tall.
Soy bajo/a.	I am small / short.
Tengo el pelo largo / corto.	I have long / short hair.
Tengo el pelo rubio / marrón / negro / rojo.	I have blonde / brown / black / red hair.
Tengo los ojos marrones / azules / grises / verdes.	I have brown / blue / grey / green eyes.
Uso / Llevo gafas.	I have / wear glasses.
delgado/a	slim
feo/a	ugly
fuerte	strong
gordo/a	fat
guapo/a	good-looking

Soy bastante … y tengo el pelo … .
I am quite … and I have … hair.
Mi hermano y yo tenemos los ojos …
pero mi madre tiene los ojos … .
My brother and I have … eyes but my mother has … eyes.

Mis hermanas llevan gafas.
My sisters wear glasses.

Adjectival agreement

Grammar page 95

Adjectives describe nouns. They must agree with the noun in gender (masculine or feminine) and number (singular or plural).

	Singular	Plural
Adjectives ending in -o		
Masculine	alto	altos
Feminine	alta	altas
Adjectives ending in -e		
Masculine	verde	verdes
Feminine	verde	verdes
Adjectives ending in a consonant		
Masculine	azul	azules
Feminine	azul	azules

Using tener

Grammar page 102

Tener is a common verb. Here it is in the present tense.

tengo	I have
tienes	you (singular) have
tiene	he / she / it has; you (formal, singular) have
tenemos	we have
tenéis	you (plural) have
tienen	they / you (formal, plural) have

Worked example

 READING Target grade **2**

Your friend, Diego, sends you a text with a photo.

Aquí estoy con unos amigos. Llevo una camiseta azul y Julia tiene el pelo rojo. A su lado está Cris, con la camiseta blanca, y Alba es la chica con las gafas.

What is the name of the girl with red hair? Write the correct letter in the box.

A	Alba
B	Cris
C	Julia

C (1 mark)

Now try this

LISTENING TRACK **2** Target grade **2**

 Listen to the recording

Mateo is describing himself. What does he say? Write the **three** correct letters in the boxes.

A	He is quite tall.	D	He has black hair.
B	He is the tallest in the family.	E	He has brown eyes.
C	He wears his hair long.	F	He does not wear glasses.

☐ ☐ ☐ (3 marks)

With reading comprehensions like this one, you can skim-read the text until you find the Spanish words you are looking for: **pelo rojo** (meaning 'red hair'). Then read around the words to find the correct answer.

Character descriptions

Digital
resources

¿Cómo es su personalidad?

Es …	He / she is …
aburrido/a	boring
activo/a	active
agradable	pleasant
alegre	cheerful
animado/a	lively
divertido/a	fun, enjoyable
feliz	happy
listo/a	clever
negativo/a	negative
nervioso/a	nervous
optimista	optimistic
positivo/a	positive
responsable	responsible
simpático/a	nice, friendly
trabajador/a	hard-working
tranquilo/a	calm
triste	sad
serio/a	serious
Soy una persona …	I am a … person
y tengo una	and I have a …
actitud … .	attitude.
fiel	loyal

Ser and estar (to be)

Grammar
page 103

The verb ser

This verb is used with adjectives that are characteristics – qualities of a person that won't change overnight.

Mi hermana es alegre y simpática.

My sister is cheerful and nice.

The verb estar

This verb is used with adjectives to describe a temporary state or condition.

Estoy nervioso porque tengo un examen.
I am nervous because I have an exam.

Ser	Estar	Present tense
soy	estoy	I am
eres	estás	you (singular) are
es	está	he / she / it is; you (singular / formal) are
somos	estamos	we are
sois	estáis	you (plural) are
son	están	they; you (formal, plural) are

Flexible phrases

En mi opinión … In my opinion …

Normalmente … Normally …

Mis amigos dicen que soy …
My friends say that I am …

When you use phrases like these, the adjectives you choose will agree with the words **persona** (person) and **actitud** (attitude). Both 'persona' and 'actitud' are feminine singular so the adjectives will be feminine singular, too.

In the exam you will need to write four full sentences at Foundation tier and five at Higher tier. Here some of the words have been given to get you started!

Worked example

¿Cómo es tu personalidad?
   En mi opinión, soy una persona activa y tengo una actitud positiva. Mis amigos dicen que soy divertido.

Listen to the recording

Aiming
Higher

   Normalmente soy una persona alegre y trabajadora, con una actitud responsable y optimista. No soy muy activo. Mis amigos dicen que soy listo pero un poco serio.

Now try this

Listen to the recording

Dictation

Omar is talking about himself. What does he say? Write down the missing words in the gaps provided. In each gap, write one word in **Spanish**.

1 Normalmente soy _____ y _____ .

2 Mi hermano es _____ y _____ .

3 Mis amigos _____ que soy _____ .

(6 marks)

You can improve your answer with longer sentences using connectives like **y**, **con** and **pero**. You can even say what you are not!

Digital resources

Family

Hablando de la familia

el marido	husband
la mujer	wife
la pareja	partner, couple
el padre	father
el padrastro	stepfather
la madre	mother
la madrastra	stepmother
el hermano	brother
la hermana	sister
el abuelo	grandfather
la abuela	grandmother
el tío	uncle
la tía	aunt
casarse	to marry
Me parezco a mi padre.	I look like my father.
Soy hijo único / hija única.	I am an only child.
Tengo un hermano mayor y una hermana menor.	I have an older brother and a younger sister.

Possessive adjectives

Grammar page 96

	followed by singular noun	followed by plural noun
my	mi	mis
your (one owner)	tu	tus
his / her / its / their / your (formal)	su	sus
our	nuestro, nuestra	nuestros, nuestras
your (more than one owner)	vuestro, vuestra	vuestros, vuestras

Mis padres son muy simpáticos.

My parents are very nice.

Nuestra abuela es bastante activa.

Our grandmother is quite active.

¿Cómo son tus abuelos?
What are your grandparents like?

Notice how you can pluralise the masculine form of a word to give a new meaning like this:

padre → padres (parents / fathers)
abuelo → abuelos (grandparents / grandfathers)
hermano → hermanos (brothers / brothers and sisters)

 **Worked example**

LISTENING TRACK 5

Target grade 4

Listen to Carla and write the correct letter in the box.

Listen to the recording

A veces creo que me gustaría tener una hermana. Pero tengo todo el amor de mis padres porque soy hija única.

How many brothers and sisters does Carla have?

A	none
B	one
C	two

 A

(1 mark)

Listen carefully. Carla says the words **una hermana**, but she is saying she would like a sister. Then she says she is a **hija única**.

  Now try this

LISTENING TRACK 6

Target grade 3

Listen to the recording

Natalia is talking about her family. What does she say? Write the correct letter in each box.

1 Natalia lives with her mum and …

A	dad.
B	stepdad.
C	gran.

☐ **(1 mark)**

2 She is the …

A	youngest.
B	oldest.
C	middle child.

☐ **(1 mark)**

3 She and her mum are …

A	small.
B	very different.
C	red-haired.

☐ **(1 mark)**

What makes a good friend

Digital resources

¿Cómo es un buen amigo?

el / la amigo/a	friend
la verdad	truth
allí	there
bueno/a	good
mejor	better, best
el interés	interest
la amistad	friendship
el sentido del humor	sense of humour
aceptar	to accept
apoyar	to support
ayudar	to help
compartir	to share
decir	to say, tell
escuchar	to listen
saber	to know (how to …)
tener mucho en común	to have lots in common
comprender	to understand
reírse	to laugh

The present tense of regular verbs

Grammar page 100

To make the present tense of regular verbs, remove the -ar, -er or -ir from the end of the infinitive and add:

	hablar	comer	vivir
I	hablo	como	vivo
you (sing.)	hablas	comes	vives
he, she, it	habla	come	vive
we	hablamos	comemos	vivimos
you (pl.)	habláis	coméis	vivís
they	hablan	comen	viven

Mi amigo y yo compartimos muchos intereses.
My friend and I share lots of interests.

Mis amigas me escuchan y me comprenden.
My friends listen to me and understand me.

Useful phrases

Un buen amigo …	A good friend …
está allí cuando …	is there when …
te ayuda …	helps you …
te acepta …	accepts you …
te dice …	tells you …
sabe escuchar …	knows how to listen …
comparte …	shares …

Un buen amigo te hace reír.
A good friend makes you laugh.

Worked example WRITING Target grade 6

You might need to address a point like this in a writing task.

Answer the following question in **Spanish**.

- Your opinion of what it takes to be a good friend.

¿Cómo es un buen amigo?

Use **también** or **además** to add extra information to a comment.

> Un buen amigo escucha tus problemas y te ayuda. También te acepta como eres.

Aiming Higher

> La amistad es muy importante y todo el mundo necesita un buen amigo. El amigo perfecto comparte tus intereses y te apoya cuando necesitas su ayuda. Un buen amigo es fiel pero siempre te dice la verdad. Tiene el mismo sentido del humor que tú y te hace reír.

Now try this WRITING Target grade 1-9

You are writing an article about friendship. Mention:

- why you get on with your best friend.

The use of a range of different verbs (necesitar, compartir, apoyar, decir, reír) shows a broad and impressive vocabulary.

Remember to change **te** to **me** when you want to say 'helps **me**' or 'supports **me**' etc. Mi mejor amigo **me** ayuda …

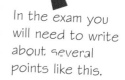

In the exam you will need to write about several points like this.

Digital resources

Relationships

¿Cómo te llevas con ...?

enojado/a	angry
el amor	love
el apoyo	support
la relación	relationship
la discusión	discussion, argument
llevarse bien / mal con	to get on well / badly with
pelearse	to fight, argue
depender de	to depend on
respetar	to respect
discutir	to argue, discuss
cuidar	to care for, look after
gritar	to shout
molestar	to annoy
tener suerte	to be lucky
divertirse	to enjoy oneself
estricto/a	strict
la igualdad	equality
el cariño	affection
la libertad	freedom
tratar	to treat

A veces discutimos.
We sometimes argue.

Generalmente nos llevamos bien.
In general we get on well.

Tengo suerte. I'm lucky.

Reflexive verbs

Grammar page 101

In Spanish there are lots more reflexive verbs than in English, and they always have the reflexive pronoun (me, te, se, etc.) with them.

The verb itself behaves as normal.

llevarse bien to get on well

me llevo bien	nos llevamos bien
te llevas bien	os lleváis bien
se lleva bien	se llevan bien

H ONLY

¿Te llevas bien con tus hermanos?
Do you get on well with your brothers?

Sí, me llevo bien con toda mi familia.
Yes, I get on well with all my family.

Notice that the reflexive pronoun goes in front of the verb, except when it's with the infinitive (llevar). Then, it goes on the end of the verb.

Se casan mañana.
They get married tomorrow.

Van a casarse pronto.
They are going to get married soon.

De vez en cuando nos peleamos.
Occasionally we fight.

Worked example

WRITING   **Target grade 8**

In the real exam you will need to write about more than one point.

You are writing a blog about your family.
Mention:
• how you get on with your family.

Normalmente nos llevamos bien, aunque a veces me peleo con mi hermana. Nunca es grave, pero me siento enojada con ella cuando lleva mi ropa o usa mis cosas. Respeto a mis padres y ellos siempre nos tratan con igualdad y cariño. Tengo mucha suerte.

You should try to expand your points with explanations and reasons. Here the student explains the reasons why she gets cross with her sister. To improve your response, using phrases like **a veces** (sometimes), **normalmente** (generally) and **siempre** (always) brings variety to your work. Words / phrases like **pero** (but) and **aunque** (although) are useful when you are introducing an opposing idea.

Now try this

SPEAKING   **Target grade 6**

You might be asked questions like this in the conversation part of your Speaking exam.

Answer these questions in **Spanish**.

1 ¿Cómo te llevas con tus amigos?
2 ¿Por qué razones discutes con tus amigos?

(4 marks)

Helping a friend

Digital resources

El problema

el comportamiento	behaviour
el error	mistake
empezar a + infinitive	to start to
fumar	to smoke
perder	to lose
romper	to break
salir	to go out
evitar	to avoid
negarse a + infinitive	to refuse to

La solución

ayudar	to help
dejar de + infinitive	to stop ...ing
intentar	to try
mostrar	to show
olvidar	to forget
equivocarse	to make a mistake
incluso	even

The preterite tense

Grammar page 105

This tense is the equivalent of the English simple past: 'I saw', 'he found', 'we helped' etc. To form it, remove the -ar, -er and -ir from the infinitive and add these endings:

	-ar verbs		-er and -ir verbs	
I	-é	visité	-í	salí
you	-aste	visitaste	-iste	saliste
he / she / it	-ó	visitó	-ió	salió
we	-amos	visitamos	-imos	salimos
you	-asteis	visitasteis	-isteis	salisteis
they	-aron	visitaron	-ieron	salieron

Note the irregular preterite forms of -zar, -gar and -car verbs in the 1st person singular: empe**c**é a I started to; me ne**gu**é a I refused to; me equivo**qu**é I made a mistake

H ONLY

Worked example

 READING   Target grade **7**

You read Sofía's story in an online magazine.

El año pasado empecé a perder interés en mis estudios y mi comportamiento cambió. Comencé a salir mucho, evité a mis amigos de siempre y pasé mucho tiempo con otros jóvenes. Incluso empecé a fumar. Un día mi amiga Lucía vino a casa, para hablar conmigo. Intentó hacerme ver mis errores, pero al principio me negué a escuchar. Me mostró fotos de momentos felices que hemos pasado juntas y finalmente acepté la verdad. ¡Gracias, Lucía, eres la mejor amiga del mundo!

Answer the following questions in **English**.

1 What does Sofía say about her behaviour last year?
It changed.

2 How did she behave towards her old friends?
She avoided them.

3 What bad habit did she pick up?
smoking

4 How did she first react to Lucía's visit?
She refused to listen.

5 What finally made her realise the truth?
seeing the photos of her and Lucía

(5 marks)

Intentó hacerme ver mis errores.
She tried to make me see my mistakes.

Now try this

 LISTENING TRACK **7**   Target grade **5** Listen to the recording

Vicente is talking in a radio phone-in.

Complete the sentences. Choose the correct answer and write the letter in each box.

1 Iván spent two months …

A	in hospital.
B	in bed.
C	at home.

☐ **(1 mark)**

2 Iván was worried about …

A	losing his notes.
B	getting bad results.
C	his bad health.

☐ **(1 mark)**

3 Vicente helped Iván …

A	revise for the tests.
B	get round the house.
C	find a job.

☐ **(1 mark)**

Digital resources

Food and drink

¿Qué vas a tomar?

el huevo	egg
el pescado	fish
el plato	plate, dish, course
el pollo	chicken
el jamón	ham
la carne	meat
la hamburguesa	burger
la manzana	apple
la mesa	table
la naranja	orange
la paella	paella
las patatas fritas	chips, fries
las tapas	tapas
la verdura	vegetable
los caramelos	sweets
el arroz	rice
¿Qué hay en … ?	What is there in … ?
Quisiera / Me gustaría … .	I would like … .

Using gustar

Grammar page 113

Gustar is an important and frequently used verb, so you need to know how to use it.

- To say 'I like … .', choose Me gusta if what you like is singular or a verb:
  Me gusta el pescado.   I like fish.
  Me gusta salir a comer.   I like eating out.

- Choose Me gustan if what you like is plural:
  Me gustan las naranjas.   I like oranges.

- Change the pronoun in front if you are talking about other people:
te gusta(n)	you (singular) like
le gusta(n)	he / she / it likes; / you (formal, singular) like
nos gusta(n)	we like
os gusta(n)	you (plural) like
les gusta(n)	they / you (formal, plural) like

- Encantar is used in the same way.
  Me encanta la paella.   I love paella.
  Me encantan los caramelos. I love sweets.

Worked example

 LISTENING TRACK 8

 Target grade 5

María and Marta are in a restaurant. What do they say? Write the **three** correct letters in the boxes.

 Listen to the recording

– ¿Tomamos un solo plato?
– Yo si, pero tomaré un café después.
– Buena idea, yo también. Pues, como plato principal, voy a tomar jamón con verduras.
– ¿No quieres compartir una paella? Es para dos personas.
– No, lo siento. No me gusta mucho el pescado.
– Vale. Entonces, me gustaría la hamburguesa.

A	They both choose a starter.
B	They plan to have coffee afterwards.
C	They decide to share a *paella*.
D	One chooses ham with vegetables.
E	One chooses a fish dish.
F	One chooses a burger.

☐ B ☐ D ☐ F   (3 marks)

Listening strategies

In the exam, you will hear the listening extracts twice. Pauses will be inserted into the recording, so do not try to write while you are still listening although you could jot down notes to help you remember. Write during the pauses and check your answers after the second hearing.

You won't always hear a straightforward comment like 'We both plan to have a coffee'. One speaker says so, and then the other agrees.
Similarly, when you hear '**¿No quieres compartir una paella?**' in the recording, notice that it isn't a statement of fact but a question, which the other person rejects.

Now try this

 SPEAKING TRACK 9

 Target grade 1-5

Prepare your own answers to the following restaurant role play prompts. Then listen to the recording of the teacher's part and say your answers in the pauses.
1 Say how many people you want a table for.
2 Say where you want to sit.
3 Say what you want to eat.
4 Say what you want to drink.
5 Ask how much it is.

 Listen to the recording

(10 marks)

Healthy eating

Digital resources

¿Tienes una dieta sana?

el agua (f)	water
el azúcar	sugar
el pan	bread
la carne roja	red meat
la dieta	diet
la fruta	fruit
la leche	milk
la sal	salt
la salud	health
la vida	life, lifestyle
las patatas fritas	chips, fries
las verduras	(green) vegetables
sano/a	healthy
tener hambre	to be hungry
tener sed	to be thirsty
vegano/a	vegan
vegetariano/a	vegetarian
dulce	sweet
equilibrado/a	balanced
sentir(se)	to feel

Para tener una dieta sana, es importante + infinitive
To have a healthy diet it is important to ... .
Para llevar una vida sana, tienes que + infinitive
To lead a healthy lifestyle you have to ... .

Useful adverbs

demasiado	too much	más	more
bastante	quite, quite a lot	menos	less, fewer

Comí demasiado ayer.
I ate too much yesterday.

Los niños comen bastante.
The children eat quite a lot.

Como más cuando estoy de vacaciones.
I eat more when I'm on holiday.

Como menos durante la semana.
I eat less during the week.

These adverbs are invariable (they do not change or agree). However, demasiado and bastante can also be adjectives. In this case, they agree with the noun they describe.

Comes demasiados caramelos.
You eat too many sweets.

Voy a comer más fruta y menos cosas dulces.
I am going to eat more fruit and fewer sweet things.

Worked example

 READING Target grade 4-9

Translate the following into **English**.

> Creo que llevo una vida bastante sana. Antes, tomaba demasiadas patatas fritas y mucha carne roja. También ponía azúcar en el café y, cuando tenía hambre, comía muchos bocadillos. Ahora, intento tener una dieta más equilibrada. Como más pescado y más frutas y verduras. Lo bueno es que me siento mucho mejor.

(10 marks)

I think that I lead quite a healthy lifestyle. Before, I used to have too many chips and lots of red meat. I also used to put sugar in coffee and, when I was hungry, I ate a lot of sandwiches. Now I try to have a more balanced diet. I eat more fish, and more fruits and vegetables. The good thing is that I feel much better.

Now try this

 LISTENING TRACK 10 Target grade 6

Alejandro is talking about his brother's diet.

 Listen to the recording

Complete the sentences. Choose the correct answer and write the letter in each box.

1 He describes his brother's current diet as ... **(1 mark)**

A	varied.
B	vegan.
C	vegetarian.

☐

2 Now, he thinks his brother is always eating ... **(1 mark)**

A	bread.
B	chips.
C	rice.

☐

Digital resources

Sport and exercise

¿Eres una persona activa?

el deporte	sport
el ejercicio	exercise
el equipo	team, equipment
el partido	match
el / la jugador/a	player
el baloncesto	basketball
el fútbol	football
la bicicleta	bicycle, bike
la piscina	swimming pool
la copa	cup, trophy
el miembro	member
el estadio	stadium
estar en forma	to be fit
dar un paseo	to go for a walk
correr	to run
jugar	to play
practicar	to practise
montar	to ride
nadar	to swim
la ropa de deporte	sportswear
la natación	swimming
caminar	to walk

Irregular first person verbs in the present tense

Grammar page 100

You will use these verbs a lot when you talk about sport and exercise:

hago	I do / make	veo	I watch / see
salgo	I go out	voy	I go

Also remember the radical-changing verbs, where a vowel in the stem changes, e→ie, o→ue, e→i:

prefiero	I prefer	puedo	I can
juego	I play	quiero	I want

Be careful which verbs you use with different activities:

Juego al baloncesto / vóleibol / tenis.

Hago ejercicio / deporte / natación.

Voy a la piscina / al gimnasio / al estadio.

Monto en bicicleta / a caballo.

Notice that you need to use 'a' after **juego** and before the sport, and remember that **a + el baloncesto = al baloncesto**

Worked example

 READING Target grade 1-5

Read Mateo's plans to keep fit.

Me gusta correr y este sábado empiezo un nuevo programa de ejercicio. A las seis de la mañana, voy a levantarme y voy a correr tres kilómetros. Si hace buen tiempo llevaré una camiseta y pantalones cortos, pero si hace un poco de frío me pondré un **chándal**.

Read the last sentence again. What is a **chándal**? Write the correct letter in the box.

A	an app
B	an item of clothing
C	a drink

B

(1 mark)

Dejé de ir al gimnasio porque me parecía muy aburrido. I stopped going to the gym because I found it very boring.

Flexible phrases

Antes practicaba ... pero ahora hago ... .
Previously I used to practise / do ... but now I do ... .

Dejé de ir a ... porque ... .
I stopped going to ... because ... .

En el futuro tengo la intención de ... .
In the future I intend to ... .

Exam alert

This type of question, found on the Reading paper, tests your ability to work out meaning from context. Note the general topic (sport and exercise) and then work out the most likely meaning judging by the rest of the sentence. Here, Mateo says he is going running (voy a correr). He says he will wear a T-shirt and shorts (camiseta y pantalones cortos) if the weather is good and a chándal if it is cold. In the context of the sentence, the word must be something you wear, so 'an item of clothing' is correct.

Now try this

SPEAKING TRACK 11   Target grade 4-9

After the photo description in the Speaking exam, you will answer questions on a broader theme. Play the audio and answer the questions on **Lifestyle and wellbeing**.

Listen to the recording

Physical wellbeing

Es importante cuidarte

cuidar	to look after
descansar	to rest
dormir, dormirse	to sleep, fall asleep
afectar	to affect
cambiar	to change
proteger	to protect
cansado/a	tired
al aire libre	outdoors, in the open air
el campo	country(side)
el paisaje	scenery
el ambiente	atmosphere
el daño	harm, damage
la energía	energy
la piel	skin
el rato	moment, while
el sol	sun
relajante	relaxing
el beneficio	benefit

Giving advice and recommendations

These phrases all take a following infinitive:

Vale la pena …	It's worthwhile … / It's worth (it) …
Hay que / Se debe …	You / One must …
Se necesita …	You need to … / One needs to …
Se puede …	You / One can …

Hay que proteger la piel cuando estás al sol.

You have to protect your skin when you are in the sun.

Worked example

Target grade 7

Read this advice from an online magazine.

Todos conocemos la famosa frase 'Eres lo que comes' pero tu salud física no solo depende de tu dieta. Para sentirte fuerte y sano también hay que dormir bien, beber suficiente agua y encontrar tiempo para descansar.

Answer the following questions in **English**.

1 What does the phrase *Eres lo que comes* mean?
(1 mark)

You are what you eat.

2 Apart from diet, what else is important for your physical health? (Give **three** details.) **(3 marks)**
sleeping well, drinking enough water, resting

Exam alert

When answering questions in English, be careful to include everything that might be needed in your response.

For instance, in the second question here, you might be tempted to write just 'sleep', 'water' and 'rest'. You can't be sure that this is enough information to gain the mark, so it is better to give a full answer. These answers contain the basic information of 'sleep', 'water' and 'rest' anyway so if that is all that is needed, you have gained the marks and lost nothing.

In the Higher tier, there are five sentences to write out in full.

Now try this

Target grade 4-9

Dictation

Write down the full sentences that you hear in the spaces provided, in **Spanish**.

1 _____ .

2 _____ .

3 _____ .

4 _____ .

5 _____ .

(10 marks)

Digital resources

Mental wellbeing

¿Cómo te sientes?

¿Qué te pasa?	What's the matter?
el consejo	advice
la presión	pressure
el cuerpo	body
el sentimiento	feeling
la felicidad	happiness
el miedo	fear
triste	sad
seguro/a	safe, secure
apoyar	to support
ayudar	to help
callarse	to be quiet

doler	to hurt
escuchar	to listen
evitar	to avoid
necesitar	to need
preocuparse	to worry
recomendar	to recommend
la salud mental	mental health
los recursos	resources
la seguridad	safety, security
expresar	to express
llorar	to cry
sufrir	to suffer

Verbs with prepositions

hablar con	to talk to (someone)
hablar de	to talk about
pensar en	to think about
depender de	to depend on
preocuparse por	to worry about
asistir a	to attend

A lot of verbs can be followed by an infinitive in Spanish. Some need a preposition in-between.

ayudar a	to help to
empezar a	to start to
aprender a	to learn to
enseñar a	to teach to
consistir en	to consist of
negarse a	to refuse to

Worked example

 READING Target grade **9**

Read this article on mental wellbeing.

Muchos jóvenes sufren presión en el instituto, y se preocupan por eventos que pasan en su vida y en el mundo. Muchos también se callan y se niegan a hablar de sus miedos. Su familia y amigos ven que están tristes, pero no saben cómo ayudar. Por eso es importante crear una situación en la que el/la joven se sienta seguro/a y pueda explicar lo que le preocupa.

What does the article say? Write the **three** correct letters in the boxes.

A	Systems at school have relieved stress.	D	People don't notice that they are upset.
B	Young people worry about world events.	E	Friends feel confident they can help.
C	Some young people keep quiet about their fears.	F	Young people need to talk.

☐ B ☐ C ☐ F

(3 marks)

Now try this

 SPEAKING TRACK **13** Target grade **4-9**

Listen to the recording

Reading aloud

You see this advice in a magazine. Read aloud the text.

Todo el mundo necesita tener alguien con quien hablar. Tenemos que aprender a escuchar a otras personas y reconocer cuando se sienten tristes. A veces no buscan consejo, solo quieren expresar sus sentimientos. No es difícil dar apoyo en estos momentos. Simplemente hay que estar allí para ellos. Para eso son los amigos.

Then play the recording to hear four questions in **Spanish** that relate to the topic of **Healthy living and lifestyle**. In order to score the highest marks, you must try to answer all four questions as fully as you can.

(15 marks)

Role models in sport

Digital resources

Los mejores modelos a seguir

el / la jugador/a	player
el concurso	competition
la copa	cup
el fútbol	football
el equipo	team
el éxito	success
la actitud	attitude
el mundo	the world
el ejemplo	example
argentino/a	Argentinian
colombiano/a	Colombian
chileno/a	Chilean
mexicano/a	Mexican
ganar	to win
seguir en Internet	to follow online
entrenar(se)	to train
el torneo	tournament
mundial (adj)	world (adj)
la igualdad	equality

Giving reasons

When you give an opinion, you need to explain why. You can introduce your reason in various ways.

porque (because)

Me gusta el jugador de tenis, Carlos Alcaraz, **porque** todavía es muy joven y creo que va a ganar muchos torneos.
I like the tennis player, Carlos Alcaraz, because he is still very young and I think he is going to win lots of tournaments.

por (for / because of), a causa de (because of)

A mí me gusta Jenni Hermoso **por** su éxito en el fútbol.
I like Jenni Hermoso for her success in football.

Mi hermano juega al baloncesto. Para mí, es el mejor modelo a seguir a causa de su actitud positiva.
My brother plays basketball. For me, he is the best role model **because of** his positive attitude.

Worked example

WRITING — Target grade 1-5

You are writing an article about your favourite sportsperson.

Write approximately **90** words in **Spanish**.

You must write something about each bullet point.

Mention:
• why they are a good role model
• what they have achieved in the past
• something they are going to do in the future.

(15 marks)

A mí me gusta el jugador de fútbol argentino, Lionel Messi, porque es un jugador genial y un hombre muy simpático. Mucha gente lo respeta. También hace mucho trabajo para ayudar a los niños pobres. Ha dado dinero y tiempo a UNICEF para ayudar a niños enfermos. Por eso creo que es un buen modelo a seguir. Ha ganado muchos premios como jugador y con su equipo, como la copa del mundo. En el futuro dice que va a volver a su pueblo, Rosario, para terminar su carrera.

Tick off each bullet point as you do it so you can be sure to have completed the full task.

Exam alert

The writing tasks of approximately 90 words appear on both Writing papers. They are the 'overlap' questions because they are targeted at the top of Foundation and the lower grades of Higher. You will have a choice of two tasks so read both carefully and make sure you have the vocabulary to write about the topic you choose.

Now try this

SPEAKING — Target grade 1-9

Describe these photos. You must say at least one thing about each photo. **(5 marks)**

In the exam, the photo will be in black and white. However, you can still talk about colours.

Digital resources

Sporting events

¿En la tele o en el estadio?

el baloncesto	basketball
el fútbol	football
el ambiente	atmosphere
el concurso	competition
la copa	tournament
el equipo	team
el partido	match
el estadio	stadium
el gimnasio	gym
el ruido	noise
cantar	to sing
ganar	to win
gritar	to shout
nadar	to swim
emocionante	exciting
la natación	swimming
el / la aficionado/a	fan
el torneo	cup
la emoción	excitement
en vivo	live (e.g. live sport)

The immediate future

Grammar page 107

This is one of the easiest tenses to learn in Spanish. It is the equivalent of 'I am / He is going to …', etc.

Take the correct part of the present tense of ir:

voy
vas
va
vamos
vais
van

+ a + infinitive

For example:

Voy a ver I'm going to watch

Vamos a ir We're going to go

You will revise the future tense later in the book, but when you want to talk about an event in the future, you can always use this tense.

El ambiente en el gimnasio va a ser increíble.
The atmosphere in the gym is going to be incredible.

Mi equipo va a ganar la copa de fútbol.
My team is going to win the football cup.

Worked example

LISTENING TRACK 14

Target grade 5

Omar and Pilar are talking about watching sport.

Answer the questions in **English**.

Listen to the recording

Omar: Me gusta ver el deporte en la tele en casa con mis amigos. Podemos hablar del partido y compartir nuestras opiniones.

Pilar: A mí me encanta ir al estadio para ver el fútbol. Me gusta el ruido de los aficionados.

1 Where does Omar like to watch sport?
(**two** details) (**2 marks**)
on TV at home

2 Why does he prefer this?
(**two** reasons) (**2 marks**)
He and his friends can discuss the match and share opinions.

3 Where does Pilar prefer to watch football? (**1 mark**)
in the stadium

4 Why does she prefer this? (**1 mark**)
She likes the noise of the fans.

Flexible phrases

Lo pasamos muy bien.
We had a great time.

Fue una experiencia que nunca voy a olvidar.
It was an experience I am never going to forget.

Nos divertimos mucho.
We really enjoyed ourselves.

Now try this

SPEAKING TRACK 15

Target grade 1-9

Think about how you would answer these general conversation questions. Then play the recording and pause after each question to give your answer.

Listen to the recording

1 ¿Qué deportes te gusta ver?

2 ¿Prefieres ver el deporte en casa o en el estadio? ¿Por qué?

3 Háblame de un evento deportivo que viste en el pasado.

School subjects

¿Qué asignaturas estudias?

la asignatura	subject
la clase	class, classroom
el dibujo	Art, drawing
la(s) ciencia(s)	Science
la educación física	PE
el español	Spanish
los estudios	studies
la historia	History, story
el idioma	language
el inglés	English
la lengua	language
las matemáticas	Maths
la música	Music
la nota	grade, mark, result
la religión	Religion, RE
la tecnología	Technology
continuar	to continue, carry on
dejar	to leave, drop (a subject)

Dejé la religión hace dos años.
I dropped RE two years ago.

El año próximo, voy a estudiar …
Next year I am going to study …

Llevo tres años estudiando …
I've been studying … for three years.

Cognates and word families

Cognates or semi-cognates are words that are the same or very similar in both Spanish and English. There are a lot of words that you will immediately recognise in Spanish, even if you have never seen them before. For example: religión, música and historia.

Word families are words that are similar to each other because they are related to the same topic. Once you know one word, you can often guess at the meaning of related words:

cocina – kitchen / cooking	viaje – journey
cocinar – to cook	viajar – to travel
cocinero/a – cook, chef	viajero/a – traveller

Mi clase favorita es ciencias.
My favourite class is Science.

Worked example

Listen to the recording

You hear a teacher is talking about her music students. Answer the questions in **English**.

1 What is Julia going to do after the exams? **(1 mark)**
She is going to drop music.

2 What is Emilio going to do next year? **(1 mark)**
Carry on with music.

3 When will Lucía decide? **(1 mark)**
When she has seen her grades.

> Julia va a dejar música después de los exámenes. Quiere estudiar ciencias en el futuro. A Emilio le encanta la asignatura y va a continuar el año próximo. Lucía no ha decidido. Va a mirar sus notas primero.

You could also answer by saying 'After she has seen her marks', 'she will wait to see her results' or 'she's going to look at her grades first'.

Now try this

Translate these sentences into **Spanish**.

1 I study Maths and Science.
2 I dropped History last year.
3 She wants to continue with Spanish and English.
4 I hope to study Art in the future.
5 We have a PE lesson at two o'clock today.

Use the regular verb **dejar** for 'to drop' and the 1st person singular of the preterite.

(10 marks)

Digital resources

School subjects – likes and dislikes

¿Cuál es tu asignatura favorita?

¿cuál(es)?	which (ones)?
¿por qué?	why?
aburrido/a	boring
difícil	difficult
divertido/a	fun, enjoyable
duro/a	hard
me encanta(n)	I love
fácil	easy
favorito/a	favourite
importante	important
imposible	impossible
interesante	interesting
más	more
menos	less
odiar	to hate
práctico/a	practical
útil	useful
aprobar	to pass
pesado/a	heavy, boring, annoying
suspender	to fail

Using -ísimo

Grammar page 97

To make an adjective really strong, you can add -ísimo to the end. This then agrees as normal.

Las matemáticas son dificilísimas.
Maths is really hard.
El inglés es facilísimo. English is really easy.

-ísimo should be used sparingly – it sounds very 'over the top' if overused.

Nunca voy a aprobar tecnología. Me parece dificilísima. I'm never going to pass Technology. I find it really difficult.

Useful phrases

La asignatura que me gusta más / menos es …	The subject I like best / least is …
Saco buenas / malas notas en …	I get good / bad marks in …
Mi mejor / peor asignatura es …	My best / worst subject is …

Worked example

 READING

 Target grade 3

Read Martín's comments about his school subjects.

> Me encanta el dibujo, es mi asignatura favorita y es muy divertida. Saco buenas notas en educación física y las clases me ayudan a estar en forma. También voy bien en inglés y creo que es una asignatura muy útil.

Be careful when you hear **educación física** – it is *Physical Education* (or *PE*) and not *Physics*.

Complete the sentences. Write the correct letter in each box.

A	Art	D	Music
B	English	E	PE
C	Maths	F	Science

1 His favourite subject is … [A]

2 He gets good marks in … [E]

3 The subject he finds useful is … [B]   **(3 marks)**

You can hear sample answers from a student working at around Grade 9 in the answer section.

Now try this

 SPEAKING   Target grade 1-9

In the general conversation part of the Speaking exam, if you are talking about school, you could be asked these questions. How would you answer them?

1 ¿Cuál es tu asignatura favorita?

2 Háblame de una asignatura que no te gusta.

The school day

Digital resources

¿Cómo es un día típico en tu instituto?

Voy al instituto / colegio ...	I go to school ...
a pie.	on foot.
en bici(cleta).	by bike.
en coche.	by car.
en autobús.	by bus.
el / la alumno/a	pupil
la clase	class, classroom, lesson
el / la compañero/a	classmate
el club	club
los deberes	homework
el / la estudiante	student
el recreo	break
el horario	timetable
la hora de comer	lunch / dinner time
el patio	yard, playground
durar	to last
empezar	to start / begin
estudiar	to study
volver a casa	to go back home

The shortening of adjectives
Grammar page 95

Some adjectives go before the noun instead of after them and a few of them shorten in that position:

These adjectives shorten before a **masculine singular noun**, and lose the final -o:

primero → el primer día (the first day)
tercero → el tercer club (the third club)
ninguno → ningún recreo (no break)
alguno → algún día (some day)
bueno → un buen estudiante (a good student)
malo → mal tiempo (bad weather)

Note how algún and ningún acquire an accent.

The adjective grande shortens before both a masculine and a feminine singular noun:

un gran colegio   a great school
una gran profesora a great teacher

Notice that in Spanish the article **el** is always used with **colegio** and **recreo**. However, we always leave 'the' out in English with 'school' and 'break'. Remember that when **el** follows **a**, it joins to become **al**.

Durante el primer recreo, tomo un bocadillo.
During first break, I have a sandwich.

Worked example

Target grade 1-5

Translate these sentences into **English**.
1 Voy al colegio en bici.
I go to school by bike.

2 Tenemos nuestra primera clase a las ocho y cuarto.
We have our first class at quarter past eight.

3 Las clases duran cuarenta y cinco minutos.
The lessons last for forty-five minutes.

4 Durante el recreo como un bocadillo.
During break, I eat a sandwich.

5 Ayer volví a casa a las tres y media.
Yesterday I went back home at half past three.   (10 marks)

Volver means 'to return' but it can be translated as 'to come back' or, like here, 'to go back'.

Now try this

Listen to the recording

You hear Hugo talking to his mother. Answer the following questions in **English**.
1 What is Hugo looking for?
2 What will he be doing in his first class today?
3 What does he ask his mother?
4 Why doesn't he want to cycle to school?

(4 marks)

Digital resources

School facilities

¿Qué hay en tu instituto?

el edificio	building
la biblioteca	library
el bolígrafo	pen
el papel	paper
el libro	book
el equipo	team, equipment
la clase	class, classroom
el campo de deportes	sports field
el / la director/a	head teacher
el patio	yard, playground
el gimnasio	gym
el ordenador	computer
el programa	programme
la actividad	activity
la pantalla	screen
moderno/a	modern
antiguo/a	old
el aula de informática	IT room
el laboratorio	lab, laboratory
el portátil	laptop
el diseño	design
los recursos	resources

Nouns with unexpected genders
Grammar page 94

Some commonly used nouns have a different gender to what you might expect from their ending. You will need to learn these:

Masculine

el problema	problem
el idioma	language
el programa	programme
el clima	climate
el tema	theme, topic
el día	day
el planeta	planet

Feminine

la mano	hand
la foto	photo
la modelo	(female) model

This answer is from a student working at around a Grade 9.

Worked example SPEAKING TRACK 18   Target grade 1-9   Listen to the recording

¿Cómo es tu instituto?

Mi instituto es bastante grande. Tiene una biblioteca y un gran campo de deportes. Algunas clases son un poco viejas pero los recursos para las ciencias son muy modernos. En mi opinión, el gimnasio es un poco pequeño y sería guay tener una piscina. El edificio está limpio, tenemos muchos ordenadores y todos los libros que necesitamos.

Tenemos un gran campo de deportes.
We have a large sports field.

Now try this LISTENING TRACK 19   Target grade 9   Listen to the recording

You hear a teacher talking about resources. What **three** things does she say? Write the correct letters in the boxes.

A	They use computers a lot in all lessons.
B	They are useful for listening activities.
C	They still rely on paper versions of course books.
D	She wishes she had a screen to show presentations.
E	Students use pens and paper much less.
F	She wonders whether all this technology is a good thing.

☐ ☐ ☐   **(3 marks)**

School uniform

Digital resources

¿Cómo es el uniforme de tu instituto?

el uniforme	uniform
la chaqueta*	jacket, blazer
la camisa	shirt
la camiseta	T-shirt
la corbata*	tie
los zapatos	shoes
la falda	skirt
los pantalones	trousers
los pantalones cortos	shorts
el vestido	dress
amarillo/a	yellow
azul	blue
blanco/a	white
gris	grey
marrón	brown
negro/a	black
rojo/a	red
verde	green
llevar	to wear

*These words are not on the AQA vocabulary list but will be useful when talking about uniform.

Revising adjectives

Grammar page 95

Remember that all adjectives must agree with the noun they describe, whether they are right next to the noun, at the other end of the sentence or not even in the same sentence.

	singular		plural	
	Masculine	Feminine	Masculine	Feminine
	rojo	roja	rojos	rojas
	verde	verde	verdes	verdes
	azul	azul	azules	azules

La falda que llevo al instituto es negra.
The skirt I wear for school is black.

Necesito zapatos nuevos. Tienen que ser marrones.
I need new shoes. They have to be brown.

Llevo una corbata roja y negra.
I wear a red and black tie.

Llevamos una camisa azul, una falda o pantalones grises y una corbata negra y azul.
We wear a blue shirt, a grey skirt or trousers and a black and blue tie.

Worked example

WRITING

Target grade 1-5

You are writing an article about your school uniform.

Write approximately **90** words in **Spanish**. You must write something about each bullet point.

Mention:
- a description of the uniform
- what you wore in school when you were little
- what you will wear at the weekend. **(15 marks)**

En mi instituto llevamos una chaqueta verde, una camisa blanca, una falda gris o pantalones grises, zapatos negros y una corbata verde y amarilla.

No me gusta mucho, pero es cómodo.

Cuando era pequeño, llevábamos uniforme en mi colegio también. Llevaba pantalones cortos grises, una camiseta blanca y una pequeña corbata roja. Siempre tenía los zapatos sucios.

El fin de semana hay una fiesta especial para el cumpleaños de mi amiga. Voy a llevar un vestido nuevo que es negro y blanco. Compré el vestido el sábado pasado.
(89 words)

Now try this

LISTENING TRACK 20

Target grade 2

Raúl is talking about his school uniform. Complete the sentences. Write the correct letter in each box.

Listen to the recording

1 Raúl wears a grey …

A	shirt.
B	jacket.
C	tie.

☐

2 The jacket is too …

A	big.
B	small.
C	old.

☐

3 The trousers are too …

A	long.
B	short.
C	tight.

☐

(3 marks)

Digital resources

Activities in class

¿Qué haces en las clases de ...?

actividad física	physical activity
el concurso	quiz, competition
los deberes	homework
escuchar	to listen
hablar	to talk, speak
escribir	to write
leer	to read
buscar información	to look for information
hacer ejercicios	to do exercises
discutir	to discuss
usar el ordenador	to use the computer
resolver problemas	to solve problems
estudiar	to study
hacer deporte(s)	to do sport(s)
contestar preguntas	to answer questions
pintar	to paint
explicar	to explain
ayudar	to help
aprender	to learn
trabajar ... en grupos	to work ... in groups
... con un compañero/a	... with a classmate

Possessive pronouns — Grammar page 96

These are words like 'mine' or 'hers' where they replace the noun. For example: That's my book. Where is **yours**?

	singular		plural	
	Masculine	**Feminine**	**Masculine**	**Feminine**
mine	el mío	la mía	los míos	las mías
yours	el tuyo	la tuya	los tuyos	las tuyas
his, hers	el suyo	la suya	los suyos	las suyas
ours	el nuestro	la nuestra	los nuestros	las nuestras
yours	el vuestro	la vuestra	los vuestros	las vuestras
theirs	el suyo	la suya	los suyos	las suyas

Note that these pronouns agree with the noun they replace, **not** the person who owns the item.

Tengo mi libro. ¿Dónde está el tuyo?
I've got my book. Where is yours?
Leave out the article (el, la, los, las) after ser:

¿De quién son estos libros? Son míos.
Whose are these books? They are mine.

Worked example   Target grade 6

Read Leya's email about her science classes.

Mi amiga no está en mi clase de ciencias; está en otra y no le gusta su profesor. Dice que no explica bien. El nuestro es excelente y hacemos muchas actividades interesantes, a veces en grupos y otras veces con un compañero. Resolvemos problemas, utilizamos los ordenadores para buscar información y hacemos actividades prácticas. Lo único negativo – ¡la cantidad de deberes que nos pone!

La profesora me ayuda si tengo un problema. The teacher helps me if I have a problem.

Which **three** statements are correct? Write the correct letters in the boxes.

A	Leya and her friend are in the same class.
B	Leya has a good science teacher.
C	They sometimes do work in pairs.
D	They don't use the computers in class.
E	There is practical work in their lessons.
F	The teacher doesn't set much homework.

☐ B   ☐ C   ☐ E   **(3 marks)**

Now try this   Target grade 4-9

Translate the following sentences into **Spanish**.

1 In our classes the teachers explain things.
2 Then we do exercises or answer questions in the text book.
3 Afterwards we work in groups to solve problems.
4 Yesterday, we watched a video in the history class.
5 It was good fun and we learned a lot.

(10 marks)

To say 'good fun', remember that 'fun' is the adjective **divertido** so add **muy** in front of it.

School rules

Digital resources

Las reglas del instituto

la regla	rule, regulation, ruler
Está prohibido ...	It is forbidden ...
No se puede ...	You may not ...
usar el móvil en clase.	use your phone in class.
mandar mensajes.	send messages.
llegar tarde.	arrive late.
correr en el edificio.	run in the building.
hablar cuando habla el / la profesor/a.	talk when the teacher is talking.
tirar basura.	drop litter.
Hay que ...	You must ...
traer el equipo necesario a clase.	bring the necessary equipment to class.
hacer los deberes.	do your homework.
respetar a tus profesores y compañeros.	respect your teachers and class mates.
llevar el uniforme correcto.	wear the correct uniform.
cuidar el edificio y los recursos.	look after the building and resources.

No hay que llegar tarde al instituto. **You must not** arrive late for school.

Using negatives

Grammar page 112

To make a verb negative, put no before it.

No está permitido. It is not allowed.

The words for 'nobody' (nadie) and 'never' (nunca) can go before or after the verb like in English:

Nadie quiere trabajar. Nobody wants to work.

No vi a nadie allí. I didn't see anyone there.

Nunca rompo las reglas.
I never break the rules.

No rompo las reglas nunca.
I never break the rules.

(You must put 'no' before the verb if it is followed by a negative word).

Nada is used for 'nothing' and 'anything' (when the sentence implies **not** anything).

No he hecho nada mal.
I have done **nothing** wrong. / I **haven't** done **anything** wrong.

Also note:

ninguno/a	none, not any
sin	without
jamás	never
ya no	no longer, not any more

Worked example

LISTENING TRACK **21**

Target grade 6

School rules

Listen to a head teacher explaining the school rules.

What does she mention? Write the **three** correct letters in the boxes.

Es muy importante cuidar el edificio y no se debe tirar basura. Siempre hay que respetar a todos los miembros del colegio. Nunca se debe llegar tarde a clase.

A	arriving late
B	doing homework on time
C	dropping litter
D	respecting others
E	wearing the correct uniform
F	using mobile phones

Listen to the recording

A C D

(3 marks)

You may be asked to talk about your school rules during the general conversation part of the speaking exam. Practise this question then listen to the sample answer from a Higher tier student in the Answer section.

Now try this

SPEAKING

Target grade 1-9

¿Qué piensas de las normas en tu instituto?

You could mention that some rules are too strict – **demasiado estrictas** – but you could show a balanced view by mentioning others that are fair – **justas**.

Digital resources

The good and the bad about school

Lo bueno y lo malo del colegio

el / la director/a	head teacher
el error	error, mistake
el examen	exam
el éxito	success
la presión	pressure
la prueba	test
aprender	to learn
aprobar	to pass
entender	to understand
gritar	to shout
hacer preguntas	to ask questions
molestar	to annoy
preparar	to prepare
sacar buenas / malas notas	to get good / bad grades
asistir	to attend
la cantidad	quantity, amount
la enseñanza	teaching
estricto/a	strict
la igualdad	equality
el nivel	level

The personal 'a'

When the object of a verb is a **person**, the word a is inserted after the verb and before the person.

Voy a ver a la directora.
I'm going to see the head teacher.

> The subject of a verb is who is doing the action of the verb. The object of a verb is what or whom the action is being done to.

The personal a is **not** used when the object of a verb is a **thing**:

Voy a ver la película.   I am going to see the film.

> Note that you don't need the personal 'a' after hay or tener or when another preposition is required: **Voy a hablar con la directora.**

Flexible phrases

Me molesta mucho cuando ...
It really annoys me when ...

Un aspecto que me gusta mucho es que ...
An aspect that I really like is that ...

Lo mejor es que ...
The best thing is that ...

Worked example

 LISTENING TRACK 22

Target grade 7

You hear Jorge talking about school. What does he say? Listen to the recording and complete the sentences. Write the correct letter in each box.

Listen to the recording

> Me molesta mucho cuando otros chicos en la clase hacen ruido y no se puede oír al profesor. Sin embargo, lo bueno es que hay un club de deberes durante la hora de comer y puedo ir a ver al profesor para hacer preguntas si me hace falta.

1   Jorge is annoyed by ...

A	poor teaching.
B	noisy classmates.
C	strict tutors.

B

(1 mark)

2   He appreciates ...

A	being able to seek help outside class.
B	getting time to relax at lunch.
C	his friend helping with homework.

A

(1 mark)

Now try this

 LISTENING TRACK 23

Target grade 7

Continue listening to Jorge and complete the sentences. Write the correct letter in each box.

Listen to the recording

1   Jorge is not happy about ...

A	the amount of testing.
B	the quantity of homework.
C	his tiring part-time job.

☐ **(1 mark)**

2   Jorge thinks that ...

A	his exam results were good.
B	he would like to work as a teacher.
C	the standard of teaching is good.

☐ **(1 mark)**

School clubs and activities

¿Qué clubs y actividades hay en tu colegio?

el club	club
la actividad	activity
el arte	art
el teatro	theatre, drama
divertido/a	fun, enjoyable
educativo/a	educational
la excursión	trip, excursion
el deporte	sport
el gimnasio	gym
la música	music
después de las clases	after school
durante la hora de comer	during the lunch hour
durar	to last
participar	to participate
pintar	to paint
actuar	to act, perform
asistir a	to attend
la orquesta	orchestra
privado/a	private

The gender of nouns

Grammar page 94

It is helpful to know the patterns of nouns that do not end in -o or -a-, but whose gender is obvious from their ending.

- Nouns that end in **-dad** are feminine:

la sociedad	society
la personalidad	personality
la universidad	university
la realidad	reality

Note also how the **-dad** ending is the equivalent of -ty in English.

- Nouns that end in **-ión** are feminine (except avión – 'plane')

la situación	situation
la información	information
la educación	education
la televisión	television

Note that -**ción** corresponds with -tion in English and -**sión** corresponds to -sion.

Me encanta ser parte de la orquesta del instituto.

I love being part of the school orchestra.

Worked example

 WRITING

 Target grade 1-9

You are writing to your friend about your school clubs. Write approximately **90** words in **Spanish**.
You **must** write something about each bullet point.
Mention:
- the clubs and activities in your school
- what club you went to last week
- what activity you will do after school this week. **(15 marks)**

This response uses good **connectors** to introduce reasons. It also develops the answer by giving **extra** information. It ensures the verbs are in the correct tenses – **past** tenses for bullet point 2 and **future** tenses for bullet point 3.

En mi instituto hay varios clubs después de las clases y algunas actividades durante la hora de comer. Me gusta especialmente el club de teatro **porque** me encanta actuar y, además, este año voy a tener un papel en una obra del instituto.

La semana pasada, **fui** al club de deberes durante la hora de comer **porque tenía** un problema con las matemáticas y **necesitaba** ayuda.

Este jueves, **voy a ir** a la reunión para los estudiantes que **participarán** en la excursión a Madrid. Vamos a recibir información importante. **(85 words)**

Now try this

 SPEAKING

 Target grade 1-9

¿Qué actividades y clubs hay en tu instituto?

You could mention clubs and activities and when they take place. You could talk about some you attend, or attended, and a club you would like to have at school. Listen to a sample answer from a student working at around Grade 9 by scanning a code in the answer section.

Digital resources

How to be a good student

Cómo ser un(a) buen(a) estudiante.

el ejercicio	exercise
una tarea	task, job, homework
el horario	timetable
aprender	to learn
buscar información	to look for information
descansar	to rest
dormir	to sleep
entender	to understand
escribir	to write
escuchar	to listen
hacer preguntas	to ask questions
pedir ayuda	to ask for help
practicar	to practise
repetir	to repeat
asistir (a)	to attend
la manera (de)	way, manner (of / to)
entregar	to submit, hand in
vale la pena (+ infinitive)	it's worth it (to)
hace falta (+ infinitive)	it is necessary (to)

Ways of expressing 'have to / must'

- **tener que + infinitive (to have to …)**
  Put tener into the appropriate tense and person, add que and the infinitive:
  Tuve que hacer los deberes.
  I had to do my homework.
  Tienes que practicar. You have to practise.

- **hay que + infinitive (one must / it is necessary to)**
  This is a general expression and cannot take a subject.
  Para entender, hay que hacer preguntas.
  In order to understand, one must ask questions.

- **deber + infinitive (must)**
  Put deber into the appropriate tense and person and add the infinitive.
  Debemos llevar uniforme. We must wear uniform.
  OR use se debe which is impersonal like hay que:
  Siempre se debe escuchar en clase.
  One must always listen in class

Worked example

 READING Target grade **5**

Read Rosalía's advice to her students.

Nunca se debe dar los deberes a tu profesor o profesora sin terminar. Siempre puedes resolver problemas. Puedes hacer preguntas a un compañero, pedir ayuda a tu profesor o buscar la solución en un libro. Muchas veces, puedes encontrar las cosas que necesitas online.

Answer the following questions in **English.**

1 What should you never do? **(1 mark)**

hand in unfinished homework

2 Which two people could you ask for help? **(2 marks)**

a classmate or a teacher

3 In which two places could you find help? **(2 marks)**

a book and online

A veces tengo que pedir ayuda a mi padre. Sometimes **I have to** ask my father for help.

Now try this

 READING Target grade **7**

Continue reading Rosalía's advice.

También siempre recomiendo no dejar los deberes hasta el último momento. Si tienes un problema, y debes entregar los deberes el día después, entonces no tienes ninguna oportunidad de pedir ayuda para resolver la dificultad. El estudiante organizado debe escribir un horario de deberes para evitar esto.

Answer the following questions in **English**.

1 What does she tell you to avoid doing? **(1 mark)**

2 What problem arises if you ignore this advice? **(1 mark)**

3 What should an organised student create? **(1 mark)**

Options at 16

Digital resources

¿Qué vas a hacer el septiembre próximo?

el resultado	result
el examen	exam
la opción	option
la asignatura	subject
el trabajo	job
el fin de semana	the weekend
la carrera	career, university degree
continuar (con)	to carry on (with)
depender (de)	to depend (on)
escoger	to choose
preparar(se)	to prepare
sacar buenas / malas notas	to get good / bad grades
seguir estudiando	to continue studying
la formación	training
profesional	professional, vocational

Using the infinitive

H ONLY

In English, we often use the present participle (or gerund) where, in Spanish, the infinitive is used. This is the case with the following expressions:

after ... -ing   después de + infinitive
Después de recibir mis notas, decidí continuar con mis estudios.
After getting my grades, I decided to carry on with my studies.

before ... -ing   antes de + infinitive
No voy a tomar una decisión antes de saber mis notas.
I am not going to make a decision **before knowing** my grades.

Flexible phrases

Voy a esperar los resultados de los exámenes.
I'm going to wait for the exam results.

Voy a continuar con mis estudios.
I'm going to carry on with my studies.

La formación profesional parece ideal para mí.
Professional / vocational training looks ideal for me.

Vamos a hablar de tus opciones para el año próximo.
We're going to talk about your options for next year.

Worked example

 SPEAKING TRACK 24

 Target grade 1-5

 Listen to the recording

¿Cuáles son tus planes para el año próximo?

Voy a continuar con mis estudios aquí en el instituto, pero quiero esperar los resultados de los exámenes para escoger mis asignaturas. Me gustaría seguir con el español, pero depende de mis notas.

You may be asked a question like this in the general conversation part of the Speaking exam. Try to answer fully to demonstrate the Spanish you know.

Good use of more complex structures like **para** + infinitive and correct prepositions (**seguir con, depender de**).

Now try this

 WRITING

 Target grade 1-5

Write an email about your plans for study and work next year.

Write approximately **50** words in **Spanish**. You must write something about each bullet point.

Mention:

- options
- school
- subjects
- how you will decide
- part-time work.

(10 marks)

25

Digital resources

Future study plans

Tus estudios en el futuro

el trabajo	work
el dinero	money
la universidad	university
la carrera	career, university course
el examen	exam
el éxito	success
el resultado	result
la lengua	language
al / en el extranjero	abroad
la intención	intention
aprobar	to pass
depender de	to depend on
estudiar	to study
la formación	training
suspender	to fail
el título	qualification

Si saco las notas necesarias, espero …
If I get the necessary grades, I hope …

Si apruebo los exámenes, quiero …
If I pass the exams, I want …

Adverbs ending in '-ly'

Adverbs that end in '-ly' in English (like 'quickly' and 'happily') are very easy to form in Spanish.

❶ Take an adjective, such as rápido (quick).

❷ Make it feminine singular → rápida

❸ Add -mente → rápidamente (quickly)

Remember that adjectives that end in -e or a consonant, like triste (sad) and feliz (happy) do not change when feminine so the suffix -mente goes straight on the end:

tristemente – sadly   felizmente – happily

Con estos resultados, probablemente estudiaré ciencias en la universidad.
With these results I will probably study science at university.

Worked example

 READING   Target grade 6

Read Omar's letter.

> Mis opciones para el año próximo dependen de si saco buenas notas o no. Espero continuar con mis estudios en el instituto. Tengo la intención de hacer un curso en ciencias y tecnología que dura dos años. Además de las asignaturas relacionadas con este programa, también tengo que seguir estudiando varias asignaturas obligatorias* como la educación física y la lengua española.

*obligatorias – compulsory

Answer the following questions in **English**.

1 What do Omar's options depend on? **(1 mark)**
getting good grades

2 What course does he hope to do? **(1 mark)**
science and technology

3 How long does the course last? **(1 mark)**
2 years

4 Name **one** of the two compulsory subjects he will study? **(1 mark)**
PE

 You could also have answered 'Spanish language' in question 4.

Now try this

 READING   Target grade 7

Read the rest of Omar's letter.

> Al final del año, tengo la intención de ir a la universidad. En este momento, no tengo la menor idea de la carrera que quiero hacer. Hay tantas posibilidades, es increíble, y muchas decisiones para tomar. Por lo menos tengo los próximos dos años para buscar la información y tomar una decisión.

Complete these sentences. Write the letter for the correct option in each box.

1 At the end of the year, Omar …

A	plans to go to university.
B	wants to learn a foreign language.
C	will travel abroad.

☐

2 At the moment, he …

A	thinks there are not too many options.
B	also wants to keep his part-time job.
C	doesn't have to make his mind up.

☐

(2 marks)

Future plans

Digital resources

¿Qué planes tienes para el futuro?

Spanish	English
la vida	life
el trabajo	work
la experiencia laboral	work experience
la cuenta	bill, account
la ciudad	city
el piso	flat
la carrera	career, course
los amigos	friends
al / en el extranjero	abroad
el éxito	success
el país	country
el dinero	money
el novio / la novia	boyfriend / girlfriend
el sueño	dream
casarse	to get married
conocer	to get to know
ganar	to earn
viajar	to travel
la independencia	independence
la aventura	adventure

Using the present subjunctive after cuando

 Grammar page 111

The present subjunctive tense is used after cuando when the following verb has not yet happened. For example: I will make my decision **when I have** my results.

You need to know the 1st, 2nd and 3rd persons **singular** of these verbs only:

	First person singular	Second person singular	Third person singular
hacer	haga	hagas	haga
tener	tenga	tengas	tenga
venir	venga	vengas	venga
ser	sea	seas	sea
ir	vaya	vayas	vaya

Cuando sea mayor, quiero tener mi propio piso.
When I am older, I want to have my own flat.

Tendré más independencia **cuando** vaya a la universidad.
I will have more independence **when I go** to university.

Useful phrases

Cuando sea mayor, me gustaría …
When I am older I would like …

Algún día, mi sueño es …
Some day, my dream is …

Para mí, lo más importante es …
For me, the most important thing is …

Cuando tenga veinte años, espero viajar.
When I am twenty, I hope to travel.

Worked example

Pilar and Mario are talking about their future plans. Complete the sentence. Choose the correct answer and write the letter in the box.

Listen to the recording

No sé si voy a casarme, solo estoy pensando en encontrar un trabajo y ganar bastante dinero para tener mi propio piso en la ciudad.

1 Pilar's main aim is to …

A	get married.
B	earn a fortune.
C	get a place of her own.

C (1 mark)

Now try this

Now listen to what Mario has to say about his future plans. Complete the sentence in **English**.

Write **one** word in each space.

2 Mario says that after _____ he wants to _____ and save money.
(2 marks)

Pilar mentions all three of these things, but she is not sure whether she will marry and she doesn't talk about earning lots of money, just enough for her own flat. So a place of her own is the main aim.

Digital resources

Part-time jobs and money

¿Tienes un trabajo los fines de semana?

el trabajo	work
el dinero	money
la hora	hour, time
el euro	euro
el restaurante	restaurant
el café	café
la comida rápida	fast food
la tienda	shop
la caja	till, checkout
el supermercado	supermarket
el / la compañero/a	colleague
el / la jefe/a	boss
ahorrar	to save
comprar	to buy
empezar	to start
ganar	to earn
gastar	to spend
pagar	to pay
terminar	to finish
trabajar	to work

Revising numbers

Grammar page 117

uno	1	catorce	14	veintisiete	27
dos	2	quince	15	veintiocho	28
tres	3	dieciséis	16	veintinueve	29
cuatro	4	diecisiete	17	treinta	30
cinco	5	dieciocho	18	cuarenta	40
seis	6	diecinueve	19	cincuenta	50
siete	7	veinte	20	sesenta	60
ocho	8	veintiuno	21	setenta	70
nueve	9	veintidós	22	ochenta	80
diez	10	veintitrés	23	noventa	90
once	11	veinticuatro	24	cien	100
doce	12	veinticinco	25	mil	1000
trece	13	veintiséis	26	un millón	1 million

Multiple of hundreds: add -cientos to the number: doscientos, (200), trescientos (300).

There are three irregulars: quinientos (500), setecientos (700) and novecientos (900)

Worked example

 READING Target grade **6**

Read Rosalía's article on part-time work for students.

Tengo un nuevo trabajo en el supermercado. I've got a new job at the supermarket.

> Cuando yo tenía diecisiete años trabajaba ocho horas los sábados, sirviendo a los clientes en un café de las nueve a las cinco. Ganaba un poco de dinero y también tenía suficiente tiempo para mis estudios.

Complete these sentences. Write the letter for the correct option in each box.

1 Rosalía used to work …

A	all weekend.
B	as a waitress.
C	a nine-hour day.

B (1 mark)

2 She says that she …

A	was paid very badly.
B	struggled with her studies.
C	had enough time to study.

C (1 mark)

Now try this

 READING Target grade **7**

Continue reading Rosalía's article.

> Ahora, soy profesora y muchos de mis estudiantes trabajan no solo los fines de semana sino algunas tardes durante la semana también. Esto pasa mucho con los que tienen trabajos en restaurantes de comida rápida o en supermercados. El resultado es que sus estudios sufren y no pueden dar el tiempo suficiente a sus deberes.

Answer the following questions in **English**.
1 Why does Rosalía complain about her students' work hours? **(1 mark)**
2 In which jobs does this happen most? **(2 marks)**
3 How does this affect the students? Mention **one** thing. **(1 mark)**

Opinions about jobs

¿Qué buscas en un trabajo?

el salario	salary
la empresa	company, firm
la carrera	career
el / la policía	police officer
el / la profesor/a	teacher
el / la director/a	director, head teacher
la oportunidad	opportunity
el / la modelo	model
el / la jefe/a	boss
el / la artista	artist
el / la escritor/a	writer
el médico / la médica	doctor
el / la enfermero/a	nurse
el / la periodista	journalist
el actor / la actriz	actor
el / la científico/a	scientist
los medios	media
la industria	industry
el empleo	employment, job
ganar	to earn
la responsabilidad	responsibility
el diseño	design

Using the article

Grammar page 94

The article is usually omitted after ser when it is followed by a job / profession.

Mi madre es médica y mi padre es profesor. Yo soy estudiante.

My mother is a doctor and my father is a teacher. I am a student.

However, when an adjective is added, the article is included.

Mi madre es una médica excelente.

My mother is an excellent doctor.

When generalising, the article is used in Spanish but is omitted in English.

Los policías ganan un buen salario.

Police officers earn a good salary.

De momento, no sé qué quiero hacer en el futuro. At the moment, I don't know what I want to do in the future.

Worked example

 LISTENING TRACK 27

 Target grade 6

Miguel is talking about jobs. What aspects does he say are important to him?

Listen to the recording

El salario no es el aspecto más importante en mi opinión. Claro que quiero ganar bastante, pero tienes que disfrutar del trabajo que haces. Me gustaría ser parte de un equipo y llevarme bien con mis compañeros. Sería excelente tener oportunidades de viajar también.

Write

    A if only statement **A** is correct

    B if only statement **B** is correct

    A+B if both statements are correct.

1 He would like to …

A	have a good salary.
B	be part of a nice team.

A+B (1 mark)

Useful phrases

Para mí, el aspecto más importante de un trabajo es …
For me, the most important aspect of a job is …

Me gustaría trabajar en el turismo / el diseño / la industria …
I would like to work in tourism / design / industry …

Quiero usar mis conocimientos de idiomas / ciencias / matemáticas.
I want to use my knowledge of languages / science / maths.

 H ONLY

Now try this

 SPEAKING

 Target grade 1-9

¿Qué tipo de trabajo te gustaría?

You may be asked a question like this in the general conversation part of the Speaking exam.

Digital resources

The pros and cons of different jobs

¿Qué tal el trabajo?

el salario	salary
las horas	hours
el horario	schedule
las vacaciones	holidays
la presión	pressure
demasiado/a	too much
el peligro	danger
la violencia	violence
el equipo	team, equipment
el / la compañero/a	colleague
la regla	rule
el uniforme	uniform
el viaje	journey
el edificio	building
la oportunidad	opportunity
apoyar	to support
la responsabilidad	responsibility
la formación	training

Masculine and feminine jobs

Grammar page 94

Masculine	Feminine	English
actor	actriz	actor, actress
profesor	profesora	teacher
director	directora	head teacher, director
médico	médica	doctor
modelo	modelo	model
jefe	jefa	boss, manager
escritor	escritora	writer
artista	artista	artist
científico	científica	scientist
policía	policía	police officer
camarero	camarera	waiter / waitress
peluquero	peluquera	hairdresser

Worked example

 READING Target grade 6

Read Sofía's email.

> Mi hermana mayor, Ana, es policía desde hace solo seis meses. Es cierto que al principio no tiene mucha responsabilidad y el salario es bastante bajo, pero le gusta mucho el trabajo y aprecia el apoyo de su jefe. Más que nada disfruta de la compañía de sus compañeros. Dice que el horario podría ser mejor, pero tendrá la oportunidad de cambiar sus horas de trabajo en el futuro.

What does Sofía say about these aspects of Ana's new job?

Complete the sentences. Write the correct letter in each box.

A	colleagues
B	hours
C	pay
D	holidays
E	support

1 Ana appreciates her … .   **E** (1 mark)

2 Most of all she likes her … .   **A** (1 mark)

3 In the future she may have different … .   **B** (1 mark)

Useful phrases

Tienes que trabajar muchas horas.
You have to work many hours.

El salario aumenta.
The salary goes up.

Las oportunidades son excelentes.
The opportunities are excellent.

Now try this

 READING Target grade 6

Read the rest of Sofía's email.

> Mis padres se preocupan un poco por Ana porque dicen que puede haber peligro en el trabajo. Piensan que ella debería trabajar en una biblioteca u otro lugar tranquilo y seguro. Pero Ana dice que prefiere tener un empleo con riesgos que dormirse en un trabajo aburrido.

Complete the following sentences in **English**.

1 Ana's parents worry about the _____ .   **(1 mark)**

2 They would prefer her to _____ .   **(1 mark)**

3 However, Ana prefers a job with some _____ .   **(1 mark)**

Digital resources

Job adverts

Se busca gente …

la gente	people
la entrevista	interview
el éxito	success
la experiencia	experience
trabajador/a	hard-working
responsable	responsible
la actitud	attitude
el teléfono	telephone
el correo electrónico	email
buscar	to look for
llamar	to call
mejorar	to improve
necesitar	to need
capaz	capable
el derecho	right; law (subject of study)
el / la experto/a	expert
la igualdad	equality
la independencia	independence
el título	qualification
lograr	to achieve, manage

Using the subjunctive after para que

Grammar page 111

The present subjunctive is also used after para que (so that).

You need to know the 1st, 2nd and 3rd persons singular of these verbs only.

	First person singular	Second person singular	Third person singular
hacer	haga	hagas	haga
tener	tenga	tengas	tenga
venir	venga	vengas	venga
ser	sea	seas	sea
ir	vaya	vayas	vaya

Ofrecemos formación **para que tengas** el conocimiento necesario.

We provide training **so that you have** the necessary knowledge.

Los trabajos se ven en línea y en el periódico.
Jobs are seen online and in the newspaper.

Worked example

 TRACK 28   Target grade 7

Antonio is talking about a job advert he has seen. What does the advert mention?

Listen to the recording and write the **three** correct letters in the boxes.

 Listen to the recording

> Una empresa tiene un trabajo que me interesa. Buscan a una persona trabajadora y responsable, capaz de trabajar en equipo, para ayudar a decidir los productos que van a vender.
>
> Se necesita hablar inglés y poder viajar al extranjero a veces para visitar empresas en otros países.

A	the personality required
B	the hours
C	the start date
D	skills in another language
E	willingness to travel
F	the location of the company

[A] [D] [E]

(3 marks)

Now try this

 TRACK 29   Target grade 7

Continue listening to Antonio talking about applying for the job. What does he say? Listen to the recording and write the correct letter in each box.

Listen to the recording

1 Interviews will be held …

A	next month.
B	in early December.
C	in the New Year.

☐

(1 mark)

2 He first needs to …

A	phone the company.
B	email the firm.
C	write a letter to express his interest.

☐

(1 mark)

Digital resources

Applying for jobs

Cómo encontrar trabajo

el periódico	newspaper
la oficina	office
el empleo	employment
el aspecto	aspect
la personalidad	personality
la carta	letter
la compañía	company
la empresa	firm
el correo electrónico	email
la razón	reason
la experiencia	experience
buscar	to look for
decir la verdad	to tell the truth
escribir	to write
explicar	to explain
llamar	to call
mandar	to send
pedir	to ask for
preguntar	to ask

Double consonants in Spanish

It is not always easy to remember spellings, but this rule will often come in useful.

There is a very famous Spanish poet and playwright called Lorca; if you remember his name, you will remember the only consonants in Spanish that can be double letters.

LORCA:

ll – calle (street), llamar (to call), silla (chair)

rr – perro (dog), cerrar (to shut), aburrido (boring)

cc – acción (action), accidente (accident), dirección (direction, address)

You may come across a word with a rare double 'n' but none of these words are on the prescribed AQA list.

Hay varios sitios donde puedes buscar trabajo. There are several places where you can look for work.

Worked example

 READING   Target grade **8**

Read this advice for job seekers.

> Cuando solicitas* trabajo, no debes inventar tu experiencia y cuando hablas de tus títulos, siempre hay que decir la verdad. Si no, puedes estar seguro de que, en algún momento, descubrirán que has dicho una *falsedad*.

solicitar – to apply for

Answer the following questions in **English**.

1 What should you **not** do? **(1 mark)**
invent your experience

2 What should you always do? **(1 mark)**
tell the truth

3 Read the last sentence again. What is a *falsedad*? Write the correct letter in the box.

A	quality
B	lie
C	reply

[B] **(1 mark)**

The text tells you not to exaggerate in your application and to always tell the truth, as you can be sure any **lie** will be discovered.

Useful phrases

Quiero ser ... porque ...	I want to be ... because ...
Me gustaría trabajar en ...	I would like to work in ...
Tengo experiencia en ...	I have experience in ...
He trabajado como ...	I have worked as ...

Now try this

LISTENING TRACK **30** Target grade **2**

You hear Marta giving advice for job seekers. What **three** things does she say? Choose the three correct answers and write the letter in each box.

Listen to the recording

A	See your school careers advisor.
B	Go to the job office.
C	Look at newspapers.
D	Talk to people you know.
E	Listen to local radio adverts.
F	Go online.

☐ ☐ ☐ **(3 marks)**

Preparing for interviews

Cómo prepararte para una entrevista

la entrevista	interview
el / la jefe/a	boss
llegar a tiempo	to arrive on time
la empresa	firm
la compañía	company
el comportamiento	behaviour
nervioso/a	nervous
el interés	interest
la confianza	confidence
buscar información	to look for information
contestar	to answer
hacer preguntas	to ask questions
llevar	to wear
preparar	to prepare
responder	to reply
sonreír	to smile
vestirse	to dress
natural	natural

Gracias por venir. Estaré en contacto pronto.
Thank you for coming. I'll be in touch soon.

A further use of the infinitive

We often use the ...ing part of the verb where in Spanish the infinitive would be used.

Cuando te presentas para una entrevista, llegar temprano es muy importante.
When you go for an interview, **arriving** early is very important.

En una entrevista, hacer preguntas muestra tu interés.
In an interview, **asking** questions shows your interest.

Sonreír muestra una actitud positiva.
Smiling shows a positive attitude.

Useful phrases

Intenta ... Try to ...

... responder con confianza.
... reply with confidence.

... dar ejemplos de tus aspectos positivos.
... give examples of your positive aspects.

... actuar de manera natural.
... act naturally.

Worked example

Target grade **6**

Read Alba's email about her interview.

> Llegué un cuarto de hora antes para evitar el estrés de llegar tarde. Luego la jefa me invitó a su oficina. Me hizo muchas preguntas sobre mi título universitario. Contesté a todo, pero estaba un poco nerviosa.

Answer the questions in **English**.

1 When did Alba arrive for the interview? **(1 mark)**
quarter of an hour early

2 Where did the interview take place? **(1 mark)**
the boss's office

3 What did the boss ask about? **(1 mark)**
Alba's degree

4 How was Alba feeling? **(1 mark)**
a bit nervous

Now try this

Target grade **7**

Continue reading about Alba's interview.

> Creo que logré actuar de manera natural y cuando me preguntó sobre mi experiencia, pude dar ejemplos de varios éxitos que he tenido en mi trabajo actual. Al final hice algunas preguntas también sobre el trabajo y el número de personas que trabajan para la empresa. Me van a llamar el viernes para decirme si tengo el trabajo o no.

Answer the following questions in **English**.

1 How does Alba think she acted?
2 What examples did she give?
3 What did Alba ask about, as well as the job itself?
4 How will she know whether she has got the job?

(4 marks)

Digital resources

Working to help others

¿Qué haces para ayudar a otras personas?

la gente	people
pobre	poor
enfermo/a	ill, unwell
mayor	larger, older, main
los / las niños/as	children
la calle	street
el / la vecino/a	neighbour
el cuidado	care
el hospital	hospital
ayudar	to help
cuidar	to look after
descansar	to rest
ganar experiencia	to gain experience
necesitar	to need
trabajar	to work
los / las ancianos/as	the elderly
el banco de alimentos	food bank
el hogar	home
pasear	to walk

Using llevar + time H ONLY

Use llevar in the present tense, then the period of time, then the present participle.

Llevo dos semanas trabajando aquí.
I have been working here for two weeks.

Lleva tres días ayudando en la cocina.
He / she has been helping in the kitchen for three days.

Lleva seis meses cuidando a su abuela.
He / she has been looking after her grandmother for six months.

Desde hace is another way of dealing with the structure 'has / have been ...ing for' + time. (See page 78 to learn more.)

Llevo tres meses trabajando en el banco de alimentos.
I've been working at the food bank for three months.

Worked example READING Target grade 6

Read Omar's blog about his voluntary work.

En el futuro, quiero ser médico y trabajar en un hospital. Para ganar experiencia, ayudo en un hogar de ancianos. Sirvo la comida a los residentes y hago bebidas calientes.

Complete the sentences.
Write the letter for the correct option in each box.

1 Omar works in a ...

A	hospital.
B	doctor's surgery.
C	home for the elderly.

C

(1 mark)

2 Omar helps with ...

A	healthcare.
B	food and drink preparation.
C	office work.

B

(1 mark)

Study strategies

Learning vocabulary is one of the best ways to ensure you can prepare yourself for the exam.

- ✓ Learn 20 words at a time regularly.
- ✓ Read them, memorise, cover the English and write down the Spanish.
- ✓ Ask someone to test you.
- ✓ Record a list of English words, play it back and say the Spanish.
- ✓ Do the opposite – record the Spanish and say the English.

Now try this WRITING Target grade 4-9

Translate the following into **Spanish**.

I have been helping in the food bank for three months and I like it a lot. My colleagues are hard-working and fun and I love knowing that our work makes a difference. We receive food from several places, but mainly supermarkets, and we organise it into boxes for our customers.

(10 marks)

Digital resources

Free-time activities

¿Qué haces en tu tiempo libre?

el dibujo	drawing
el deporte	sport
la música	music
la novela	novel
la actividad	activity
aburrido/a	boring
interesante	interesting
activo/a	active
divertido/a	fun, enjoyable
práctico/a	practical
emocionante	exciting
artístico/a	artistic
dar un paseo	to go for a walk
ir al cine	to go to the cinema
jugar a los videojuegos	to play videogames
leer	to read
pintar	to paint
salir con amigos	to go out with friends
ver la televisión	to watch TV
la lectura	reading
cocinar	to cook
actuar	to act
la obra	a play
el / la aficionado/a	fan
relajante	relaxing

Expressing different opinions

- You can use gustar and encantar to talk about how much or how little you like an activity.

no me gusta nada	I don't like it at all
no me gusta	I don't like it
no me gusta mucho	I don't like it much
me gusta	I like it
me gusta un poco	I like it a bit
me gusta bastante	I quite like it
me gusta mucho	I like it a lot
me encanta	I love it

- You can use odiar if you hate something:
  Odio hacer deportes de equipo.
  I hate doing team sports.

- You can use interesar if something interests you or does not interest you:
  Me interesa la música, pero no me interesa nada ver la televisión.
  I'm interested in music, but I'm not at all interested in watching TV.

  If you are using gustar, encantar or interesar, add an -n if the following noun is plural:
  Me interesan las actividades culturales.

These verbs can be followed by an infinitive:
Me gusta / Me interesa / Odio leer novelas largas. Or they can be followed by a noun:
Me gusta / Me interesa / Odio el dibujo.

Worked example

 SPEAKING TRACK 31   Target grade 1-9

Answer the following question in **Spanish**.

¿Qué te gusta hacer en tu tiempo libre?

Me gusta mucho hacer deporte. Juego al fútbol todos los fines de semana y soy miembro del equipo del instituto.

Me encanta leer y mis novelas favoritas son las de ciencia ficción. También me gustan las actividades artísticas como pintar y el dibujo. Sin embargo, no tengo mucho tiempo libre porque tengo muchos deberes en este momento.

Listen to the recording

You might be asked a question like this in the conversation part of your exam.

Me encanta ir al cine con mis amigos.
I love going to the cinema with my friends.

A detailed and accurate Higher tier response that gives examples, reasons, extra information and points out a problem.

Now try this

 LISTENING TRACK 32   Target grade 3

Listen to the recording

Luisa and Emilio are talking about their free time. Complete the sentences in **English**.

1 Luisa loves to _____ because it is very _____ .

2 Emilio likes to _____ because it is very _____ .   (2 marks)

Digital resources

Music and dance

El mundo de la música y el baile

el baile	dance
la canción	song
el / la cantante	singer
el flamenco	flamenco
el grupo	group
el instrumento musical	musical instrument
la letra	words, lyrics
la música	(pop / classical / rock)
(pop / clásica / rock)	music
la voz	voice
la guitarra	guitar
aprender a + infinitive	to learn to
bailar	to dance
cantar	to sing
escuchar	to listen (to)
tocar	to play (an instrument)
la banda	band
la orquesta	orchestra
la radio	radio

Un día voy a tocar la guitarra en una banda famosa.
One day I am going to play the guitar in a famous band.

Talking about hopes for the future

These are some ways of expressing **future** hopes by using verbs in the **present tense**:

Quiero …	I want …
Espero …	I hope …
Tengo la intención de …	I intend to …

In addition, to vary your verbs you can use:

Me gustaría …	I would like …
Quisiera …	I would like …

You could talk about an instrument you play, like **la guitarra** (the guitar), or **el piano** (the piano), even if it is not on the AQA vocabulary list.

Flexible phrases

Un día voy a ser (+ noun) …
One day I am going to be …

En el futuro espero (+ infinitive) …
In the future I hope to …

Cuando sea mayor, tengo la intención de (+ infinitive) …
When I am older I intend to …

Worked example

 READING   Target grade 3

Read Hugo's text.

En mi tiempo libre me encanta tocar la guitarra. Normalmente mi amigo Dani y yo tocamos juntos. Esperamos escribir canciones también un día.

Complete these sentences. Write the letter for the correct option in each box.

1 Hugo likes to play the …

A	guitar.	**B**	piano.	**C**	violin.	A

2 He plays with his …

A	brother.	**B**	friend.	**C**	band.	B

3 In the future they hope to …

A	make a record.
B	give a concert.
C	write songs.

C

(3 marks)

Exam alert

The questions on the Reading paper have varying degrees of difficulty. There are challenging ones dotted around throughout the paper. So if you come up against a more difficult one, don't panic, the next one may be easier. The ones at the beginning of the paper are designed to get you going and give you confidence.

Most questions have options to choose from, and so if you are stuck, make an educated guess!

Now try this

 WRITING   Target grade 1-5

Translate the following sentences into **Spanish**.

1 I like to dance to rock music.
2 One day I hope to learn to play the piano.
3 She has a lovely voice and she sings well.
4 I wrote the words for the song.
5 We listen to music online.

(10 marks)

Music and dance events

Digital resources

¿Tienes tus entradas?

el ambiente	atmosphere
la entrada	(entry) ticket
el espectáculo	show
la fiesta	festival, party
alegre	happy, cheerful
emocionante	exciting
especial	special
guay	cool
divertido/a	fun, enjoyable
musical	musical
el grupo	group
pasarlo bien	to have a good time
ver	to watch
actuar	to act, perform
la cola	queue
el evento	event
latino/a	Latin American, Latin
asistir (a)	to attend
divertirse	to enjoy oneself
la banda	band

Expressions of time

Grammar page 117

lunes	Monday	To say **on**
martes	Tuesday	+ day of the week:
miércoles	Wednesday	el lunes — on Monday
jueves	Thursday	los martes — on Tuesdays
viernes	Friday	los sábados — on Saturdays
sábado	Saturday	
domingo	Sunday	

Days of the week in Spanish do **not** have capital letters. Only sábado and domingo have a plural form.

To say 'in the morning/afternoon' and so on:
por la mañana – in the morning
por las tardes – in the afternoons/evenings
los domingos por la mañana – on Sunday mornings

BUT use de after time:
a las diez **de** la noche at ten o'clock at night

El concierto fue guay y nos divertimos mucho.
The concert was cool and we had a great time.

Worked example

SPEAKING TRACK 33

Target grade 4-9

Háblame de un evento musical que viste recientemente.

Listen to the recording

El sábado pasado asistí a un festival de música con mis amigos. Había mucha gente y colas largas, pero la música fue excelente. Vi a varios grupos y mi banda favorita tocó las canciones que me gustan más. Había un ambiente alegre y lo pasamos muy bien.

Flexible phrases

Some useful verbs to talk about the past:
había	there was / there were
fui a	I went to
vi	I saw
Lo pasamos muy bien.	We had a really good time.

You might be asked a question like this in the conversation part of your Speaking exam. This answer is from a student working at Grade 9.

Now try this

READING

Target grade 6

Read this advert in a music magazine.

El viernes por la tarde se publican las fechas de la gira* de la estrella de pop Alba del Río. La cantante va a hacer una serie de conciertos por España, empezando el once del próximo mes. Si quieres entradas, recomendamos comprarlas pronto porque se venderán muy rápido.

*gira – tour

What does the advert say? Write the **three** correct letters in the boxes.

A	Alba del Río is a pop group.	D	The first concert is on the 11th next month.
B	Alba del Río is about to go on tour.	E	Fans should not delay getting their tickets.
C	The concert dates come out on Thursday.	F	Alba del Río is touring around several countries.

☐ ☐ ☐

(3 marks)

Digital resources

Reading

¿Te gusta leer?

el amor	love
la ciencia ficción	science fiction
divertido/a	fun, enjoyable
gracioso/a	funny
emocionante	exciting
el final	ending
la historia	story, history
el humor	humour
el mensaje	message
la novela	novel
la página	page
el personaje	character
el principio	beginning
el libro electrónico	e-reader
el tema	theme
leer	to read
perderse	to lose oneself
el estilo	style
la lectura	reading
la obra	play
imaginar	to imagine
decepcionante	disappointing
relajante	relaxing

Extending your range of adjectives

Grammar page 95

The adjectives aburrido and interesante are perfectly good, but they are very overused. Your language will be much more impressive if you use a wider range of descriptive words.

El personaje principal es muy complicado.
The main character is very complicated.

La novela tiene un tema muy serio.
The novel has a very serious theme.

La historia comunica un mensaje muy fuerte.
The story conveys a very strong message.

La novela cuenta una historia maravillosa.
The novel tells a wonderful story.

Creo que es un libro increíble.
I think it's an incredible book.

OR

Es una novela pesada y demasiado larga.
It's a boring book, and too long.

La acción es muy lenta, parece que no pasa nada.
The action is very slow, it's like nothing happens.

Esta novela es pesada y demasiado larga.
This novel is boring and too long.

Quiero ver qué pasa al final.
I want to see what happens at the end.

Worked example

LISTENING TRACK 34

Target grade 2

Sofía is telling you about the books she likes to read. What types of book does she mention? Write the **three** correct letters in the boxes.

Listen to the recording

Me encantan las novelas históricas porque aprendes mucho cuando las lees. No me gustan mucho los libros de humor, prefiero historias más serias. Odio las historias de amor – nunca las leo.

A	action	D	historical
B	funny	E	romance
C	comedy	F	science fiction

D   B   E

(3 marks)

Now try this

READING

Target grade 8

Read what Indra thought of the novel she has just finished. What is her opinion of it? Write the correct letter in the box.

El estilo era natural y los personajes parecían muy auténticos. Al principio, disfruté perdiéndome en la historia. Tengo que criticar el final, que fue muy decepcionante en mi opinión.

A	positive
B	negative
C	positive and negative

(1 mark)

Television

¿Qué te gusta ver en la tele?

la cocina	cooking
la ciencia ficción	science fiction
el deporte	sport
educativo/a	educational
extranjero/a	foreign
la historia	history
la música	music
la naturaleza	nature
las noticias	news
el país	country
el papel	role
la película	film
el personaje	character
el principio	beginning
el programa	programme
la serie	series
la televisión	television
la temporada	season
el canal	channel
el documental	documentary
el sonido	sound
internacional	international
nacional	national

Phrases of frequency

When talking about free-time activities, you need to know ways of expressing how often you do things.

Nunca veo la televisión. I **never** watch TV.

No veo las películas extranjeras casi nunca.
I **hardly ever** watch foreign films.

A veces veo una serie con mis padres.
I **sometimes** watch a series with my parents.

Veo programas de cocina con frecuencia.
I **frequently** watch cooking programmes.

He visto el programa muchas veces.
I have **often** watched the programme.

Siempre veo los documentales sobre la naturaleza.
I **always** watch nature documentaries.

El problema es que no nos gustan los mismos programas. The problem is that we don't like the same programmes.

This question could be asked in the conversation section of the exam.

Worked example

SPEAKING TRACK 35 · **Target grade 1-9**

Listen to the recording

¿Qué te gusta ver en la televisión?

Me gustan las comedias y los programas de música.

Aiming Higher Siempre veo los programas de deporte. A veces veo las noticias para ver qué pasa en el mundo y anoche vi una película de acción con mi padre. Esta noche voy a ver un documental sobre la historia de la música rock.

Aiming higher

The first response in the Worked example is a good Foundation tier answer. It would be credited for being relevant and clear to understand.

The second response is a great Higher tier answer. It would be credited for being relevant and easy to understand, with developed ideas, a wide range of vocabulary and more complex language, such as successful use of past, present and future time frames, and consistently accurate use of language.

Now try this

LISTENING TRACK 36 · **Target grade 7**

Listen to the recording

You hear Cris and Gaby talking about what to watch. Complete the sentences by writing the correct letters in the boxes.

1 Cris wants to watch …

A	an action movie.
B	a comedy film.
C	a sci-fi adventure.

☐ **(1 mark)**

2 Gaby wants to watch …

A	a cooking programme.
B	a dance show.
C	a drama series.

☐ **(1 mark)**

Digital resources

The cinema

¿Quieres ir al cine?

la acción	action	la entrada	ticket
el actor	actor (m)	la estrella	star
la actriz	actor (f)	famoso/a	famous
el amor	love	el final	ending
gracioso/a	funny	el papel	role
divertido/a	fun, enjoyable	la película	film
		el precio	price
de miedo	frightening	el premio	prize, award
la bebida	drink	el principio	beginning
el cine	cinema	costar	to cost
la historia	story, history	ganar	to win
		la aventura	adventure
emocionante	exciting	el sonido	sound

¿Te gusta ir al cine?
Do you like going to the cinema?

Role play: asking questions

In the role play, one of the five tasks at both Foundation and Higher is a question. This is made clear by a question mark in the margin (?) and the task tells you to ask your friend a question about something.

Here are some useful questions about:

- what someone likes: ¿Te gusta(n) ... ? Do you like ... ?
- what someone thinks about something: ¿Qué piensas de ... ? What do you think of ... ?
- the opinion someone has about something: ¿Cuál es tu opinión de ... ? What is your opinion of ... ?
- what a person/place/thing is like: ¿Cómo es / son ... ? What is / are ... like?

¡Me encanta ir al cine!
I love going to the cinema!

Worked example

 SPEAKING TRACK 37

 Target grade 1-5

Role play

You are with a friend. Your teacher will play the part of your friend and will speak first. You should address your friend as **tú**.

Listen to the recording

When you see a question mark (?) in the margin you will have to ask a question.

Teacher: ¿Qué quieres hacer este fin de semana?

1 Say when you want to go to the cinema.
Quiero ir al cine el sábado.

Teacher: ¿Qué tipo de películas te gusta?

2 Say what type of films you prefer?
Prefiero las películas de acción.

Teacher: Muy bien. ¿A qué hora prefieres ir?

3 Say what time you want to go.
Vamos a las ocho.

Teacher: De acuerdo. ¿Dónde vamos a comer?

4 Say where you want to eat.
Quiero comer en un restaurante.

Teacher: Yo también.

? – 5 Ask a question about food.
¿Te gusta la comida mexicana?

Teacher: Sí, mucho.   **(10 marks)**

Now try this

 LISTENING TRACK 38

 Target grade 7

You hear Hugo talking about a film he wants to see. What **three** things does he mention?

Listen to the recording

Write the correct letters in the boxes.

A	It's the director's first film.
B	It has won a prize.
C	The main character is a woman.
D	The star of the film is from Chile.
E	The film is based on historical events.
F	The film is a comedy.

☐ ☐ ☐

(3 marks)

What's the story?

Digital resources

¿De qué se trata … ?

la historia	story
la novela	novel
el papel	role
el personaje	character
principal	main
el final	ending
el principio	beginning
la serie	series
seguir	to follow
el evento	event
la obra	play
tratar(se) de	to be about
verdadero/a	true
el título	title
contar	to tell
ocurrir	to happen, occur

La historia empieza cuando …
The story begins when …

Tiene un final feliz / triste.
It has a happy / sad ending.

La película / la novela trata de …
The film / novel is about …

Se trata de … It's about …

The present continuous

Grammar page 104

This tense is used to describe what is happening right now. It is essential for describing a picture in your Speaking or Reading exam.

		present tense of estar	+	present participle
I		estoy		hablando (speaking)
you		estás		
he / she / it		está	+	
we		estamos		comiendo (eating)
you		estáis		
they		están		

Add -ando for -ar verbs

Add -iendo for -er / -ir verbs

Está trabajando.   She is working.
Están viendo.   They are watching.
Estoy leyendo. (irregular) I am reading.

Tiene un final muy triste.
It has a really sad ending.

Worked example

  Target grade 7

Read this review of a film.

★★★☆☆

La película trata de un joven español, Mario, que está trabajando durante el verano en una biblioteca en Buenos Aires. Una actriz famosa entra para esconderse de unos aficionados que están siguiéndola. Mario no la reconoce, porque no ha visto muchas películas argentinas, y la actriz disfruta hablando con él porque la trata como a una persona normal y no como a una estrella. Así empieza esta historia de amor.

Answer the following questions **in English**.

1 Where has Mario got a summer job?   (1 mark)
in a library in Buenos Aires

2 Why does the actor go into the building?   (1 mark)
to hide from fans who are following her

3 Why doesn't Mario recognise her?   (1 mark)
He hasn't seen many Argentinian films.

4 Why does she enjoy talking to Mario?   (1 mark)
He treats her like a normal person,
not like a star.

5 What type of film is it?   (1 mark)
a love story

Exam alert

Giving complete answers

It is always worth giving a full answer if you know all the details rather than risk losing a mark by missing out information that you know.

You can use different words to communicate the correct answer. For example, in Question 2, you could write 'To get away from fans chasing her', and that would also be correct.

Now try this

SPEAKING Target grade 4-9

Háblame de tu película favorita.
¿De qué se trata?

Questions like this could arise in the general conversation section of the Speaking exam.

Digital resources

Everyday life

Un día típico

coger el autobús	to catch the bus
despertarse (ie)	to wake up
dormirse	to fall asleep
escuchar música	to listen to music
hablar	to speak
hacer los deberes	to do homework
ir a la cama	to go to bed
jugar a los videojuegos	to play videogames
lavarse	to have a wash
levantarse	to get up
salir de casa	to leave the house
tomar el desayuno	to have breakfast
ver la televisión	to watch television
vestirse (i)	to get dressed
acostarse	to go to bed

Radical-changing verbs

Grammar page 100

The following spelling changes affect certain verbs in the present tense.

	e → ie querer – to want, love	o → ue mostrar – to show	e → i pedir – to ask for
I	quiero	muestro	pido
you	quieres	muestras	pides
he / she / it	quiere	muestra	pide
we	queremos	mostramos	pedimos
you	queréis	mostráis	pedís
they	quieren	muestran	piden

The **endings** are exactly the same as regular verbs; it is only the **stem** that is affected.

Flexible phrases

Normalmente durante la semana, … .
Normally during the week, … .

Los sábados, suelo … .
On Saturdays, I usually … .

Sin embargo, el fin de semana pasado … .
However, last weekend … .

Depende. It depends.

Suelo is actually a verb and is always followed by the infinitive.

Por las tardes, **suelo jugar** juegos en mi móvil.
In the evenings I **usually play** games on my phone.

Worked example

 SPEAKING TRACK 39

Target grade 1-9

Listen to the recording

¿Cómo es un día típico en tu casa?

Tomo el desayuno a las ocho y voy al instituto a las nueve. Vuelvo a casa a las cuatro, ceno con la familia y hago mis deberes. Voy a la cama a las diez.

This answer is accurate and shows a good range of verbs including the irregular **hago** and the stem changing **vuelvo**.

Aiming Higher

Depende. Durante la semana me levanto a las siete, pero los fines de semana suelo dormir hasta las diez. Si voy al instituto, salgo de casa sobre las ocho para llegar a las ocho y media. Las clases terminan a las tres. Normalmente tomo un bocadillo porque no cenamos hasta las siete. Hago los deberes antes de cenar y, después, leo o veo la tele.

This response shows ways of extending sentences (**pero …**), reasons (**porque …**) and sequences (**antes, después**). It has some more unusual vocabulary (**depende, suelo**) and good use of infinitives (**para +** infinitive, **antes de** + infinitive).

Now try this

 LISTENING TRACK 40

Target grade 5

Listen to the recording

Paula is talking about her sister's day. What does she say? Answer in **English**.   **(4 marks)**

1 At what time did Andrea wake up?
2 What did she do immediately afterwards?
3 What did she leave without?
4 What did she realise when she got to school?

Meals at home

Comer en casa

el agua (f)	water
el café	coffee
el desayuno	breakfast
el pescado	fish
el pollo	chicken
grande	big
la bebida	drink
la carne	meat
la cena	evening meal
la comida	meal, food, lunch
la ensalada	salad
las verduras	vegetables
ligero/a	light
pequeño/a	small
beber	to drink
comer	to eat
hacer	to make, do
preparar	to prepare
cocinar	to cook
el arroz	rice

Describing when

por la mañana	in the morning
por las tardes	in the afternoons / evenings
durante la semana	during the week
los fines de semana	at weekends
los domingos	on Sundays

Telling the time

Grammar page 117

- To say 'it is' + o'clock:
  es la una, son las dos, son las nueve, son las diez
- To say 'at' + time:
  a las doce, a la una
- If it's minutes **past** the hour, add:
  y cinco, y diez, y cuarto, y veinte, y veinticinco, y media
- If it's minutes **to** the hour, add:
  menos cinco, menos diez, menos cuarto, etc.

Son las doce y media.	It's half past twelve.
A la una y diez.	At ten past one.
Son las diez menos cuarto.	It's a quarter to ten.
Sobre las seis.	At about six.

Los domingos comemos en casa de mis abuelos.
On Sundays we have lunch at my grandparents' house.

Worked example

  WRITING · Target grade 1-5

What is in the photo? Write **five** short sentences in **Spanish**. **(10 marks)**

1 Hay cuatro personas.
2 Están los padres y los hijos.
3 La familia está en la cocina.
4 Están comiendo pollo y ensalada.
5 Son felices.

Concentrate on making the sentences clear and accurate. It's nice to use different verbs, but for this type of question, if you're stuck, you can reuse **hay**. You don't need to write much – the instruction says 'short sentences'.

Now try this

  WRITING · Target grade 1-5

Write an email to your Spanish friend about meals at home.

Write approximately **50** words in **Spanish**. You must write something about each bullet point.
You must include the following points:

- meal times
- where you eat
- who prepares the meals
- what you eat
- a meal you don't like.

(10 marks)

Digital resources

Celebrations

¿Cómo celebras las ocasiones especiales?

el baile	dance
el cumpleaños	birthday
la canción	song
la tarjeta	card
organizar una fiesta	to organise a party
preparar una comida	to prepare a meal
recibir	to receive
sacar una foto	to take a photo
salir a cenar	to go out to eat
abrir	to open
bailar	to dance
cantar	to sing
celebrar	to celebrate
comprar regalos	to buy presents
invitar a la familia	to invite the family
la ocasión	occasion

Saqué una foto de la cena.
I took a photo of the meal.

Asking questions

Grammar page 115

Most question words are invariable (they don't change).

¿Qué?	What?
¿Cuándo?	When?
¿Dónde?	Where?
¿Por qué?	Why?
¿Cómo?	How?

Some have plural forms:

¿Quién / Quiénes?	Who?
¿Cuánto/a?	How much?
¿Cuántos/as?	How many?
¿Cuál / Cuáles?	Which (one, ones)?

Notice the word order:

¿Qué hace Daniel?	What is Daniel doing?
¿Dónde vive tu amigo?	Where does your friend live?

Also notice that all question words have an accent on them.

Worked example

WRITING

Target grade 4-9

You are writing an email to your friend about a special occasion that you are planning.
Write approximately **90** words in **Spanish**.
You must write something about each bullet point.
Mention:
• what you think about the occasion
• how you celebrated last time
• what you are planning this time.   **(15 marks)**

El mes próximo es el cumpleaños de mi padre. Va a tener cincuenta años así que es un día especial y va a ser muy emocionante. El año pasado salimos a cenar a un restaurante, pero esta vez vamos a organizar una fiesta en casa. Vamos a preparar una gran cena y mi madre va a hacer toda su comida favorita. Invitaremos a mis tíos y a mis abuelos. Yo voy a hacerle una tarjeta y todos vamos a comprarle regalos.

You do not have to write the same amount on each bullet point but you **must** cover all three bullet points in order to access the full range of marks.

Exam alert

Question 1 on the Higher Writing paper includes past, present and future tenses, so make sure you are confident with these.

It also requires you to express an opinion, so you will need to know a range of adjectives and expressions of liking and disliking.

Here, the adjectives are especial (special) and emocionante (exciting).

Now try this

SPEAKING TRACK 41

Target grade 1-5

Listen to the questions about celebrations and special occasions and pause after each one to give yourself time to answer.

Listen to the recording

You might meet questions like these in the general conversation which follows the discussion of the photo card in the exam.

Customs and festivals

Digital resources

Las fiestas en España y Sudamérica

el pueblo	village
la comunidad	community
la cultura	culture
el concierto	concert
el puesto	stall
la fiesta	festival, party
la plaza	square
el espectáculo	show
alegre	lively, happy
al aire libre	in the open air, outdoors
el desfile	parade
el disfraz	costume, fancy dress
los fuegos artificiales	fireworks
la Nochevieja	New Year's Eve
las Fallas	The Fallas festival
la Tomatina	The Tomatina festival
El Día de Muertos	Day of the Dead
El Día de Reyes	Epiphany, 6th January
Semana Santa	Easter week
atraer	to attract

Using se to form the passive

Grammar page 116

The passive in English consists of the verb 'to be' followed by a **past participle**. For example:

Eggs **are sold** on the market.
Music **will be played** during the parade.

One of the most common forms of the passive in Spanish is to use se with the appropriate person and tense of the verb.

Se venden huevos en el mercado.
Eggs are sold on the market.
Se tocará música durante el desfile.
Music will be played during the parade.
Se preparó la paella al aire libre.
The paella was prepared outdoors.

En la ciudad de Córdoba, los patios se llenan de flores.
In the city of Córdoba, the patios **are filled** with flowers.

Worked example

 READING   Target grade 6

You read this description of the Fallas festival on a visitor website.

> Las fallas son figuras que se diseñan y se construyen poco a poco durante todo el año. Representan personas famosas o historias antiguas; algunas son divertidas, pero todas son hermosas y artísticas. Los cientos de fallas se ponen en las calles de Valencia durante las primeras semanas de marzo. El diecinueve de marzo, se queman todas las fallas entre las diez y las once de la noche. Es un espectáculo de fuegos artificiales. La fiesta empezó como una celebración de la llegada de la primavera.

Which **three** statements are correct? Write the correct letters in the boxes. The *fallas* …

A	do not take long to make.	D	appear on the streets on March 19.
B	are sometimes amusing.	E	are burned at midnight.
C	often represent celebrities.	F	event was originally a spring festival.

[B] [C] [F]

(3 marks)

Now try this

 SPEAKING   Target grade 1-9

¿Qué piensas de las fiestas españolas?

You might be asked a question like this in the general conversation section of the Speaking exam. Think how you would answer it.

Digital resources

Spanish festivals

Las fiestas españolas

los fuegos artificiales	fireworks
la música	music
el baile	dance
la Nochevieja	New Year's Eve
la uva	grape
los Sanfermines	San Fermín festival
la plaza de toros	bullring
los Reyes Magos	the Three Kings
el desfile	parade
el disfraz	costume, fancy dress
los caramelos	sweets
el regalo	gift, present
la suerte	luck
tirar	to throw
la banda	band

 Verbs with an irregular first person singular preterite

Grammar page 105

Some verbs change their spelling in the first person singular of the preterite in order to retain the correct pronunciation and follow usual spelling patterns.

- Verbs that end in -gar:
  llegar → llegué   pagar → pagué
  (The letter 'u' is added to keep the hard 'g' sound.)

- Verbs that end in -car:
  buscar → busqué   tocar → toqué
  ('c' changes to 'qu' to keep the hard 'k' sound.)

- Verbs that end in -zar:
  empezar → empecé   comenzar → comencé
  ('z' changes to 'c' to follow normal spelling patterns.)

Los Reyes Magos llevan disfraces llenos de detalle.
The Three Kings wear costumes full of detail.

Worked example

 READING   **Target grade 6**

Read Leo's account of a local fiesta.

> El cinco de enero cada año, mi familia y yo vamos a ver el desfile de los Reyes Magos cuando pasan por el pueblo. Llegan en barco al puerto por la tarde y mientras suben la calle hasta el centro, forman una larga procesión con música y baile. Los tres reyes, vestidos con disfraces estupendos, tiran caramelos para los pequeños y los niños corren a recogerlos.

Answer the questions in **English**.

1 When does Leo watch the festival?

5 January every year

2 Where do the Three Kings arrive?

at the port

3 Where does the procession go?

up the street to the centre

4 How are the Kings dressed?

in lovely costumes

5 What do the Kings do during the parade?

throw sweets for the children

(5 marks)

Now try this

LISTENING   TRACK 42   **Target grade 3**

You hear Laura talking about New Year's Eve. Complete the sentences. Write the correct letter in each box.

Listen to the recording

1 Laura and her family …

A	eat out.
B	play games.
C	visit relatives.

☐

2 At eleven thirty they …

A	go outside.
B	turn off the lights.
C	put the television on.

☐

3 The city squares …

A	are full of people.
B	are lit up.
C	show events on a big screen.

☐

4 At midnight they …

A	sing a traditional song.
B	eat 12 grapes.
C	make a wish.

☐

(4 marks)

Latin American festivals

Digital resources

Unas fiestas de Sudamérica

el disfraz	costume, fancy dress
antiguo/a	old
religioso/a	religious
el espectáculo	show
celebrar	to celebrate
dar gracias a	to give thanks to
durar	to last
estar lleno/a de	to be full of
llevar	to wear, take, carry
permitir	to allow
recordar	to remember
el cultivo	crop
asistir	to attend
crecer	to grow
estar cubierto/a de	to be covered in
ofrecer	to offer

Tuve la suerte de visitar ...
I was lucky enough to visit ...

Expressions with tener

Grammar page 102

There are expressions that in English use 'to be', but in Spanish use the verb tener.

tener suerte	to be lucky
tener calor / frío	to be hot / cold (of a person)
tener hambre	to be hungry
tener sed	to be thirsty
tener razón	to be right / correct

Where 'very' is used in English, mucho/a is used in Spanish.

I am very cold. Tengo mucho frío.
I am very hungry. Tengo mucha hambre.

La gente lleva disfraces.
The people wear costumes.

Worked example

 READING   Target grade 5

Read Javier's account of his visit to friends in México.

El año pasado tuve la suerte de visitar a unos amigos que viven en México durante el Día de Muertos, que la gente celebra el primero de noviembre. La fiesta es para recordar a los seres queridos que han muerto. En la casa pusieron un altar con fotos y velas* en honor de los miembros que la familia ha perdido. Por la tarde llevamos flores al cementerio** y vimos que las calles estaban llenas de gente con disfraces de esqueletos***.

*la vela – candle   **el cementerio – cemetery   ***el esqueleto – skeleton

Complete the sentences. Write the correct letter in each box.

1 The Day of the Dead is ...

A	on 31 October.
B	on 1 November.
C	at the end of November.

B

2 The festival is ...

A	for those who died in wars.
B	held in the local church.
C	for loved ones who have died.

C

3 In the evening they ...

A	took flowers to the cemetery.
B	joined in the parade.
C	looked at old family photos.

A

4 In the streets they saw ...

A	people dancing.
B	people in fancy dress.
C	people selling toys.

B

(4 marks)

Now try this

 LISTENING TRACK 43   Target grade 7-8

Listen to the recording

Lucía is giving a presentation in school about a festival in Perú.
Answer the questions in **English**.

1 What did people do during the festival?
2 How long did the original celebrations last?
3 When is the festival held these days?
4 Approximately how many people attend the event?

(4 marks) **47**

Digital resources

My favourite celebrity

La persona famosa que más me gusta

el actor / la actriz	actor
el / la cantante	singer
el / la jugador(a)	player
la personalidad	personality
el grupo	group
famoso/a	famous
conocido/a	well-known
guapo/a	good looking
el / la seguidor/a	follower
las redes sociales	social networks
el vídeo	video
la película	film
el concierto	concert
la música	music
la letra	lyrics, words
la estrella	star
bailar	to dance
cantar	to sing
estar de moda	to be fashionable
tocar	to play
la banda	band
el / la deportista	sportsperson
el talento	talent

Nationality

Grammar page 95

Many adjectives of nationality end in **-o** in the masculine singular and behave just like normal **-o** type adjectives.

	Singular	Plural
Masculine	chileno	chilenos
Feminine	chilena	chilenas

británico	British
colombiano	Colombian
cubano	Cuban
europeo	European
mexicano	Mexican

The adjective for 'Spanish' behaves differently as it ends in -l.

	Singular	Plural
Masculine	español	españoles
Feminine	española	españolas

También escribe la letra de sus canciones.
She also writes the words of her songs.

Worked example

 LISTENING TRACK 44

 Target grade 6

Natalia is describing a celebrity she admires.

Write
  A if only statement **A** is correct
  B if only statement **B** is correct
  A+B if both statements **A and B** are correct.

Listen to the recording

> La persona famosa que más me gusta es una actriz inglesa de pelo rojo que se hizo famosa en un concurso de talento en la tele. No solo actúa, sino que canta muy bien también y ha sido la estrella de varias películas y obras de teatro musicales.

1 The celebrity …

A	is a blonde actress.
B	was in a TV talent show.

B

(1 mark)

2 The celebrity …

A	is also a good singer.
B	has starred in musical theatre.

A + B

(1 mark)

Useful phrases

Es el cantante principal de una banda.
He is the lead singer of a band.

Toca la guitarra en un grupo de rock.
He / she plays the guitar in a rock group.

Es uno de los mejores jugadores del mundo.
He is one of the best players in the world.

Es una actriz con mucho talento.
She is a very talented actor.

Now try this

 READING

 Target grade 1-5

Translate these sentences into **English**.

1 David es un jugador de fútbol argentino.
2 Mi cantante favorito francés escribe todas sus canciones.
3 Es un actor mexicano muy guapo con muchos seguidores.
4 Me gusta leer la letra cuando veo los vídeos.
5 Es un influencer en las redes sociales españolas.

(10 marks)

Profile of a celebrity

Digital resources

Te presento a ...

el nombre	name
la edad	age
el premio	prize, award
soltero/a	single, unmarried
guapo/a	good-looking
la carrera	career
la entrevista	interview
la estrella	star
la imagen	image
la revista	magazine
la serie	series
el anuncio	advert
el carácter	character, personality
el papel	role
el personaje	character (film, book)
el / la seguidor/a	follower
casarse	to get married
divorciarse	to get divorced
estar casado/a	to be married
grabar	to record, to film
nacer	to be born
presentar	to introduce
separarse	to separate
tener éxito	to be successful

Using the third person preterite and imperfect

Grammar page 105, 106

Use past tenses to describe someone's career and early days.

Use the **preterite** to describe actions that are complete and in the past:

Recibió un premio. She received an award.

The 3rd person endings for the preterite are:

-ar verbs:

-ó (3rd person sing.), -aron (3rd person plural)

-er and -ir verbs

-ió (3rd person sing.), -aron (3rd person plural)

Use the **imperfect** to describe actions that people used to do:

Tenía un papel en una serie de televisión.

He used to play a role in a TV series.

The 3rd person endings for the imperfect are:

-ar verbs:

-aba (3rd person sing.), -aban (3rd person pl.)

-er and -ir verbs

-ía (3rd person sing.), -ían (3rd person pl.)

At Foundation tier, you do not need to know the plural endings for the imperfect tense.

Worked example

  READING · Target grade 6

Read this article about the actress Maribel Verdú.

> Maribel Verdú nació en Madrid en 1970 y es una famosa actriz española. Empezó su carrera como modelo en revistas de deportes y de moda. A la edad de trece años, escogieron a Maribel para hacer un papel en una serie de televisión y desde entonces ha estado en muchas películas. Ha ganado cuatro premios de cine.

What does the article tell us about Maribel? Write the **three** correct letters in the boxes.

A	her partner	D	her acting awards
B	her first job	E	when she was born
C	her hobbies	F	her parents

[B] [D] [E]

(3 marks)

Empezó su carrera como modelo.
She began her career as a model.

Now try this

  LISTENING TRACK 45 · Target grade 6

Julio is talking about his favourite sportsman: Pau Gasol.

Complete the sentences in **English**. Write **one** word in each space.

Listen to the recording

1 Pau was born in the year _____ .

2 Pau's parents played _____

3 He was also interested in _____

4 He initially wanted to be a _____ .

5 He left university to go professional after _____

6 He retired from professional sport in _____ .

7 Marc Gasol is Pau's _____

(7 marks)

Digital resources

Celebrities as role models

¿Es un buen modelo a seguir?

el modelo (a seguir)	role model
el ejemplo	example
rico/a	rich
el dinero	money
famoso/a	famous
joven	young
popular	popular
el público	public
los medios de comunicación	the media
la carrera	career
la entrevista	interview
la estrella	star
la imagen	image
de moda	fashionable
la personalidad	personality
la relación	relationship
el éxito	success
apoyar	to support
ayudar	to help
respetar	to respect

Using de to indicate belonging / possession

In English, we use an apostrophe to indicate possession (for example, 'my friend's group'), but there are no apostrophes in Spanish.

Instead, we would say 'the group of my friend' – el grupo de mi amigo/a.

Some examples are:

la cantante principal de la banda
the band's lead singer

la imagen del jugador the player's image

el éxito del actor the actor's success

Flexible phrases

Lo hizo por una buena causa.
He / She did it for a good cause.

Es un buen / mal ejemplo a seguir.
He / She is a good / bad role model.

Worked example

LISTENING TRACK 46

Target grade 5

Listen to the recording

Ángela and Jorge are talking about celebrities. Answer the following questions in **English**.

1 What example of good behaviour does Jorge mention?

giving money to the poor (1 mark)

2 What does he think is a bad example?

taking drugs (1 mark)

3 What does Ángela describe as a negative example?

smoking (1 mark)

4 What positive example does she give?

helping good causes (1 mark)

> **Jorge:** Un ejemplo de buen comportamiento es cuando una persona famosa da dinero a la gente pobre. Si los famosos toman drogas, entonces dan un mal ejemplo porque eso es muy peligroso.
>
> **Ángela:** También pueden dar un ejemplo negativo si fuman. Respeto a los famosos que ayudan a las buenas causas porque dan un ejemplo muy positivo.

Notice the different ways of indicating 'good' and 'bad':
good → bueno / positivo / respeto
(respeto = I respect)
bad → malo / negativo / peligroso
(peligroso = dangerous)

La sigo en las redes sociales.
I follow her on social networks.

Now try this

READING

Target grade 5-9

Translate these sentences into **English**.

1 Muchas personalidades famosas son excelentes modelos a seguir para los jóvenes.

2 Un jugador de fútbol español ayudó a sus vecinos después de un desastre natural.

3 Conozco a una cantante colombiana que ayuda a los niños pobres.

4 Son ejemplos muy buenos y merecen nuestro respeto.

5 Hay otros que tienen una imagen negativa en los medios de comunicación.

(10 marks)

TV reality shows

Digital resources

¿Qué piensas de los programas de telerrealidad?

el concurso	competition
el / la cantante	singer
la carrera	career
los medios de comunicación	the media
el programa	programme
el espectáculo	show
el público	public
el apoyo	support, backing
la relación	relationship
buscar	to seek, look for
ganar	to win, earn
preferir	to prefer
querer	to want
votar	to vote
el talento	talent
enamorarse (de)	to fall in love (with)

Some irregular verbs in the preterite tense

Just like in English, there are a number of verbs that have an irregular pattern in the preterite. Here are six of them:

hacer (to do, make)	tener (to have)	poner (to put)
hice	tuve	puse
hiciste	tuviste	pusiste
hizo	tuvo	puso
hicimos	tuvimos	pusimos
hicisteis	tuvisteis	pusisteis
hicieron	tuvieron	pusieron
traer (to bring)	**venir** (to come)	**querer** (to want)
traje	vine	quise
trajiste	viniste	quisiste
trajo	vino	quiso
trajimos	vinimos	quisimos
trajisteis	vinisteis	quisisteis
trajeron	vinieron	quisieron

Don't be put off by the irregular verbs. Each has a stem that stays the same (apart from one in hacer) and all share the same set of endings.

Worked example

 LISTENING TRACK 47

 Target grade 4

Martina, Toni and Isabel are talking about different TV reality series. Which show is each one describing? Write the correct letter in the boxes.

– Hola. Soy Martina. En la tele hay una serie sobre un grupo de jóvenes que pasan tiempo en una isla buscando el amor e intentando crear una relación con una de las otras personas.

– Me llamo Toni. Anoche tuvieron que preparar dos tipos de pan. Uno olvidó la sal completamente, y otro puso azúcar en lugar de sal. Horrible.

– Soy Isabel. Reciben consejos de cantantes profesionales y luego cantan. El público vota al artista que le gusta más.

Muchos cantantes buscan una carrera en la industria musical.

Many singers are seeking a career in the music industry.

A	a cooking competition
B	a painting competition
C	a singing contest
D	arranging a wedding
E	finding love on an island
F	learning to dance

Listen to the recording

Now try this

 LISTENING TRACK 48

 Target grade 7

Isabel is talking about TV reality shows. Complete the sentences in **English**. Write one word in each space.

Listen to the recording

1 Some reality show contestants manage to be _____ in the _____ . **(2 marks)**

2 To win a singing contest, a lot depends on getting the _____ of the _____ . **(2 marks)**

Martina ☐ E ☐ Toni ☐ A ☐ Isabel ☐ C ☐ **(3 marks)**

Digital resources

The good and the bad of being famous

Lo bueno y lo malo de ser famoso

el dinero	money
rico/a	rich
la entrevista	interview
el periodista	journalist
el periódico	newspaper
la revista	magazine
la imagen	image
las noticias	news
la ropa	brand, make
la marca	clothes
el premio	prize, award
el comportamiento	behaviour
la ventaja	advantage
la desventaja	disadvantage
hacer fotos	to take photos
tener cuidado	to be careful
la prensa	the press
el diseño	design
la vida privada	private life
el beneficio	benefit

Revising object pronouns – him, her, it, them

Grammar page 99

- If you want to refer to 'him' or 'it' use lo.

  El cantante es famoso ahora. Lo vi en una revista.

  The singer is famous now. I saw **him** in a magazine.

  La actriz ganó un premio. Lo recibió en una ceremonia ayer.

  The actor won an award. She received **it** in a ceremony yesterday.

- For feminine singular (her, it) use la.

  ¿La viste en esa serie?

  Did you see **her** in that series?

  Es una película genial. La vi ayer.

  It's a great film. I saw **it** yesterday.

- For masculine plural (them) use los and for feminine plural (them) use las.

  Son chicos simpáticos y los respeto.

  They are nice boys and I respect **them**.

  Estas son mis bandas favoritas; las veo en YouTube.

  These are my favourite bands; I watch **them** on YouTube.

Worked example

 TRACK 49

 Target grade 5-9

Role play

¿Cuál es tu persona famosa favorita?

Listen to the recording

1 Say which famous person you like. (Give **one** detail.)

Me gusta mucho el jugador de fútbol, Marcus Rashford.

¿Por qué te gusta?

2 Say why they are a good role model. (Give **two** details.)

Intenta ayudar a otras personas, especialmente a los niños.

¿Cuáles son las ventajas de ser famoso?

3 Give **two** advantages of being famous.

Puedes comprar lo que quieres y tener muchas vacaciones.

¿Y las desventajas?

4 Give **two** disadvantages of being famous.

La prensa te sigue y es difícil tener una vida privada.

? – 5 Ask a question about being famous.

¿Te gustaría ser famoso?

No, no me gustaría nada.

Now try this

 READING

 Target grade 6

You read this article about being famous.

No me gustaría nada ser famosa; es demasiada presión. Cada vez que sales de casa tienes que estar perfecta. Tienes que pensar en cada aspecto de tu ropa, tu pelo y tu maquillaje*.

Todo el mundo quiere tocarte y hacer fotos, y tienes que sonreír y aceptar todo. No está permitido estar de mal humor ni decir "déjame en paz". Lo odiaría.

*maquillaje – make-up

Complete these sentences. Write the letter for the correct option in each box.

1 The writer thinks being famous is …

 A great. B stressful. C boring. ☐

2 You always have to think about your …

 A appearance. B fans. C behaviour. ☐

3 You always have to be …

 A funny. B calm. C cheerful. ☐

(3 marks)

Plans for the holidays

Digital resources

¿Cuáles son tus planes para las vacaciones?

Voy a …	I am going to
Tengo (la) intención de …	I intend to
Espero …	I hope to …
leer más	read more
ir a la piscina al aire libre	go to the open-air pool
descansar	rest
salir con mis amigos	go out with friends
salir en bicicleta	go out on my bike
levantarme tarde	get up late
visitar a familia	visit family
hacer camping	go camping
ir a un festival de música	go to a music festival
jugar al fútbol	play football
trabajar en un café	work in a café
ir de excursión a …	go on a trip to …
pasar una semana en …	spend a week in …

Plurals of nouns

Grammar page 94

The basic rule for making nouns plural is very straightforward:

add -s to a vowel
sitio → sitios, biblioteca → bibliotecas
add -es to a consonant
plan → planes, ciudad → ciudades

Final z – changes to a c before adding -es
vez → veces, actriz → actrices

-ón at the end of a noun – remove the accent
excursión → excursiones, millón → millones

Las vacaciones de verano son una buena oportunidad para descansar y leer más. The summer holidays are a good opportunity to rest and read more.

Worked example

 SPEAKING TRACK 50

 Target grade 1-9

¿Qué vas a hacer durante las vacaciones de verano este año?

Listen to the recording

Creo que seguiré trabajando en el café los fines de semana, y posiblemente otros días si me necesitan. Es una buena oportunidad de ganar un poco de dinero. No voy de vacaciones con mis padres, pero saldré con mis amigos y esperamos ir al festival de música en agosto.

Flexible phrases

Normalmente no tengo tiempo, pero durante las vacaciones …
Normally I don't have time, but during the holidays …

Las vacaciones son una buena oportunidad para …
The holidays are a good opportunity to …

You could be asked a question like this in the conversation part of your Speaking exam.

 This student is working at around a Grade 7.

 seguiré trabajando is a Higher tier expression that will impress. It uses the verb **seguir** plus the present participle (**-ando / -iendo**). It means 'to carry on / keep on …ing'. So here, it means 'I will carry on working'.

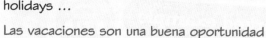

Now try this

 WRITING

 Target grade 1-5

Write an article about somewhere you like to go in the school holidays.

Write approximately **50** words in **Spanish**.

You must write something about each bullet point. Mention:

- a description of the place
- when you go
- your opinion of the place
- who you go with
- what else you do during the holidays.

(10 marks)

Had a look ☐　Nearly there ☐　Nailed it! ☐

Holiday preferences

 Digital resources

¿Adónde prefieres ir?

el campo	country(side)
el país	country
en el / al extranjero	abroad
la costa	coast
la playa	beach
las montañas	mountains
la ciudad	the city
el viaje	journey
España	Spain
Sudamérica	South America
pasar	to spend
viajar	to travel
el destino	destination
la arena	sand

For Foundation tier, you only need the first three parts of the tense.

The conditional

Grammar page 108

You use the conditional to say what you would do. You can form it in Spanish by adding these endings to the infinitive:

Endings	Examples	
ía	hablaría	I would speak
ías	viajarías	you (sing.) would travel
ía	vería	he / she would see
íamos	comeríamos	we would eat
íais	viviríais	you (plural) would live
ían	recibirían	they would receive

When 'would' really means 'used to' then use the imperfect.

Cuando era pequeño, íbamos a la costa.

When I was little, we **would** / **used to** go to the coast.

Some verbs have an irregular stem in the conditional; these are listed on page 108.

Me encantaría viajar por Sudamérica. I would love to travel through South America.

Worked example

TRACK 51

Target grade 3

Paula is talking about holidays. Which **three** places would she like to visit?

Listen to the recording

Write the correct letters in the boxes.

En primavera me gustaría ir a las montañas porque las vistas son bonitas. En otoño, lo ideal sería ir a la costa porque hay menos gente que en verano. Este invierno, me encantaría ir al sur de España. Allí, las temperaturas son bastante altas en diciembre y tienen muchos días de sol.

A	city	D	mountains
B	coast	E	south America
C	countryside	F	south of Spain

☐ B ☐ D ☐ F **(3 marks)**

Now try this

LISTENING TRACK 51

Target grade 3

Listen to the recording again and complete the sentences. Write the correct letter in each box.

 Listen to the recording

1 Paula wants to go to the mountains because …

A	she likes skiing.
B	the views are lovely.
C	it is so peaceful.

☐

2 The coast is ideal in autumn because …

A	it is a little cooler.
B	hotels are cheaper.
C	there are fewer people.

☐

3 The south of Spain is a good choice in winter because …

A	there is so much to do.
B	the weather is warm.
C	there are good deals on flights.

☐

(3 marks)

As you listen, you can tick the options that you think are correct. Then at the end of the recordings, you can make your final decision and complete the boxes.

Types of holidays

¿Qué tipo de vacaciones te gusta?

el campo	country(side)
el sol	sun
la playa	beach
cultural	cultural
la cultura	culture
activo/a	active
la actividad	activity
tranquilo/a	peaceful, quiet
el mar	sea
la piscina	swimming pool
el edificio	building
antiguo/a	old, ancient
histórico/a	historic
el museo	museum
la arquitectura	architecture
la fiesta	festival
la tradición	tradition
el arte	art
la fiesta	festival
hacer camping	to go camping
probar	to try, taste, sample
tomar el sol	to sunbathe
relajante	relaxing

Giving reasons and justifications

Whether you are speaking or writing in Spanish, you will be credited for developing your answers and for giving reasons for your opinions and statements.

Use the following connectors to introduce your reasons:

- **porque** (because)

  Me gustan las vacaciones activas **porque** es aburrido si tomas el sol todo el tiempo.

  I like active holidays **because** it's boring if you sunbathe all the time.

- **dado que** (given that)

  Dado que estudio historia y dibujo, me gustan más las vacaciones culturales.

  Given that I study history and art, I like cultural holidays best.

This is part of a typical writing task on both the Foundation and Higher papers. The full task includes three bullet points and you need to write a total of about 90 words.

Worked example

Target grade **5**

You are writing an email to your friend about holidays.

You **must** write something about each bullet point.

Mention:

- your favourite type of holiday
- what you did during your last holiday.

Prefiero pasar las vacaciones en un país donde hace bastante calor porque puedes hacer muchas actividades diferentes, sin el problema del mal tiempo.

Sobre todo me encanta nadar en el mar. El año pasado fui a la costa en el sur de mi país y visitamos unos pueblos y un castillo antiguo. También jugamos al tenis y fuimos a la playa.

Me encanta aprender sobre las tradiciones y fiestas de otro país. I love learning about the traditions and festivals of a different country.

Note that the responses to both bullet points contain an explanation or reason for the preference stated. The word **porque** is used to introduce the reasons.

Now try this

Target grade **5**

This is the remaining bullet point in the task given in the worked example. Write approximately 30 words to complete this part of the task:

- a holiday activity you would like to try in the future.

Digital resources

Where to stay

¿Dónde vas a quedarte?

el alojamiento	accommodation
el baño	bathroom, bath
el camping	campsite, camping
la estrella	star
la habitación	room
las instalaciones	facilities
limpio/a	clean
la maleta	suitcase
vistas (a)	view (of)
decidir	to decide
escoger	to choose
esperar	to wait, hope
llegar	to arrive
quedarse	to stay (accommodation)
alquilar	to hire, rent
el ascensor	lift
el lujo	luxury

Using different tenses in speaking and writing tasks

Grammar pages 100, 105, 107

Certain tasks in the exam require the **present tense only**:

- the four follow-up questions for the reading aloud task
- the Foundation role play
- the photo card at Foundation tier
- Foundation writing Questions 1 and 2.

Future time frames are needed in other speaking and writing tasks. You can use:

- the future tense
- the immediate future
- verbs in the present tense that express future ideas: espero + infinitive (I hope to), tengo (la) intención de + infinitive (I intend to), me gustaría + infinitive (I would like to).

The most important **past tense** is the preterite but at Higher tier you could demonstrate your range of language by using the perfect and imperfect tenses too.

Listening and Reading tasks may feature all these three forms of the past tense at both tiers.

Un piso en la costa. An apartment on the coast.

Worked example

 READING   Target grade **6**

Read Marta's email.

> Acabamos de volver de las vacaciones en la costa. El hotel estaba muy limpio y teníamos dos habitaciones muy cómodas con vistas al mar. También había un concurso de baloncesto para los jóvenes y un club para los niños con actividades organizadas cada día. Por eso, mi marido y yo logramos descansar al lado de la piscina, sabiendo que nuestros hijos estaban seguros y contentos también. Pasamos dos semanas muy felices.

Complete these sentences. Write the correct letter in each box.

1 The hotel was …

A	clean.
B	huge.
C	excellent.

A

2 The rooms were …

A	spacious.
B	comfortable.
C	next to each other.

B

3 The rooms overlooked the …

A	sea.
B	gardens.
C	pool.

A

4 For teenagers, there was a …

A	nightclub.
B	basketball competition.
C	games room.

B

(4 marks)

Now try this

READING Target grade **1-5**

Translate these sentences into **English**.

1 Las instalaciones en el hotel son geniales.
2 Nuestra habitación tiene vistas a las montañas.
3 Decidimos quedarnos en un piso.
4 Había una piscina y un centro de deportes.
5 Vamos a escoger un hotel de tres estrellas.

(10 marks)

Booking accommodation

Digital resources

¿Quiere reservar una habitación?

¿cuándo?	when?
¿cuánto/a/os/as?	how much / many?
el hotel	hotel
el piso	apartment
la habitación	room
para	for
la noche	night
el desayuno	breakfast
la cena	evening meal
la maleta	suitcase
con vistas a	with a view of
la piscina	swimming pool
la playa	beach
cerca de	near to, close to
al lado de	next to
abrir	to open
el ascensor	lift

Quisiera reservar …
I would like to book / reserve …

¿A qué hora se abre … ?
What time does … open?

a + el / de + el

Grammar page 94

When you use a (at / to) and it is followed by the masculine singular definite article el, then the two combine to form al.

Llegamos al hotel a las cuatro.
We arrived **at the** hotel at four o'clock.

Fuimos al restaurante del hotel.
We went **to the** hotel restaurant.

A similar thing also happens when de (of / from) is followed by el.

Las habitaciones del hotel son cómodas.
The rooms **of the** hotel are comfortable.

La distancia del hotel al mar no es un problema.
The distance **from the** hotel to the sea is not a problem.

This only happens with these two particular combinations.

Buenos días. ¿En qué puedo ayudarle?
Good morning. How can I help you?

Worked example

 LISTENING TRACK 52

 Target grade 4

Listen to the recording

Rosalía is booking a hotel room. What does she say? Write the correct letter in each box.

– Buenos días. ¿En qué puedo ayudarle?
– Quisiera reservar una habitación para dos noches.
– Muy bien. ¿Quiere desayuno?
– Sí, pero salgo a cenar con amigos.
– De acuerdo. ¿Quiere una habitación con vistas a los jardines o a la piscina?
– A los jardines. Creo que será más tranquilo.

Don't confuse **dos** and **doce**. There are two syllables with the word **doce** (pronounced 'do-thay').

1 Rosalía wants …

A	a room for 12 nights.
B	a room for 2 nights.
C	two rooms for one night.

☐ B

2 She asks for …

A	bed and breakfast.
B	all meals included.
C	no meals, just the room.

☐ A

3 She wants a view of the …

A	sea.
B	pool.
C	gardens.

☐ C

(3 marks)

Now try this

 LISTENING TRACK 53

 Target grade 6

Listen to the recording

Continue listening to Rosalía and answer the following questions in **English**.

1 What does Rosalia first want to know?

2 What would she like to do?

3 What does the receptionist offer?

4 What does Rosalía need to know next?

(4 marks)

Digital resources

Holiday activities

¿Qué vamos a hacer hoy?

dar un paseo	to go for a walk, ride
dar un paseo en bicicleta	to go for a bike ride
jugar al fútbol	to play football
jugar al baloncesto	to play basketball
montar a caballo	to go horse riding
nadar	to swim
visitar	to visit
el jardín	garden
el edificio	building
histórico/a	historic
antiguo/a	old, ancient
hacer una excursión	to go on a trip
el barco	boat
la montaña	mountain
el castillo	castle
el mercado	market
la fiesta	festival
el desfile	parade
el espectáculo	show
el baile	dance
el flamenco	flamenco
alquilar	to rent, hire

Using time phrases

Grammar pages 100, 107

Time phrases can help you to identify when something is happening.

Past	
ayer	yesterday
anoche	last night
hace + time	time + ago
recientemente	recently
el año / mes pasado	last year / month
la semana pasada	last week
en el pasado	in the past
Present	
hoy	today
en este momento	at the moment
ahora	now
actualmente	currently, presently
Future	
mañana	tomorrow
esta tarde	this afternoon
este viernes / jueves	this Friday / Thursday
el domingo próximo	next Sunday
en el futuro	in the future

Flexible phrases

Hace dos días fuimos a ... Two days ago we went to ...
Hoy esperamos visitar ... Today we hope to visit ...

Este viernes vamos a ver un espectáculo de baile flamenco.
This Friday we are going to see a flamenco dance show.

Worked example

 READING   Target grade 6

Read Mario's email.

> Lo estamos pasando muy bien aquí en la costa y en este momento estamos tomando el sol en los jardines del hotel. Hace tres días alquilamos un barco para hacer una excursión en el mar. Fue muy divertido. Esta noche vamos a ver un espectáculo de baile aquí en el hotel.

Answer the following questions in **English**.

1 Which activity took place in the past? **(1 mark)**
a boat trip

2 What is Mario doing now? **(1 mark)**
sunbathing

3 What activity is planned for tonight? **(1 mark)**
a dance show

Now try this

 LISTENING TRACK 54   Target grade 5

Listen to the recording

Ana is talking about her holiday. Answer the questions in **English**.
1 When will Ana go to the market?
2 When is Ana going sightseeing?

3 When did Ana watch the festival parades?

(3 marks)

Trips and visits

Digital resources

¿Adónde vas a ir?

reservar	to book, reserve
el billete	ticket (transport)
la entrada	ticket (entry)
el puente	bridge
el castillo	castle
la plaza	square
la isla	island
el puerto	port, harbour
el viaje	journey
la excursión	trip, excursion
¿A qué hora … ?	What time … ?
llegar	to arrive
salir	to leave, go out
tardar + time	to take + time
ver	to see
visitar	to visit
la oficina de turismo	tourist office
cruzar	to cross

Key prepositions

Vocabulary page 118

a (at, to)

Vamos a la plaza. We are going **to** the square.

El concierto es a las ocho.

The concert is **at** eight.

But llegar a = to arrive in

El tren llega a Granada a la una.

The train arrives **in** Granada at one.

en (in, on)

Estamos en la playa. We are **on** the beach.

Comimos en la plaza. We ate **in** the square.

But

Lo compré en el supermercado.

I bought it **at** the supermarket.

So, when we say 'at + a place', 'at' in Spanish is en.

de (of, from)

Este es el tren de Barcelona.

This is the train **from** Barcelona.

Las vistas del puente son increíbles.

The views **from / of** the bridge are incredible.

Worked example

READING   Target grade **3**

Read this advert.

Los viajes en barco para visitar la isla salen del puerto tres veces al día. El viaje dura una hora y se pueden comprar bebidas y bocadillos en el barco. En la isla se puede visitar el antiguo castillo, dar un paseo por el bosque y subir la montaña para ver las hermosas vistas.

Answer the following questions in **English**.

1 How often are the trips to the island?

three times a day

2 Where do the trips leave from?

the port

3 How long is the crossing?

one hour

4 What can you buy if you are hungry?

sandwiches

5 What historic building can you visit?

the castle

6 Where can you walk?

the woods

(6 marks)

Tengo muchas ganas de visitar el famoso castillo en Segovia.

I'm very keen to visit the famous castle in Segovia.

Flexible phrases

Me interesa + infinitive
I'm interested in …

Tengo ganas de + infinitive
I am keen to …

Me gustaría + infinitive
I would like to …

Now try this

WRITING   Target grade **1-5**

Translate the following sentences into **Spanish**.

1 The journey to the island is interesting.
2 The bus arrives in one hour.
3 I love the views from the castle.
4 We have tickets to visit the stadium.
5 Yesterday the boat left at two o'clock.

(10 marks)

59

Digital resources

Giving and asking for directions

Por favor … .

a la derecha	on the right
a la izquierda	on the left
al lado de	next to
antes de	before
después de	after
hasta	up to, as far as
a unos metros	a few metres away
estar cerca (de)	to be near / close (to)
estar lejos (de)	to be far (from)
la esquina	(street) corner
la plaza	square
el puente	bridge
la calle	street
la carretera	road
el final	the end
a pie	walking
bajar	to go down
coger	to catch
continuar	to continue
salir	to leave
seguir	to follow, carry on
subir	to go up
tomar	to take
cruzar	to cross
caminar	to walk

Giving instructions

Grammar page 110

When talking to one person, remove the s from the second person singular of the verb (bajas becomes baja):

Toma la primera calle.	Take the first street.
Cruza el puente.	Cross the bridge.
Sigue esta calle.	Follow this street.
Coge el autobús en la plaza.	Catch the bus in the square.

For irregular imperatives, see page 110.

The plural form has these endings -ad, -ed, -id
-ar verbs ➔ tomad
-er verbs ➔ coged
-ir verbs ➔ seguid

H ONLY

Por favor ¿hay un supermercado por aquí?
Excuse me, is there a supermarket round here?

Useful phrases

¿Por dónde se va a … ?   How do you get to … ?

¿Hay un / una … por aquí?
Is there a … round here?

Por favor ¿sabe dónde está(n) …
Excuse me, do you know where … is / are?

Worked example

LISTENING TRACK 55

Target grade 6

Listen to these directions. Complete the sentences. Choose the correct answer and write the letter in each box.

Listen to the recording

Primero, continúa por esta calle hasta el final. Allí, toma la calle a la derecha.

1 To start with, you should …

A	continue over the bridge.	
B	go to the end of the street.	B
C	take the first road on the left.	

2 Then you need to …

A	take the street to the right.	
B	go straight on.	
C	follow the road to the corner.	A

(2 marks)

Now try this

LISTENING TRACK 56

Target grade 5

Listen to the second part of the directions. Complete the sentences. Choose the correct answer and write the letter in each box.

Listen to the recording

1 What must you do next?

A	Go over the bridge.	
B	Cross the square.	
C	Take the next left.	

2 Where is the library?

A	to the right	
B	in the shopping centre	
C	on the corner	

(2 marks)

Tourist information

¿Qué hay para los turistas?

el plano	(street) plan, map
el sitio de interés	place of interest
el barrio antiguo	the old quarter
la lista	list
el hotel	hotel
el camping	campsite
la estación	station
la excursión	trip
el horario	timetable
la tienda	shop
el centro comercial	shopping centre
la bicicleta	bicycle, bike
la piscina	swimming pool
al aire libre	open air
el público	public
abierto/a	open
cerrado/a	closed
reservar	to book
alquilar	to hire

Using se puede

When you want to ask if something is possible, you can use se puede + infinitive. It is like saying 'Can one … ?' or 'Can you … ?'

¿Se puede coger un tren de aquí a Barcelona?
Can you get a train from here to Barcelona?

¿Se puede alquilar bicicletas en el pueblo?
Can you hire bikes in town?

Se puede ir de excursión a estos sitios.
You can go on a trip to these places.

Se puede usar la piscina del camping de al lado.
You can use the pool in the campsite next door.

Worked example LISTENING TRACK 57 Target grade 6

 Listen to the recording

You hear Paula talking to the assistant in the tourist office. Answer the following questions in **English**.

Paula: Hola. ¿Tienes un plano de la ciudad?
Assistant: Sí, mira. Este plano es el mejor porque tiene una lista de sitios de interés en el otro lado.
Paula: Perfecto. Busco una piscina al aire libre. ¿Se puede usar la piscina en el camping?

1 What docs Paula ask for?   **(1 mark)**
a street map of the city

2 What is good about the one she is given?   **(1 mark)**
It has a list of places of interest.

3 What is Paula trying to find?   **(1 mark)**
an open air pool

Now try this LISTENING TRACK 58 Target grade 6

 Listen to the recording

Listen to the rest of the conversation in the tourist office and answer the questions in **English**.

1 What does the assistant tell Paula about the cost of using the pool?   **(1 mark)**

2 Why is Paula concerned about the pool's location? Give **two** reasons.   **(2 marks)**

3 How can Paula get to the pool?   **(1 mark)**

4 What does the assistant give to Paula?   **(1 mark)**

Digital resources

Tourist attractions

¿Adónde vamos hoy?

el castillo	castle	el arte	art
la isla	island	la arquitectura	architecture
la plaza	square	la plaza de toros	the bullring
la foto	photo		
el espectáculo	show	el río	river
el desfile	parade	el barco	boat
la fiesta	festival, party	el parque temático	theme park
el museo	museum	disfrutar	to enjoy
el concierto	concert	la exposición	display, exhibition
el baile	dance		
el caballo	horse	la fuente	fountain
el edificio	building	el parque acuático	water park
la cultura	culture		

¿Qué hay en la región para …	What is there in the area for …
los turistas?	tourists?
los jóvenes?	young people?
los niños?	children?

Using acabar de + infinitive (H ONLY)

This verb is used in Spanish when, in English, we would say 'has / have just …ed'. Conjugate the verb acabar as usual in the present tense, add de + infinitive.

acabo de llegar	I have just arrived
acabas de comprar	you have just bought
acaba de salir	he / she has just left
acabamos de ver	we have just seen
acabáis de mandar	you have just sent
acaban de dar	they have just given

¿Qué sitios de interés recomiendas? What places of interest do you recommend?

Worked example

  SPEAKING TRACK 59 · Target grade 1-9

¿Qué hay en tu región para los turistas?

Mi ciudad es muy interesante. Se puede visitar el museo y además hay muchos restaurantes y tiendas en el centro.

Listen to the recording

Aiming Higher
Mi ciudad es muy interesante y cuando se pasea por el barrio antiguo, se puede ver que está llena de edificios históricos. Es muy popular entre los turistas porque tiene mucha historia y era una ciudad importante hace varios siglos. Puedo recomendar el museo porque acabo de visitarlo y fue excelente. Además, vale la pena ver el paisaje de la región porque es muy bonito.

This is an example of one question you might be asked during the conversation task in your Speaking exam.

Aiming higher

The conversation which follows the picture task at the end of the Speaking exam is worth 20 of the 50 marks available for this component.

The second response here demonstrates many of the criteria that examiners are looking for in order to award top marks:

- an extended sequence of speech
- development of the conversation
- justification of thoughts and opinions
- reference to events in more than one time frame, which is one way of using more complex language.

Now try this

 SPEAKING · Target grade 1-9

Think about how you would answer this question in the Speaking exam:

Háblame de un sitio interesante que visitaste recientemente.

Remember to try to include the four bullet points in the Aiming higher box.

Holiday problems

Tenemos un problema

el aeropuerto	airport
el vuelo	flight
el baño	bathroom, bath
la comida	food
enojado/a	angry, cross
la maleta	suitcase
frío	cold
limpio/a	clean
sucio/a	dirty
la luz	light
el billete	ticket
la recepción	reception
funcionar	to work, function
pedir	to ask for, order
perder, perderse	to lose, get lost
robar	to steal
romper	to break
tardar	to delay
la llave	key
quejarse (de)	to complain (about)
arreglar	to repair, fix
el retraso	delay

The perfect tense

Grammar page 109

In English, the perfect tense is the past tense that contains 'has' or 'have', for example:

I have listened / we have found / she has broken

The part of the verb that follows 'has' or 'have' is called the **past participle**.

In Spanish, the verb haber is used for 'to have' and is conjugated like this:

he
has
ha **+ past participle**
hemos
habéis
han

> The **past participle** is formed by removing the infinitive ending and adding:
> -ado (to -ar verbs)
> -ido (to -er or -ir verbs)

Put the two verbs together:

he comprado	I have bought
ha comido	he / she has eaten
han salido	they have gone out

For a list of irregular past participles, see page 109.

Worked example

 LISTENING TRACK 60 **Target grade 7**

You hear Sebastián talking about a holiday problem. Complete the sentences and write the correct letter in each box.

Listen to the recording

> Acabo de llegar en el vuelo de Barcelona, y ya han bajado todas las maletas. He esperado hasta el final, pero mis maletas no están. ¿Dónde pueden estar?

1 Sebastián is …

A	at the hotel reception.
B	at the airport.
C	at the police station.

B (1 mark)

2 The problem is that …

A	his rucksack was stolen.
B	he has lost his credit card.
C	his luggage is missing.

C (1 mark)

Este no es el plato que he pedido.
This isn't the meal I have ordered.

Now try this

 LISTENING TRACK 61 **Target grade 7**

You hear Rosalía at the hotel reception. Complete the sentences and write the correct letter in each box.

Listen to the recording

1 Rosalía says that …

A	the bathroom light isn't working.
B	their room needs cleaning today.
C	the chair in their room is broken.

(1 mark)

2 Rosalía would like …

A	room service.
B	a spare key.
C	to book a table.

(1 mark)

Digital resources

Accommodation problems

Quiero hablar con el jefe / la jefa.

la cuenta	bill
la mesa	table
la cama	bed
la ventana	window
el piso	apartment, flat
la habitación	room
el jardín	garden
el patio	patio, yard
el baño	bathroom
limpio/a	clean
sucio/a	dirty
el camping	campsite
el ruido	noise
la vista	view
la falta	lack
el teléfono	phone
la silla	chair
la actividad	activity
la carta	menu, letter
el sitio	place, room
el plato	plate, dish
dormir	to sleep
arreglar	to repair, fix

Pronouns after prepositions

H ONLY

Grammar page 98

When you need a pronoun (e.g. me, him, it, them) after a preposition (e.g. for, with, without), then a special set of pronouns are needed:

mí (me)	nosotros, -as (us)
ti (you)	vosotros, -as (you)
él (him)	ellos (them, masc.)
ella (her)	ellas (them, fem.)
usted (you, formal)	ustedes (you, formal)

Examples

Es para ti.   It's for you.

No voy a ir sin ella.
I won't go without her.

Quiere hablar con nosotros/as.
He / She wants to talk to us.

¿Quieres venir conmigo?
Do you want to come with me?

Note the irregular forms:

conmigo ➡ with me
contigo ➡ with you

¡Quiero hablar con la jefa!
I want to talk to the manager!

Worked example

 READING

 Target grade 6

Read this customer review of a holiday villa.

La casa no era la que pedimos. Era demasiado pequeña para nosotros y no había bastante espacio. Tenía vistas al pueblo, no al mar y, debido a su posición, ni el patio ni el jardín recibían sol durante el día. Tampoco había mucho que hacer para los niños.

What **three** things does the customer complain about? Write the correct letters in the boxes.

A	lack of space
B	noise from local children
C	not having enough to do
D	the apartment's shady position
E	the distance from the town
F	the views over the pool

[A] [C] [D]

(3 marks)

The customer does complain about the view, but not the view of the pool. Don't be misled by the one word **vista**.

Useful phrases

No estamos contentos con el / la / los / las ...
We are not happy with the ...

Hay un problema con el / la / los / las ...
There is a problem with the ...

No es lo que pedimos cuando reservamos.
It's not what we asked for when we booked.

Now try this

 READING

 Target grade 4-9

Translate these sentences into **English.**

1 El piso que alquilamos en la costa era bonito.
2 No había mucho espacio y los dormitorios eran muy pequeños.
3 En el patio, la única mesa estaba sucia.
4 Una de las sillas se rompió cuando me senté en ella.
5 La zona es hermosa, pero no hay mucho que hacer para los turistas.

(10 marks)

Eating out

Digital resources

¿Qué vais a tomar?

la mesa	table
para cuatro personas	for four people
para las ocho	for 8 o'clock
para esta noche / martes	for tonight / Tuesday
al lado de la ventana	by the window
el plato principal	main course
primero	first
segundo	second
el pan	bread
el agua (f)	water
la fruta	fruit
el pescado	fish
la carne	meat
el pollo	chicken
el jamón	ham
las patatas fritas	chips
la hamburguesa	burger
la paella	paella (rice and seafood dish)
la verdura	vegetable
para beber	to drink
reservar	to book
fuera	outside
dentro	inside
el arroz	rice

H ONLY — Irregular preterite verbs

Grammar page 105

The following verbs change their stem from an e to an i in the preterite third person singular and plural:

sentir (to feel) → sintió, sintieron
pedir (to ask for) → pidió, pidieron
seguir (to follow) → siguió, siguieron
repetir (to repeat) → repitió, repitieron
elegir (to choose) → eligió, eligieron
preferir (to prefer) → prefirió, prefirieron

One verb changes an o to a u:
dormir (to sleep) → durmió, durmieron

Some verbs add a y:
leer (to read) → leyó, leyeron
(also construir, caer, creer, sustituir)

The first and second person singular and plural preterite are regular in these verbs.

Agua is feminine but it uses the article for masculine nouns (el). That is because it begins with a stressed a and is difficult to say when it follows la. This happens with other feminine nouns that begin with a stressed a or ha, like el hambre (hunger).

¿Qué quiere tomar?
What would you like?

Worked example

READING — Target grade 2

Read this menu.

> **Menú del Día €16**
> 1º Ensalada mixta
> 2º Hamburguesa (con patatas fritas)
> 3º Fruta
> Pan y agua

Answer the following questions in **English**.

1 What is the first course? **(1 mark)**
mixed salad

2 What is the burger served with? **(1 mark)**
chips / fries

3 What is the third course? **(1 mark)**
fruit

4 What else is included in the price? **(2 marks)**
bread and water

Now try this

SPEAKING — TRACK 62 — Target grade 1-5

Reading aloud

Read aloud the following text in **Spanish**.

> Ayer cené con mi familia en un restaurante. Yo tomé pollo con verduras. Mi hermano escogió una hamburguesa con ensalada. Todos bebimos agua y después tomamos café. La comida estuvo muy rica y bien preparada.

Play the recording to hear four questions in **Spanish** that relate to the topic of **Travel, Tourism and Places of interest**. Try to answer all four questions as fully as you can.

Listen to the recording

(15 marks)

65

Digital resources

Opinions about food

¿Qué tal la comida?

Está muy bueno/a.	It's very good.
Está muy rico/a.	It's very tasty.
Soy vegetariano/a.	I am a vegetarian.
Soy vegano/a.	I am a vegan.
está frío/a	it is cold
está caliente	it is hot
con	with
sin	without
caro/a	expensive
barato/a	cheap
dulce	sweet
tiene …	it has …
demasiado azúcar	too much sugar
demasiada sal	too much salt
disfrutar	to enjoy
probar	to try

More irregular preterite verbs

Here are six more irregular preterite tense verbs.

Grammar page 105

ser and ir	dar	estar
fui	di	estuve
fuiste	diste	estuviste
fue	dio	estuvo
fuimos	dimos	estuvimos
fuisteis	disteis	estuvisteis
fueron	dieron	estuvieron
hacer	**poder**	**decir**
hice	pude	dije
hiciste	pudiste	dijiste
hizo	pudo	dijo
hicimos	pudimos	dijimos
hicisteis	pudisteis	dijisteis
hicieron	pudieron	dijeron

¿Cuáles son los platos veganos?
Which are the vegan dishes?

Don't be put off by the irregular verbs. When you look closely at them, each of them has a stem that stays the same throughout (apart from one in **hacer**) and all of them share the same set of endings.

Worked example

 READING

 Target grade **5**

Read Sara's account of an awkward customer.

Ayer una mujer vino al restaurante donde yo trabajo. Me pidió pescado con patatas fritas y dijo que no tenía mucho tiempo porque tenía que coger un tren. El chef hizo la comida rápidamente y yo la puse en la mesa delante de ella. Entonces, dijo que no quería comerla porque no estaba muy caliente. Luego, salió sin pagar. ¡Algunos clientes son muy difíciles!

Complete the sentences. Write the correct letter in each box.

1 Sara works …

A	as a chef.
B	as a waitress.
C	in customer services.

B **(1 mark)**

2 The customer ordered …

A	fish and chips.
B	a vegan dish.
C	an omelette.

A **(1 mark)**

Now try this

 READING

 Target grade **5**

Read Sara's account again. Write the correct letter in each box.

1 Why was the customer in a hurry?

A	She had to get back to work.
B	She had to get a train.
C	She was going to a concert.

☐ **(1 mark)**

2 What was her reaction to the food?

A	She asked for something else.
B	She sent it back.
C	She refused to eat it.

☐ **(1 mark)**

3 What reason did she give?

A	It was too cold.
B	It wasn't vegan.
C	It wasn't cooked.

☐ **(1 mark)**

The weather

¿Qué tiempo hace?

Hace …	It is …
buen tiempo	good weather
mal tiempo	bad weather
sol	sunny
calor	hot
frío	cold
viento	windy
el grado	degree (temperature)
la temperatura	temperature
el clima	climate
el cielo	sky
gris	grey
el riesgo	risk
la lluvia	rain
fresco/a	cool, fresh
el norte	north
el sur	south
el este	east
el oeste	west
bajar	to go down
llover	to rain
subir	to go up
la nube	cloud

Using hacer in different tenses

The verb hacer is very important when talking about the weather.

If you are talking about an occasion in the past, use the preterite. For example:

Hizo frío ese día. **It was** cold that day.

If you are describing how the weather was when you were doing things, use the imperfect.
For example:

Hacía sol y salimos al campo para pasear.
It was sunny and we went into the country for a walk.

When talking about the future, you could use the future or the immediate future tense.

Mañana hará / va a hacer viento.
Tomorrow **it will be** / **it is going to be** windy.

Hace mucho viento hoy.
It's very windy today.

Worked example

  Target grade 3

Read today's forecast.

A	Mañana habrá cielos grises en el oeste.
B	En el norte va a llover.
C	Hará bastante viento en el este.

Which forecast matches each description?
Write the correct letter in each box.

1 It will be windy.   **C**   **(1 mark)**

2 It will be cloudy.   **A**   **(1 mark)**

3 It will rain.   **B**   **(1 mark)**

Exam alert

Weather expressions are very useful in the picture task if the photo shows an outside scene. Use hace if you want to use one of the expressions with hacer (e.g. hace calor – it is hot).

Use the present continuous with llover (está lloviendo – it is raining).

Now try this

 TRACK 63 Target grade 7

You hear a weather forecast. Answer these questions in **English**.

1 What will the weather be like in Barcelona?   **(2 marks)**
2 What can they expect in Madrid?   **(2 marks)**
3 What will the weather be like on the Islands?   **(2 marks)**

Digital resources

Me and my mobile

¿Podrías vivir sin tu móvil?

el móvil	mobile (phone)
la pantalla	screen
el mensaje	message
la app	app
la cámara	camera
la foto	photo
la dirección	address, direction
la información	information
el juego	game
el vídeo	video
el plano	(street) map
el contacto	contact
bajar	to download
buscar	to look for, search
compartir	to share
escuchar	to listen (to)
hacer / sacar una foto	to take a photo
llamar	to call
mandar	to send
usar	to use

Object pronouns ('it' and 'them')

Grammar page 99

Object pronouns are the little words like 'me', 'you' and 'it' that follow verbs in English:

I bought **it** last week.

I sent **them** to my friend.

To say 'it', use **lo** if 'it' refers to a masculine thing and **la** if 'it' refers to a feminine thing.

For 'them', use **los** if referring to masculine things and **las** if referring to feminine things.

Lo compré.	I bought it. (masculine singular)
La compré.	I bought it. (feminine singular)
Los compré.	I bought them. (masculine plural)
Las compré.	I bought them. (feminine plural)

In Spanish object pronouns go in front of the verb (Lo uso para …) but they can go on the end of an infinitive (Voy a usarlo para …)

Flexible phrases

por un lado	on the one hand
por otro lado	on the other hand
sin embargo	however
aunque	although
por eso	therefore
por muchas razones	for lots of reasons

Uso mi móvil todo el tiempo. Sin embargo, ahora la pantalla está rota. I use my mobile all the time. However, the screen is now broken.

You might be asked questions like this in the general conversation task (after the picture task).

Listen to the recording

Worked example

SPEAKING TRACK 64

Target grade 4-9

Answer the following questions in **Spanish**.

¿Por qué usas tu móvil?

¡Por muchas razones! Lo uso para mandar mensajes a mi familia, llamo a mis amigas y busco información en Internet. También escucho música y miro las redes sociales. Por eso no puedo imaginar la vida sin el móvil.

¿Piensas que el móvil es algo totalmente positivo, entonces?

Pues, por un lado, están todas las ventajas que estaba describiendo. Pero, por otro lado, a veces estoy con mis amigos y nadie habla porque todos estamos mirando la pantalla de nuestros móviles.

You don't have to repeat the question when you begin your answer (e.g. **Uso mi móvil para …**). This response ('For lots of reasons!') is a lively and natural way to start.

Now try this

LISTENING TRACK 65

Target grade 4

You hear Marco talking about mobile phones. Write the correct letter in the box. What feature does he find most useful?

Listen to the recording

A	accessing his emails	C	using the torch
B	getting directions		

☐ (1 mark)

Social media

Digital resources

Las redes sociales

Uso las redes sociales para ...	I use social networks to ...
compartir vídeos y fotos	share videos and photos
conocer a nueva gente	meet new people
quedarme con los amigos	arrange to meet my friends
hablar online	talk online
mandar mensajes	send messages
Para usarlas con seguridad hay que ...	To use them safely, you must ...
proteger tu información personal	protect your personal information
No hay que ...	You must not ...
subir información que debería ser privada	upload information that should be private
compartir tus contraseñas	share your passwords
prestar atención a mensajes horribles.	pay attention to horrible messages.

Object pronouns

Grammar page 99

Spanish	English
me	(to) me
te	(to) you
lo (m)	him, it
la (f)	her, it
le	(to) him, (to) her (to) you (polite singular)
nos	(to) us
os	(to) you (plural)
los (m)	them
las (f)	them
les	(to) them, (to) you (polite plural)

Nos mandó un vídeo. He sent us a video.
Le mostré las fotos.
I showed the photos to him.
Te mandé un mensaje ayer.
I sent you a message yesterday.
Para usarlas con seguridad ...
To use them safely ...

Notice the object pronoun goes on the end of the infinitive here.

Puedes usarlas para compartir vídeos y fotos.
You can use them to share videos and photos.

Worked example

 READING Target grade 7

Read this list of advantages and disadvantages of social networks. Which are the **three disadvantages**? Write the correct letters in the boxes.

A	Conexión con gente de todo el mundo
B	Pueden llegar a ser muy adictivas
C	Permiten conocer opiniones alternativas
D	Tienen un impacto negativo en nuestras emociones
E	Ofrecen oportunidades laborales
F	Riesgo de robo de datos

B D F

(3 marks)

Now try this

 WRITING Target grade 4-9

Translate the following sentences into **Spanish**.

1 I use social networks to download music and to share photos.
2 I understand that it is important to protect my personal information.
3 I never upload things that are private.
4 Yesterday I sent a message to Ana.
5 She often sends me funny videos.

(10 marks)

 Digital resources

The internet

¿Cómo usas Internet?

el artículo	article
el correo electrónico	e-mail
falso/a	false
gratis	free
la imagen	image
la información	information
la página web	web page
el periódico	newspaper
el sitio web	website
el / la seguidor/a	follower
el uso	use
afectar	to affect
apagar	to turn off
enviar	to send
hacer las compras	to do the shopping
reservar	to reserve, book
reconocer	to recognise
el / la usuario/a	user

These phrases are all followed by the infinitive.

Varying your vocabulary

You might need to say how you use the internet and why. It is a good idea to use a variety of phrases:

es bueno para …	it's good for …
es excelente para …	it's excellent for …
es perfecto para …	it's perfect for …
es ideal para …	it's ideal for …
es útil para …	it's useful for …

You can adapt these as follows:

Es ideal cuando quieres buscar información.
It's ideal when you want to look for information.
Es útil cuando tienes que enviar un correo electrónico.
It's useful when you have to send an email.
Es muy práctico cuando necesitas ver un plano.
It's very practical when you need to look at a map.

Mi madre dice que es ideal para hacer las compras de la semana.
My mother says that it's ideal for doing the weekly shop.

Varying your verbs

You can also use a variety of different verbs when introducing other people's opinions:

Mi madre dice que …	My mother says that …
Mi padrastro piensa que …	My stepdad thinks that …
Según mi abuelo, …	According to my grandad, …
Mi hermano cree que …	My brother thinks that …

Worked example

 SPEAKING TRACK 66   Target grade 4-9

Answer the following question in **Spanish**.
¿Cómo usáis Internet en tu familia?

Lo usamos mucho, todo el tiempo. Mi madre dice que es importante cuando está trabajando en casa, para mandar correos electrónicos y mantenerse en contacto con la oficina. Mi hermano piensa que es muy útil cuando tiene que hacer proyectos para el instituto. Lee artículos online y usa las imágenes en su trabajo. Según mi padre, es ideal cuando quieres organizar las vacaciones porque puedes reservar vuelos y hoteles, mirar planos y aprender frases en otro idioma.

 Listen to the recording

You might be asked a question like this in the general conversation section of your exam. This answer is from a student working at Grade 9.

Now try this

 WRITING   Target grade 4-5

You are writing a blog about the internet. Write approximately **90** words in **Spanish**. You must write something about each bullet point.

Mention:

- how you and your family use the internet
- how you used the internet in school last week
- how you will use the internet this weekend.

(15 marks)

Computer games

Digital resources

Lo bueno y lo malo de los videojuegos

lo bueno	the good thing
la acción	action
el personaje	character
divertido/a	fun, enjoyable
educativo/a	educational
emocionante	exciting
real	real
social	social
solo/a	alone
el concurso	competition
el problema	problem
el ejercicio	exercise
la falta	lack
la imagen	image
la violencia	violence
jugar	to play
resolver	to solve
la aventura	adventure
la mente	mind
desarrollar	to develop

Using lo + adjective

This expression means 'the ... thing'.

lo malo es que	the bad thing is that
lo más interesante	the most interesting thing
lo mejor de	the best thing about

The adjective and the word lo never change or agree.

The phrase lo que is also extremely handy. It means 'what' when you are not asking a question.

Es importante leer lo que dicen los expertos.
It's important to read what the experts say.

Jugar a los videojuegos puede ser una actividad social.
Playing computer games can be a social activity.

Flexible phrases

Lo mejor de todo ... The best thing of all ...
Lo que me gusta más ... What I like best ...
Lo que me preocupa ... What worries me ...
Lo peor es que hay mucha violencia.
The worst thing is that there is a lot of violence.

Worked example

 WRITING   Target grade 5-9

You are writing an article about computer games. Write your answer in **Spanish**.

You must include the following point:

- your opinion on this topic.

Me gusta jugar a los videojuegos. Son muy emocionantes. Prefiero los juegos de acción y ciencia ficción. Normalmente juego por la tarde en mi dormitorio.

Aiming Higher

No me gustan nada los videojuegos porque creo que hay mejores cosas que puedes hacer con tu tiempo. Lo que me preocupa es que los jóvenes juegan solos en su dormitorio y no hacen actividades deportivas. Lo peor es que hay mucha violencia en los juegos que podría tener un efecto negativo en el jugador.

In the exam you will need to write about more than one bullet point.

Aiming higher

First response: good Foundation level answer		Second response: high-scoring Higher level answer	
accurate	✓	longer sentences	✓
gustar	✓	complex language	✓
adjectives	✓	social impact	✓
irregular verbs	✓	impressive vocabulary	✓

Now try this

 READING Target grade 4-9

Translate these sentences into **English**.

1 Me gusta jugar a mi videojuego favorito.
2 La acción es muy emocionante y los personajes parecen muy reales.
3 Creo que algunos videojuegos pueden ser muy educativos.
4 En algunos tienes que tomar decisiones y resolver problemas.
5 Pienso que son relajantes también.

(10 marks)

Digital resources

The good and the bad of technology

¿Qué piensas de la tecnología?

la cámara	camera
lento/a	slow
rápido/a	quick, fast
la red	net, network, web
la ventaja	advantage
la desventaja	disadvantage
apagar	to turn off
dejar de + infinitive	to stop ...ing
depender de	to depend on
funcionar	to work, function
guardar	to keep, save
olvidar	to forget
preocupar	to worry, to be a worry
recordar	to remember
la contraseña	password
la duda	doubt
el beneficio	benefit
conectar	to connect
confiar	to trust

The imperfect continuous

Grammar page 104

This means 'was / were ...ing'. It is formed in Spanish like this:

estaba
estabas
estaba   + present participle
estábamos   (-ar verbs add -ando
estabais   -er / -ir verbs add -iendo)
estaban

At Foundation level, you only need to know the first three (singular) parts of estar in the imperfect tense.

Estaba haciendo mis deberes cuando se me apagó el ordenador.

I was doing my homework when the computer turned off.

Flexible phrases

No hay duda de que ...
There is no doubt that ...

Una de las cosas que me preocupa es que ...
One of the things that worries me is that ...

Worked example

 LISTENING TRACK 67   Target grade 6

Listen to Marta talking about technology. What **three** advantages does she mention? Write the correct letters in the boxes.

> Me compré un libro electrónico el año pasado y me parece muy práctico porque es fácil bajar novelas rápidamente. No hay duda de que uso menos papel también; todas las cosas que necesito están guardadas en el ordenador. La gran ventaja para mí es que puedes encontrar toda la información del mundo en un solo segundo.

A	communication with others
B	games and entertainment
C	going paperless
D	rapid access to information
E	shopping takes less time
F	using an e-reader

 Listen to the recording

[C] [D] [F]

(3 marks)

Now try this

 LISTENING TRACK 68   Target grade 6

Problems with technology

Alejandro is talking about technology. Write the correct letter in each box.

Listen to the recording

1 What does Alejandro say about technology?

A	Life would be boring without it.
B	It is more reliable than before.
C	We rely on it too much.

☐ **(1 mark)**

2 What has Alejandro done?

A	Forgotten to save his work.
B	Downloaded a file with a virus.
C	Written his project by hand.

☐ **(1 mark)**

Places in town

Digital resources

Por favor, ¿dónde está(n) … ?

las afueras	outskirts
el banco	bank
el café	café
la calle	street
el castillo	castle
la iglesia	church
el centro comercial	shopping centre
la ciudad	city
la esquina	(street) corner
la estación	station
el gimnasio	gym
el jardín	garden
el mercado	market
la piscina	swimming pool
la plaza	square
el pueblo	village, town
el puerto	port, harbour
los servicios	toilets
el supermercado	supermarket
el teatro	theatre
la tienda	shop
la fuente	fountain
la oficina de turismo	tourist office

Hay mucho que hacer en mi ciudad.
There is a lot to do in my town / city.

No hay nada que hacer para los jóvenes.
There is nothing to do for young people.

Using estar for location

Grammar page 103

Whenever you are talking about where someone or something is, you will need the verb estar for 'to be'.

¿Dónde está Manuel?	Where is Manuel?
Está en el banco.	He is at the bank.
¿Dónde están los servicios?	Where are the toilets?
Están allí a la derecha.	They are there, on the right.

Adverbs of place used with estar

al lado de	next to	detrás de	behind
cerca de	near / close to	entre	between
lejos de	far from	a la derecha	on the right
delante de	in front of	a la izquierda	on the left

Hay muchos edificios históricos en mi ciudad. There are lots of historic buildings in my city.

Now try this

 SPEAKING

 Target grade 1-9

Talk about the content of these photos. You must say at least one thing about each photo. **(5 marks)**

Worked example

WRITING

Target grade 1-5

Write an email to your Mexican friend about the town / village where you live. Write approximately **50** words in **Spanish**. You must write something about each bullet point.

Mention:

- its size
- the buildings
- the green spaces
- the people
- your opinion of the place. **(10 marks)**

Vivo en un pueblo muy grande. En la calle principal hay edificios históricos, una iglesia, muchas tiendas y un supermercado. También hay un parque para los niños. La gente es muy simpática y tengo muchos amigos aquí. Me gusta el pueblo porque es bonito y tranquilo, pero aburrido a veces.

The word count means that you need to write just ten words per bullet point. However, it is fine to write more about one thing and less about another, as long as you cover all points in the list.

Digital resources

Things to do

¿Qué vamos a hacer?

ir ...   to go ...
  al centro comercial   to the shopping centre
  al centro deportivo   to the sports centre
  de compras   shopping
  al cine   to the cinema
  al museo   to the museum
  a la piscina   to the swimming pool
  al teatro   to the theatre
cenar en un restaurante   to eat in a restaurant
jugar al fútbol en   to play football in
  el parque   the park
dar un paseo en los   to go for a walk in
  jardines   the gardens
tomar algo en el café   to go for something to eat/
                                     drink at the café

El próximo fin de semana iremos a ...
Next weekend we'll go to ...
La semana que viene cenaremos en ...
Next week we'll eat in ...
Este sábado jugaremos al ...
This Saturday we'll play ...

The future tense

Grammar page 107

This is the equivalent of 'will':
We **will arrive** around four o'clock.
You form it by taking the infinitive and adding the following endings (the same for all verbs). For Foundation, you only need to know singular forms.

Infinitive	Ending	Examples
-ar -er + -ir	é ás á emos éis án	hablaré I will speak darás you will give verá he / she will see comeremos we will eat viviréis you will live irán they will go

There are some **irregular** stems:
tener (to have) → tendré, tendrás, etc.
hacer (to do, make) → haré, harás, etc.
poder (to be able) → podré, podrás, etc.
poner (to put) → pondré, pondrás, etc.
habrá = there will be

La semana que viene cenaremos en un restaurante en la ciudad.
Next week we'll eat out in a restaurant in town.

Worked example

 WRITING   Target grade 4-9

You are writing a letter to your friend. You must write in **Spanish** something about the following point:

• what you will do in town next week.

El viernes por la noche iré al teatro con mis amigas porque hay una obra que quiero ver. El sábado trabajaré en el café en el centro porque tengo un trabajo allí los fines de semana. El domingo mi familia y yo comeremos en un restaurante con los abuelos.

This is a model answer to the final bullet point in a Higher Writing question. The whole task has four bullet points and 130–150 words.

Now try this

 READING   Target grade 4

You read Javier's email to his friend.

Llovió mucho ayer y decidimos no ir al parque para dar un paseo con el perro. Fuimos al centro comercial para mirar las tiendas. Dicen que va a hacer buen tiempo mañana; entonces iré a la piscina al aire libre y volveré a casa para comer.

Answer the following questions. Write the correct letter in each box.

1 Why did Javier change his plan yesterday?

A	transport issue
B	weather problem
C	sport cancellation

☐ (1 mark)

2 Where did they end up going?

A	shopping centre
B	park
C	beach

☐ (1 mark)

3 Where will he go tomorrow?

A	restaurant
B	countryside
C	swimming pool

☐ (1 mark)

Shopping for clothes

Digital resources

¡Vamos de compras!

la tienda	shop
el centro comercial	shopping centre
el tamaño	size
la ropa	clothes
la camiseta	T-shirt
la camisa	shirt
la falda	skirt
el vestido	dress
los pantalones	trousers
los zapatos	shoes
demasiado	too
grande	big
pequeño/a	small
corto/a	short
largo/a	long
más grande	bigger
más pequeño/a	smaller
de otro color	in another colour
comprar	to buy
costar	to cost
devolver	to take back
ir de compras	to go shopping
pagar	to pay (for)
probarse	to try on
la cola	queue

¿Tiene uno / una más grande / pequeño/a?
Have you got a bigger / smaller one?

¿Puedo probármelo / probármela?
Can I try it on?

Lo / la / los / las compro.
I'll buy it / them.

Demonstrative adjectives and pronouns
Grammar page 98

These are the grammatical names for the simple words 'this', 'that', 'these' and 'those'.

	Masculine	Feminine	
Singular	este	esta	this (one)
Plural	estos	estas	these (ones)
Singular	ese	esa	that (one)
Plural	esos	esas	those (ones)

Compraré esta camiseta porque esa es demasiado grande.

I'll buy this T-shirt because that one is too big.

On the Higher papers, you might also come across these words, which mean 'that' / 'those':
aquel / aquella / aquellos / aquellas

¿Puedo probármela?
Can I try it on?

Worked example

 READING Target grade 8

Read this article about internet shopping.

> Las ventajas de comprar por Internet son claras: evita hacer colas y se puede comprar artículos que no se encuentran en tu país. Pero comprar por Internet también tiene sus desventajas. Algunas de ellas son el proceso de pagar y lo difícil que es devolver artículos. Sin embargo, cada año más gente empieza a hacer sus compras de esta manera y la seguridad mejora todo el tiempo.

Answer the following questions in **English.**

1 Give two advantages of buying online.
You avoid the queues, you can buy things you can't get in your country.

2 Give two disadvantages of online shopping.
The payment process and the difficulties of returning things.

(4 marks)

Now try this

SPEAKING TRACK 69   Target grade 1-5

Reading aloud

Read aloud the following text in **Spanish.**

> El jueves voy al centro comercial. Quiero comprar un vestido. Voy a llevarlo a la fiesta de cumpleaños de mi amiga. Vi unos zapatos que no cuestan mucho.
> No sé si los tienen en mi tamaño.

Then listen to the recording of four questions in **Spanish** that relate to the topic of **The environment and where people live**. In order to score the highest marks, you must try to answer all four questions as fully as you can.

Listen to the recording

(15 marks)

Had a look ☐   Nearly there ☐   Nailed it! ☐

Digital resources

Transport

¿Qué tal el transporte en tu región?

el autobús	bus
el tren	train
el avión	plane
el barco	boat
la bicicleta	bicycle
el coche	car
la estación	station
el metro	metro, underground
el kilómetro	kilometre
rápido/a	quick, fast
práctico/a	practical
cómodo/a	comfortable
barato/a	cheap
caro/a	expensive
durar	to take / last + time
ir a pie	to go on foot
llegar	to arrive
salir	to leave, depart
caminar	to walk

Comparatives and superlatives

Grammar page 97

In English, we use the comparative form of the adjective: for example, 'more comfortable', 'less expensive' or 'faster'.

To do this in Spanish, use más for 'more', menos for 'less', and que for 'than'.

El coche es más rápido que la bicicleta.

To say 'as ... as', use tan ... como around the adjective:

El tren es tan barato como el autobús.

The train is as cheap as the bus.

Note these irregulars:

better → mejor   older → mayor

worse → peor   younger → menor

To say the fastest, the cheapest, etc., add the article.

El tren es el más rápido.

The train is the fastest.

Estos billetes son los más baratos.

These tickets are the cheapest.

H ONLY

Worked example

 READING

 Target grade **6**

Read the results of a transport survey. Complete the tables in **English**.

Resultados del voto

Los vecinos de la ciudad han votado por su transporte favorito. Aquí están los resultados. En último lugar está el sistema de trenes que la gente describió como 'el peor de todos' porque están sucios y siempre llegan tarde. En segundo lugar, está el sistema de autobuses que la gente encuentra bastante práctico y no muy caro. En primer lugar, tenemos el sistema de metro porque la gente dice que es rápido y barato.

Es más cómodo viajar en tren.
It's more comfortable travelling by train.

Transport in last place	trains
Reason (Give **one** detail.)	dirty

Transport in second place	buses
Reason (Give **one** detail.)	practical

Transport in first place	underground
Reason (Give **one** detail.)	quick

(6 marks)

Now try this

 LISTENING TRACK **70**

 Target grade **3**

You hear Juan and Paula discussing how to travel.

Complete the following sentences in **English**.

Listen to the recording

1 Juan does not like the idea of travelling by _____ . **(1 mark)**

2 Juan likes the idea of travelling by _____ . **(1 mark)**

3 Paula does not like the idea of travelling by _____ . **(1 mark)**

4 Paula likes the idea of travelling by _____ . **(1 mark)**

Travelling on public transport

Digital resources

¿Adónde quieres ir?

el horario	timetable
el billete	ticket
la estación de trenes / de autobuses	train / bus station
hay	there is / are
el vuelo	flight
la maleta	suitcase
la ventana	window
la mesa	table
primera clase	first class
segunda clase	second class
bajar de	to get off
cambiar de trenes	to change trains
llegar	to arrive
salir	to leave, depart
pagar	to pay (for)
subir a	to get on
sentarse	to sit

¿A qué hora sale el … ?
What time does the … leave?
¿A qué hora llega? What time does it arrive?
¿De dónde sale? Where does it leave from?

Using por and para

Grammar page 114

Use por for:
- **exchange**
  Pagué €30 por este billete,
  I paid €30 for this ticket.
- **reason – because of**
  El vuelo salió tarde por el mal tiempo.
  The flight left late because of the bad weather.

Use para for:
- **purpose (in order to / for)**
  Voy a usar mi tarjeta para pagar los billetes.
  I'm going to use my card to pay for the tickets.
- **destination (time, people, place)**
  Ese billete es para mañana.
  That ticket is for tomorrow.
  Tengo los billetes para los niños.
  I've got the tickets for the children.
  Salió para Barcelona.
  She left for Barcelona.

Always look at the instructions and setting because, if you ever need to do any educated guesswork, your guess needs to make sense in the context.

Dos billetes para Barcelona por favor.
Two tickets to Barcelona please.

Worked example LISTENING TRACK 71 Target grade 5

At the train station

Listen to the recording

You hear Julia and Malek talking at the train station. Complete the sentences in **English**.

Julia: Aquí viene el tren. ¿Dónde vamos a sentarnos? A mí me gusta sentarme al lado de la ventana para mirar el campo. ¿Y tú?

Malek: Prefiero tener una mesa si hay una libre. Necesito hacer trabajo en mi portátil.

1 Julia prefers to sit ...<u>by the window</u>... so she can look ...<u>at the countryside.</u>...

(2 marks)

2 Malek prefers to sit ...<u>at a table</u>... because he has to ...<u>work on his laptop.</u>...

(2 marks)

Now try this READING Target grade 4

A phone message

Hugo gets this alert on his phone.

> Hoy no hay vuelos del aeropuerto por los vientos fuertes que están afectando los aviones.

What does the alert say? Write the correct letter in the box.

There are no flights today due to the …

A	rain.
B	high temperatures.
C	wind.

☐

(1 mark)

Digital resources

My region – the good and the bad

¿Cómo es la región donde vives?

las afueras	outskirts
el barrio	area, district
bonito/a	pretty
el campo	country(side)
la capital	capital
la carretera	road
cerca de	near to
la ciudad	city, town
el edificio	building
el espacio	space
histórico/a	historic
la industria	industry
el paisaje	scenery, landscape
el parque	park
el pueblo	village, small town
el ruido	noise
tranquilo/a	peaceful, quiet
la zona	area, region
construir	to build
el camino	path, way, route

Using desde hace

On their own desde means 'since / from' and hace means 'ago'. Together they mean 'for', in this specific construction.

Vivo en Barcelona desde hace diez años.
I have been living in Barcelona for ten years.
Trabaja en Madrid desde hace seis meses.
She has been working in Madrid for six months.
Esta casa está aquí desde hace siglos.
This house has been here for centuries.

Notice that the verb 'has / have been' or 'has / have been …ing' is in the present tense in Spanish.

Preferiría vivir en el campo.
I would prefer to live in the countryside.

Worked example

Target grade 6

Read this text about the Spanish region of Valencia.

La comunidad de Valencia es una zona con una gran variedad de paisajes. En el este tiene su larga costa, desarrollada para el turismo y llena de casas y hoteles. Al oeste están los campos verdes de arroz, para la famosa paella, y los árboles llenos de naranjas. Vale la pena visitar sus hermosas ciudades históricas y no se debe perder la oportunidad de caminar por los pueblos más pequeños y tranquilos.

Which **three** statements are true, according to the text? Write the correct letters in the boxes.

The Valencia region …

A	has a range of different landscapes.
B	has a long western coastline.
C	does not get much tourism.
D	grows different produce.
E	has modern cities which are worth a visit.
F	has quiet villages that are a must-see.

☐ A   ☐ D   ☐ F

(3 marks)

Useful phrases

La gran ventaja de vivir aquí es que …
The big advantage of living here is that …

No me gustaría vivir en ningún otro sitio.
I wouldn't want to live anywhere else.

Lo bueno de mi región es que …
The good thing about my area is that …

Lo malo de mi barrio es …
The bad thing about my neighbourhood is …

Now try this

Target grade 6

Read the text on **The region of Valencia** again. Answer the questions in **English.**

1 What two products are grown in the west of the region? **(2 marks)**

2 What famous dish from the area uses one of these products? **(1 mark)**

My region in the past

Digital resources

¿Cómo era tu región?

Había mucha industria y contaminación.
There was a lot of industry and pollution.

El aire no estaba limpio.
The air was not clean.

Era mucho más tranquilo.
It was a lot quieter.

Era solo un pueblo pequeño.
It was just a little village.

Había poco tráfico.
There wasn't much traffic.

Había campos donde ahora hay casas.
There were fields where now there are houses.

Teníamos más espacios verdes.
We had more green spaces.

Todo el mundo se conocía.
Everyone knew each other.

Había mucho humo de la industria.
There was a lot of smoke from the industry.

The imperfect tense

Grammar page 106

Use this tense to describe how things used to be or what was ongoing or occurring regularly at the time.

	-ar **verbs**	-er / -ir **verbs**
	• Remove -ar from the infinitive • Add these endings:	• Remove -er/-ir from the infinitive • Add these endings:
I	-aba hablaba	-ía comía
you	-abas hablabas	-ías comías
he / she / it	-aba hablaba	-ía comía
we	-ábamos hablábamos	-íamos comíamos
you	-abais hablabais	-íais comíais
they	-aban hablaban	-ían comían

Note also: había (there was / there were)
See page 106 for the irregular forms of ser, ir and ver.

En el pasado era solo un pueblo pequeño.
In the past it was just a small village.

For Foundation tier, you only need to know the singular parts of the verb (the first three parts). For Higher tier, you need to know all forms.

Worked example

LISTENING TRACK 72 · **Target grade 5**

You hear Juan talking about his town.

Mi abuelo dice que el pueblo era muy tranquilo en el pasado y que, un día, vio un perro dormido en el centro de la calle. Dice que ahora no se puede tener una conversación en la calle principal por el ruido del tráfico.

Listen to the recording

Answer the questions in **English**.

1 What did Juan's grandfather see one day?
a dog asleep in the road

2 What can't you do any more on the high street
have a conversation

3 Why is this impossible?
because of the noise from the traffic

(3 marks)

You can use different words as long as the meaning is correct. For example, answering 'The traffic is so loud' for Question 3 would also be correct.

Now try this

LISTENING TRACK 73 · **Target grade 7**

Juan is talking about his town again. Complete the sentences by writing the correct letter in each box.

Listen to the recording

1 Juan's grandfather says that the neighbours …

A	got on well.
B	all knew each other.
C	looked after each other's children.

☐ **(1 mark)**

2 The neighbours did **not** …

A	have much money.
B	have holidays.
C	lock their doors.

☐ **(1 mark)**

3 Juan says that his grandfather's memories are …

A	really interesting.
B	possibly inaccurate.
C	something he often talks about.

☐ **(1 mark)**

Had a look ☐   Nearly there ☐   Nailed it! ☐

 Digital resources

Town or country?

¿Dónde prefieres vivir?

agradable	nice, pleasant
el aire	air
el árbol	tree
la arquitectura	architecture
el banco	bank, bench
bonito/a	pretty
el campo	countryside, field
la ciudad	city
el espacio	space
la flor	flower
el paisaje	scenery, landscape
el parque	park
la planta	plant
el río	river
el ruido	noise
(estar) sucio/a	(to be) dirty
tranquilo/a	quiet, peaceful
(estar) limpio/a	(to be) clean
los alrededores	surrounding area
el estilo de vida	lifestyle
el humo	smoke
el lago	lake
precioso/a	beautiful
puro/a	pure
relajante	relaxing

Using connectives

These words join ideas or phrases together. Simple ones are y (and), que (that), cuando (when) and donde (where).

Showing reason and cause
porque because
por eso therefore

Showing a different view / opinion
pero but
sin embargo however
aunque although
en cambio on the other hand, whereas

Flexible phrases

Creo que, en general, me gusta más ...
I think in general that I prefer ...
Pero, en cambio ...
But, on the other hand ...
Lo mejor de todo sería ...
Best of all would be ...

Lo mejor de todo sería vivir en una ciudad – pero muy cerca del campo.
Best of all would be to live in a city – but near the countryside.

Worked example

  WRITING — Target grade 1-5

Translate the following sentences into **Spanish**.

1 I love living in the city.
2 I am never bored because it is lively.
3 However, this morning there was a lot of noise.
4 Next week I am going to the countryside.
5 It is always peaceful there.

(10 marks)

1 Me encanta vivir en la ciudad.
2 Nunca estoy aburrido/a porque es animado.
3 Sin embargo, esta mañana había mucho ruido.
4 La semana próxima voy al campo.
5 Siempre es tranquilo allí.

Ser or estar?
To say 'I am never bored', you say Nunca estoy aburrido.

Now try this

  WRITING — Target grade 4-9

Translate the following sentences into **Spanish**.

1 I like living in the country.
2 On the other hand, my parents prefer life in a big city.
3 They used to live in Valencia where there were lots of facilities and transport.
4 In the future I will live in the country.
5 There are open spaces, green fields, tall trees and beautiful flowers.

(10 marks)

The environment and me

 Digital resources

¿Qué haces tú para ayudar al medioambiente?

el medioambiente	the environment
la energía	energy
la luz	light
el plástico	plastic
el agua (f)	water
la naturaleza	nature
el transporte público	public transport
ahorrar	to save
apagar	to turn out / off
cuidar	to take care of
ir a pie	to walk
ir en bicicleta	to cycle
proteger	to protect
reciclar	to recycle
separar	to separate
tirar basura	to drop litter
usar	to use
utilizar	to use
el planeta	planet

Using the verb soler + infinitive (H ONLY) — Grammar page 100

This is used to mean 'to usually + verb'.
Suelo reciclar papel y plástico.
I usually recycle paper and plastic.
The verb follows the usual pattern of stem-changing verbs:

suelo
sueles
suele } + infinitive
solemos
soléis
suelen

Solemos ir a pie. We usually walk.
¿Sueles reciclar la ropa?
Do you usually recycle clothes?

Solemos separar la basura en casa.
We usually separate the rubbish at home.

Worked example   Target grade 2

Read these comments from an internet forum. Who says what?

Write **A** for Alba
   B for Bruno
   C for Carmen

Write the correct letter in each box.

A	Yo siempre voy al instituto en bicicleta. Quiero proteger el medio ambiente. *Alba*
B	Yo apago las luces en casa. Siempre intento usar menos energía. *Bruno*
C	Yo intento usar menos agua; no llueve mucho en mi región. *Carmen*

	Who …	
1	… turns off the lights?	B
2	… tries to use less water?	C
3	… wants to protect the environment?	A
4	… mentions lack of rain?	C
5	… tries to use less energy?	B
6	… cycles to school?	A

(6 marks)

Flexible phrases

Para proteger la naturaleza, yo siempre …
To protect nature, I always …
Para ahorrar energía, intento + infinitive …
To save energy, I try to …
Para cuidar el planeta, tenemos que …
To take care of the planet, we have to …

Remember that the double 'l' sound in Spanish (as in **botella** and **llevamos**) is like the 'li' sound in 'million', or as an 'y' sound. It is not acceptable to pronounce it like the double 'l' in the English word 'yellow'.

Now try this   Target grade 1-5

Reading aloud
Read aloud the following text in **Spanish**.

En mi casa siempre reciclo el papel. Mi hermano recicla las botellas y el plástico.
Llevamos la ropa usada a una tienda de segunda mano.
Intentamos ir a pie. Es mejor para el medioambiente que ir en coche.

81

Digital resources

Local environmental issues

El medio ambiente en tu región

sucio/a	dirty
la falta	lack
el río	river
el espacio	space
verde	green
el ruido	noise
el aire	air
el jardín	garden
el bosque	wood, forest
el parque	park
la naturaleza	nature
el tráfico	traffic
el coche	car
la carretera	road
la basura	rubbish, litter
limpiar	to clean
recoger	to collect, pick up

Using seguir + present participle

H ONLY

Grammar page 104

This is the equivalent of the English 'to carry on ...ing', 'to continue to ...', 'to keep on ...ing' or 'to still be ...ing'.

Use seguir in the present tense and add the present participle:

sigo
sigues
sigue
seguimos
seguís
siguen

} + present participle (-ando, -iendo)

Seguimos destruyendo los bosques.
We keep on destroying the forests.

La industria sigue causando contaminación.
Industry continues to cause pollution.

Flexible phrases

En mi región, tenemos un problema con ...
In my area, we have a problem with ...

En mi barrio, lo peor es ...
In my neighbourhood, the worst thing is ...

Worked example

 LISTENING TRACK 74

 Target grade 6

Listen to the recording

You hear Nadim talking about his local environment. Complete the sentences. Write the correct letter in each box.

> Cuando construyen casas nuevas en mi pueblo, no piensan en crear parques o jardines entre los edificios. Entonces, hay una falta de espacios verdes. También, todos los coches que pasan por la carretera principal producen demasiado ruido.

1 Nadim complains about the lack of ...

A	affordable housing.
B	building over a park.
C	green spaces.

C (1 mark)

2 He also dislikes ...

A	the new road being built.
B	the noise from the road.
C	the pollution from cars.

B (1 mark)

Now try this

 LISTENING TRACK 75

Target grade 6

Listen to the recording

Continue listening to Nadim. Complete the sentences. Write the correct letter in each box.

1 Nadim is glad that ...

A	trees have been planted.
B	a new law was passed.
C	there are now more buses.

☐ (1 mark)

2 He is also happy about ...

A	the litter-picking campaign.
B	the river being clean.
C	the new recycling centre.

☐ (1 mark)

Global environmental issues

Problemas para el planeta

el animal	animal
el calor	heat
el cambio climático	climate change
el clima	climate
el efecto	effect
la especie	species
el fuego	fire
la lluvia	rain
ahorrar energía	to save energy
apagar	to turn off, put out
aumentar	to increase
causar	to cause
contaminar	to pollute
destruir	to destroy
amenazar	to threaten
el consumo	consumption
conservar	to preserve
contribuir	to contribute
quemar	to burn
los recursos	resources
el desastre	disaster
el incendio	wildfire

conservar los espacios naturales
to preserve natural spaces

reducir el consumo de carne
to reduce meat consumption

The passive using ser + past participle

Grammar page 116

The passive in English consists of the verb 'to be' followed by a past participle.

The resources were destroyed.

The trees are cut down.

The passive can be produced in Spanish in the same way using ser (in the appropriate tense) + past participle.

The main difference is that the past participle agrees with what it describes.

El problema fue causado por el cambio climático.

The problem was caused by climate change.

(causado agrees with problema – masc. sing.)

Los nuevos datos serán publicados mañana.

The new data will be published tomorrow.

(publicados agrees with datos – masc. pl.)

Worked example

  READING Target grade 7

You read this entry on a forum on the environment.

Fue terrible cuando las ***inundaciones*** destruyeron muchos de los campos y cultivos cerca de donde vivimos. Alguna gente tuvo que dejar sus casas cuando el agua entró por las puertas.

What caused the ***inundaciones***?
Write the correct letter in the box.

A	high winds
B	heavy rains
C	prolonged drought

B **(1 mark)**

The key clues are the fact that fields and crops were destroyed (**destruyeron muchos de los campos y cultivos**) and that water came into the houses (**el agua entró por las puertas**). So **inundaciones** are floods, caused by heavy rains.

Flexible phrases

Aún queda mucho por hacer.
There is still a lot to be done.

Now try this

  SPEAKING Target grade 1-9

¿Qué problema del medioambiente te preocupa más?

You may be asked a question like this in the general conversation part of the Speaking exam.

Use the vocabulary and ideas above to help you give your answer, then listen to a sample response from a student working at around Grade 9 in the answer section.

El cambio climático está causando una crisis mundial.
Climate change is causing a world-wide crisis.

Digital resources

Caring for the planet

¿Cómo podemos cuidar el planeta?

el agua (f)	water	la basura	rubbish, litter
la tierra	land, earth	el plástico	plastic
el animal	animal	cuidar	to look after
el pájaro	bird	evitar	to avoid
el campo	countryside	molestar	to annoy
el aire	air	prohibir	to forbid, ban
el mar	sea	proteger	to protect
la montaña	mountain	recoger	to pick up
la flor	flower	cortar	to cut
responsable	responsible	conservar	to preserve
la naturaleza	nature	la víctima	victim
la especie	species	amenazar	to threaten

Useful phraes

Tenemos que ... We have to ...

... reducir las temperaturas del planeta.
... bring down the temperatures on the planet.
... proteger los árboles y los bosques del mundo.
... protect the world's trees and forests.
... conservar todas las especies de animales y pájaros.
... preserve all the species of animals and birds.
... parar la contaminación de los ríos y mares.
... stop the pollution of rivers and seas.

Using the subjunctive **H** ONLY Grammar page 111

The present subjunctive tense is used after verbs of wishing, commanding or requesting when someone is trying to get someone else to do something.

Quiero que los animales tengan un futuro.

I want the animals to have a future.

(Literally, 'I want that the animals have a future').

Voy a decirles que no hagan un fuego.

I'm going to tell them not to make a fire.

(Literally, 'I am going to tell them that they do not make a fire').

It is also used after emotion verbs:

Me preocupa que muchos pájaros sean víctimas de la contaminación.

I am worried that many birds are victims of pollution.

Worked example

 LISTENING TRACK 76

 Target grade 6

Listen to the recording

Para proteger el planeta, hay que conservar los bosques.
To protect the planet, we must preserve the forests.

You hear a guide of a nature reserve talking to visitors. What **three** things does he say? Write the correct letters in the boxes.

Mientras estamos en el parque, no está permitido recoger las flores. Algunas de las plantas son especies amenazadas. Por favor apagad los móviles durante la visita; el ruido molestará a los pájaros. Tened cuidado de no tirar basura, puede ser peligrosa para los animales.

The two verbs ending in -ad / -ed (**apagad / tened**) are commands addressing a group of people. See page 110.

A	Stay with the group.		D	Turn off phones.
B	Do not pick the flowers.		E	Do not feed the birds.
C	Talk quietly.		F	Do not leave any rubbish.

[B] [D] [F]

(3 marks)

Now try this

 LISTENING TRACK 77

 Target grade 7

Listen to the recording

Continue listening to the guide. Answer the questions in **English**.

1 Why can't the group go any further in the park?
2 What happened last year?
84 3 Why was this a sad thing to happen?

(3 marks)

A greener future

Digital resources

Para crear un futuro verde

el sol	sun
el viento	wind
el mar	sea
la energía	energy
sucio/a	dirty
peligroso/a	dangerous
el vuelo	flight
la bolsa de plástico	plastic bag
crear	to create
cuidar	to look after
prohibir	to forbid, ban
proteger	to protect
conservar	to preserve
la ley	law
el desarrollo	development
el beneficio	benefit
quejarse	to complain
el gobierno	government

Saying what should / ought to and could happen

Use the conditional of deber for 'ought to / should':

El gobierno debería hacer más …

The government should do more …

Creo que deberías quejarte …

I think you ought to complain …

Use the conditional of poder for 'could':

Para usar menos energía, podríamos mejorar el sistema de transporte público.

To use less energy, we could improve the public transport system.

Useful phrases

Deberíamos usar la energía del sol / del viento / del mar.

We should use the energy from the sun / the wind / the sea.

Todos deberíamos comer comida que se produce en la región.

We should all eat food produced in the area.

Hay que gastar más dinero en el desarrollo de las energías alternativas.

We must spend more money on developing alternative energies.

Worked example

READING · Target grade 7

Read this entry on a forum on the environment.

Hay que reconocer que, a veces, un cambio bastante pequeño puede tener un efecto profundo. Los supermercados dejaron de dar bolsas de plástico gratis a los clientes y esto ha llevado a reducir un 98% el uso de bolsas de plástico de un solo uso.

Complete these sentences. Write the letter for the correct option in each box.

1 The supermarkets …

A	reduced packaging.
B	stopped giving free bags.
C	used recycled plastic.

B

(1 mark)

2 As a result, …

A	customers quickly got used to it.
B	fewer people shopped there.
C	there has been a reduction in single-use plastic.

C

(1 mark)

Now try this

READING · Target grade 1-5

Translate these sentences into **English**.

1 No voy a usar bolsas de plástico.

2 Los coches eléctricos son mejores para el medio ambiente.

3 Tenemos que proteger los bosques.

4 Todos somos responsables de cuidar la naturaleza.

5 Ayer ayudé a recoger la basura en el parque.

(10 marks)

Paper 1: Listening

Digital resources

Overview

Section A: Listening comprehension

Section B: Dictation

Timing: Foundation: 35 minutes; Higher: 45 minutes

Marks: The Listening exam makes up 25% of the exam total. Foundation is worth 40 marks; Higher is worth 50 marks.

✓ All the questions in the comprehension section are in English.

✓ There is a reading time of five minutes before the recording begins. Use it to familiarise yourself with the paper and perhaps jot down the Spanish word for some of the English options. Remember you might hear a related word – perhaps *viaje* instead of *excursión*.

✓ There are also two minutes at the end of the recording for you to check your work.

✓ The recordings for the comprehension section are all heard twice, and pauses are inserted to give you time to think and write. For the dictation, all sentences are heard three times.

✓ The more challenging questions are distributed among more accessible questions so that you do not hit a 'wall' after which you feel you cannot do any more.

✓ You can always jot down ideas in the pauses between recordings, or tick words in the grid even as you listen.

✓ Use the marks in brackets on the papers to guide you. One mark usually means one detail.

Multiple choice

Track 78

Sometimes these are questions where you select one of three given options and write the letter A, B or C into the answer box.

> Hoy tenemos matemáticas por la mañana y dibujo a las dos. No hay clase de ciencias hoy.
>
> What subject does Ana have this afternoon?
>
> | A | Art |
> |---|-----|
> | B | Maths |
> | C | Science |
>
> Write the correct letter in the box.   **A**

Others require you to select your answer from a grid, like this question. The answers are heard in the same order as the questions.

> Los lunes voy al gimnasio. Los jueves juego al baloncesto. El domingo es cuando voy a la piscina.
>
> | A | Basketball | D | Running |
> |---|-----------|---|---------|
> | B | Gym | E | Swimming |
> | C | Horse riding | | |
>
> What does Ana do on these days?
>
> | | | |
> |---|---------|---|
> | 1 | Monday | **B** |
> | 2 | Thursday | **A** |
> | 3 | Sunday | **E** |

Multiple choice – two details

Track 79

These questions ask for two pieces of information and, again, you will select your answers from grids.

> En julio voy a dejar mi trabajo porque mi sueño es escribir una novela.
>
> | **Job** | | **When** | |
> |---|---------|---|--------|
> | A | Actor | P | Past |
> | B | Author | N | Now |
> | C | Teacher | F | Future |
> | D | Waiter | | |
>
> | | **Job** | **When** |
> |---|---------|----------|
> | 1 | **B** | **F** |

One or both

Track 80

Here you need to decide whether one option is correct or both given options are correct. This could be an opinion question, where you listen to a recording and decide if the speaker expresses a positive opinion (**P**), a negative opinion (**N**), or both (**P + N**).

> La profesora de inglés es muy divertida pero las clases son demasiado largas.
>
> Elena's opinion of English classes.   **P + N**

The other type of question offers you two statements and you choose if just A is correct, just B is correct, or if both A and B are correct.

> | A | The English teacher is boring. |
> |---|-------------------------------|
> | B | The English lessons are too long. |
>
> **B**

Paper 1: Listening

Digital resources

Questions to answer in English

A few of the comprehension questions require you to write an answer in English.

The first type requires a short answer.

Track 81

> El viernes pasado, alquilamos bicicletas.

What did they do last Friday?
hired bikes
(1)

The second type requires you to fill in a gap with a missing word.

> Necesitamos más autobuses en las afueras.

Tomás says they need more .... buses ....
in the .... outskirts .... **(1)**

Never offer two options – this will not be awarded any marks. Make your decision and give one answer.

Dictation

On the Foundation paper, there are four sentences for you to hear and write in Spanish; on the Higher paper there are five.

Track 82

There will be 20 words in the four Foundation tier sentences, and 30 for Higher tier. On both papers, two of the words will be from outside the prescribed vocabulary list.

You hear the sentences three times: the first time as a full sentence, the second time in short sections and the third time again as a full sentence. Listen to the recording to hear an example of this.

You get marks for getting the general message across and for overall accuracy.

Tips for success

- ✓ Ensure you read the question introductions, titles and instructions. They give important information like the context and number of correct answers.
- ✓ You can make notes as you listen (ensuring you leave your answer area clear). For the dictation, you can jot down words in the first listen that you can then check and refine into sentences.
- ✓ You can make notes on the paper (ensuring you leave your answer area clear).
- ✓ When answering in English, don't waste time giving long responses when a short phrase is all that is needed to give a clear answer.

Closing time of museum
4.30

This answer is quicker to write than **The museum closes at half past four.**

- ✓ Listen for negatives like nunca or words like menos or salvo which change the meaning of the sentence.
- ✓ If you are not sure, try to work out meanings from the context. If, on the second listen (or third in the dictation), you still don't know, make a guess. Don't leave blanks.

Spelling tips

The dictation will test your spelling of the typical sounds in the Spanish language. Here are some of the 'ones to watch'.

ll	like 'li' in million, or like 'y'	llevar, calle
cu + vowel	like 'kw'	cuando, cuidar
ce / ci / z	the 'c' and 'z' are like 'th' in 'thin'	once, cita, zapato
que / qui	like 'kay' and 'key' (not kway!)	querer, quitar
ge / gi / j	the 'g' and 'j' are like 'ch' in 'loch'	general, colegio, bajo
gue / gui	hard 'g', don't pronounce the 'u'	sigue, seguir
ñ	like 'ni' in 'onion'	señor, año
v	strong, like 'b'	vivo, veces
h	silent	hotel, ahora

Small errors may not lose you marks unless the meaning of the sentence is lost.

If you make a mistake when writing a letter in an answer box, put one line through it and write the correct answer next to the box.

| A̶ | B |

Paper 2: Speaking

Digital resources

Overview

Task 1: Role play
Task 2: Reading aloud and follow-up questions
Task 3: Photo card and unprepared conversation
Timing: Preparation – 15 mins before exam; Foundation exam – 7–9 mins; Higher exam – 10–12 mins
Marks: 50 marks; 25% of the exam total

Cans and Cannots:

✓ You **can** make as many notes as you like on a sheet of paper, even full sentences if you like.

✓ You **can** use the notes during the exam.

✓ You **can** use vocabulary not on the prescribed list.

✗ You **cannot** use a dictionary.

Using the preparation time

- Start with the **role play**. Check the scenario, read the full task and write your responses on the paper provided. Just prepare what you are asked for – no developments or extras are needed.

- Next, look at the **photo card**. Jot down ideas and vocabulary about the two photos. You do not have to talk about each one for the same amount of time, but you must mention at least one thing about each photo.

- Turn to the **read aloud** task. Read it through in your head, getting an understanding of the meaning. Make notes on any notepaper of any pauses or tricky pronunciation. Think what the follow-up questions could be about.

This is **one** recommendation for how to prepare. See what works best for you when you get the chance to practise.

The role play – what to expect

☑ The role play consists of five bullet points indicating the five tasks / things you need to say. There is a total of 10 marks.

☑ At both Foundation and Higher tier, one bullet point will be a question you need to ask.

☑ All the bullet points in the tasks will be in English so you know exactly what is required of you.

☑ At the top of the card, you are reminded to use a verb in each response. Each bullet point tells you exactly how many details are needed; there is no need to give any extra information.

☑ All the role plays are informal conversations with a Spanish-speaking friend. There are no formal situations.

☑ At Foundation, all bullet points can be tackled using the present tense. At Higher, one bullet point will refer to a time in the past or the future.

Each task is awarded 2 marks if the message is relevant and clear, 1 mark if there is some lack of clarity and 0 marks if the message does not come across.

You cannot write on the role play card or the photo card, but you can make notes on the paper provided.

The role play – tips for success

Take a look at these two bullets from a Higher tier role play and a student's answers.

- Say what you do at home at the weekend. (Give **two** details.)
  Los fines de semana escucho música y ayudo a limpiar la casa.
- Say what you and your family did last weekend. (Give **one** detail.)
  Fuimos de compras a la ciudad.

This student's answers are good because:

✓ the answers are clear to understand

✓ their language is accurate and varied

✓ the required past time frame is clearly conveyed.

Keep your answers simple, but remember always to include a verb.

Paper 2: Speaking

Digital resources

The 'reading aloud' task – what to expect

All the words in the reading aloud passage come from AQA's prescribed lists. At Foundation the passage has a minimum of 35 words and at Higher a minimum of 50 words.

You can practise reading the passage silently to yourself during the preparation time. Then, your teacher will tell you when the preparation time is up and will ask you to read the passage out loud.

You can keep the card during the follow-up questions in case you wish to use something from the passage in your answers.

If you make a mistake or are not happy with how you pronounced something, you can start the reading task again.

After your reading, there are four follow-up questions on the same topic as the passage, in the present tense at both Foundation and Higher. These are not printed on the card. However, because they are on the same topic as the passage, you will be able to anticipate what sort of questions will come up and can jot some ideas down on paper.

The 'reading aloud' task – tips for success

- Take time to understand the passage during the preparation period – your intonation will improve if you know what you are saying.
- You cannot write on the reading aloud text but you can make any notes you want on paper to remind you of pauses and particular pronunciations.
- Read the text steadily and clearly. You will not sound 'more Spanish' if you try to read fast – it will just prevent the examiner from hearing your pronunciation.

For the follow-up questions the minimum requirements to access the top range of marks are as follows:
Develop two of your answers using **three** pieces of information with verbs (Veo la tele, escucho música y voy a la piscina.)
Develop one further response using **two** pieces of information with verbs (Me gusta el jamón pero no me gusta el pollo.)
You can give a less developed response as your fourth answer (El fútbol).

Photo card – what to expect

- Describing the photos – 5 marks
(1 minute at Foundation, 1.5 minutes at Higher)
- Unprepared conversation – 20 marks
(3–4 minutes at Foundation, 6–7 minutes at Higher).

The teacher will say Háblame de las fotos to invite you to talk about the photos. Remember to talk about **both** the photos. (This means that there is plenty to say and you won't run out of ideas!)

Afterwards, your teacher will lead you into a broader conversation on the themes and the topics within that theme.

Ensure your answer is relevant to the question and listen out for opportunities to develop your answers with opinions and reasons.

If you are confident with your tenses, use references to past and future events so that you demonstrate the range and complexity of your language. However, if everything you say is accurate, clear and varied, you can still score full marks if you only use the present tense.

Sample description

En la primera foto hay una chica bonita con el pelo largo y marrón. Está en la cama, en su habitación, mirando su móvil y creo que está mandando mensajes a sus amigos porque está sonriendo. En la otra foto, hay un chico que juega a un videojuego en su ordenador. Tiene el pelo corto y marrón. Creo que en el juego el chico conduce un coche a gran velocidad.

This is part of a student answer.

✓ Refers to both photos
✓ Message is always clear
✓ Develops the description with extra details, introduced by con, y, creo que, porque, and también.
✓ Good use of present continuous tense
✓ Language is accurate and varied

89

Digital resources

Paper 3: Reading

Overview

Section A: Reading comprehension
Section B: Translation
Timing: Foundation – 45 mins; Higher – 1 hour
Marks: 50 (including 10 for the translation into English); 25% exam total

✓ Titles, instructions, questions and answers are all in English. Photos used will **not** give clues to any answers but may help you understand what the text is about.

✓ The number of marks indicates how much detail you should give and how long you should spend on that answer.

✓ Questions vary in difficulty. If you find one hard, the next one may be easier.

Multiple choice questions

You need to select one of three options.

> Miguel: Tengo un examen de historia el lunes.

What does Miguel have on Monday?

A	a PE lesson
B	a History exam
C	an English trip

B   (1)

If you make a mistake, put a single line through the box and write the correct answer next to it.

Answers in English

Some texts will require short answers in English instead of selecting a letter or number from a grid.

> El problema más grande que afecta la costa en este momento es la contaminación del mar.

What is the worst problem facing the coast?
pollution in the sea   (1)

You can answer this question with a few words that are clear and to the point. A full sentence is not needed. Other questions will need a whole sentence in order to give a full response:

> No me gustó nada el hotel porque mi habitación tenía vistas a una fábrica.

Why did José dislike the hotel?
His room had a view of a factory.   (1)

A or B or both?

Some questions will offer you two options and you need to decide if one or both are correct.

> Ana: Ayer recibí un móvil nuevo para mi cumpleaños. Tiene una cámara excelente.

Ana's mobile …

A	is new.
B	has a good camera.

A + B

For this type of question, the texts do not follow the same order as the questions in the grid. You need to check back to all three texts to find the answer to each question.

Who … ?

A	Ayer evité comer carne y salí a correr con mi padre.	Cris
B	Yo fui a dar un paseo en el campo y llevé agua porque hacía calor.	Ana
C	Hoy, tomé fruta durante el recreo y jugué al fútbol en el parque.	Iván

Who …

1	… played a team sport?	C
2	… went walking?	B
3	… took water with them?	B
4	… had a meat-free day?	A
5	… had fruit for a snack?	C
6	… went out running?	A

Paper 3: Reading

Digital resources

Inference questions

There are 2 marks for inference questions on Foundation and Higher papers. The text will feature a word that is not on the prescribed list, but there are clues in the text to the meaning of the word. You are given three answer options to choose from.

Natalia:

Ayer, la familia preparó una cena con *chuletas*. Yo soy vegetariana desde hace dos años, y solo comí la ensalada y las patatas fritas.

Which of these is the best translation of *chuletas*?

A	mushrooms
B	chops
C	beans

B

Natalia:

Ayer, la familia preparó una cena con chuletas. Yo soy vegetariana desde hace dos años, y solo comí la ensalada y las patatas fritas.

Clue 1: 'I'm a vegetarian'.

Clue 2: 'I only ate the salad and chips'.

So Natalia avoided the *chuletas* because she is vegetarian. Therefore, *chuletas* must be 'chops', the only meat option out of the three possible answers.

Translation into English (Foundation)

There are five sentences to translate from Spanish, with a minimum of 35 words in total. There are 10 marks for this section.

Four sentences require the present tense, and at least one other requires a past or future tense.

Mostly first-person verbs are required ('I' or 'we') but at least one verb will probably be in the third person ('he / she / it' or 'they').

All vocabulary and grammar will be taken from the Foundation lists.

Translation into English (Higher)

There are five sentences to translate from Spanish, with a minimum of 50 words in total. There are 10 marks for this section.

Verbs will mostly be in the present, but at least one verb will refer to a time in the future or the past.

Verbs will mostly be in the first persons ('I' or 'we') but there will be probably sentences with verbs in the third person ('he / she / it' or 'they').

All vocabulary and grammar will be taken from the Foundation and Higher lists.

Marking the translation – it does not need to be perfect!

Each sentence is divided into two sections on the mark scheme, with the key translation and other versions which are acceptable. You are awarded a mark for every section for which you can get the meaning across sufficiently clearly.

So it pays to have a go at everything!

Translation tips

✓ Try to understand the sentences first, as this will help you to translate them.

✓ Consider each word in your translation, so that you don't miss anything out.

✓ Although you should consider each word, not every Spanish word will have a direct translation into English. For example, you have to translate: El hombre estaba en el extranjero. The correct way to translate this is: 'The man was abroad.' Normally, en el means 'in / on the', but it makes no sense if you include it here.

✓ There is often more than one way of translating a text. You are marked on whether your English communicates clearly the Spanish you have translated. The Spanish will be accurate, so make sure that your English version makes sense.

✓ Read through your work at the end to make sure it makes sense.

Digital resources

Paper 4: Writing

Overview

Sections:

Foundation: 3 writing tasks, 1 translation

Higher: 2 writing tasks, 1 translation

Timing: Foundation: 1 hour 10 minutes;
Higher: 1 hour 15 minutes

☑ All questions, titles and instructions are in English.

☑ All questions are related to one or more of the topics and themes:

Identity and relationships	Celebrity culture
Healthy living and lifestyle	Travel, tourism and places of interest
Education and work	Media and technology
Free-time activities	The environment and where people live
Customs, festivals and celebrations	

You can always use vocabulary that is not on the prescribed list, as long as it is correct.

You can describe the people, using hair, eyes and clothes. You can write about what they are doing, and the surroundings, including the weather (if visible). But make sure what you describe is actually on the picture.

Foundation Question 1

The first question asks you to describe a photo in five short sentences. There are 2 marks per sentence.

☑ Keep your sentences short (but make sure they **are** sentences – include a verb!). Stick to words you know.

☑ There are only marks for correct communication of relevant information. So make sure your answer is relevant (you are describing something in the photo), correct (your Spanish is accurate) and you communicate a point. There are no marks for elaborating on your answer in this question.

☑ Revise some basic verbs that will come in handy in a wide range of situations:

hay – there is / there are)

es – he / she / it is

son – they are

tiene – he / she / it has

tienen – they have

Short and simple sentences that would get you full marks.

Example:

Hay una familia.

Es una fiesta.

Es el cumpleaños del niño.

Hay regalos en la mesa.

El niño está muy contento.

Foundation Question 2

This writing task requires a response of approximately 50 words in Spanish. There are 10 marks available.

There are five bullet points to guide you on what to write. You will be marked for writing clear information on all the bullet points and for the variety and accuracy of the language.

All points can be answered in the present tense.

Write an email about school.

Mention:
- subjects
- teachers
- rules
- uniform
- break

Me gustan mis **asignaturas**, especialmente la historia. Los **profesores** son simpáticos, pero hay muchos deberes. Las **reglas** son estrictas pero necesarias. Odio el **uniforme** porque es un verde muy feo y no me gusta nada el color. El **recreo** es a las once y salimos al patio a comer un bocadillo.

(51 words)

Foundation Question 3

This is a fill-the-gap exercise where there are five sentences, each with one word missing, and three options are provided. You choose the correct one and write it in the gap in the sentence.

Mi hermano _está_ en su dormitorio.

es	está	va

(1)

You choose **está** because **estar** is the verb used for *to be* when you are describing where someone or something is.

You must copy the word exactly to get the mark – that includes accents as well.

About the exams

Paper 4: Writing

Digital resources

Writing task (90 words)

This question appears on both the Foundation paper (Question 5) and the Higher paper (Question 2). You must write a response in Spanish. There are 15 marks available.

You have a choice of two different tasks, on different themes.

There are three bullet points you must cover:

- ✓ answer in the present tense
- ✓ past event
- ✓ future event

Write a letter to your friend about holidays and tourism.

You **must** include the following points:

- what there is for tourists in your area
- what you did in the last school holidays
- a place you will visit in the future.

In the exam, tick off the bullet points as you cover them to ensure you don't miss one by mistake.

Writing task (130–150 words) Ⓗ ONLY

This writing task appears as Question 3 on the Higher paper. You must write a response in Spanish. There are 25 marks available.

You have a choice of two different tasks, on different themes.

There are two bullet points and you must cover both. One bullet point can be answered in the present tense, the other one will refer to either the past or the future.

You are writing an article for an online magazine on the environment.

Write approximately 150 words in **Spanish**. You must write something about both bullet points.

Mention:

- the positive aspect of the environment where you live
- something you did recently to help the environment.

- Do the tasks in order (it makes it clear that you have covered all points).
- Avoid repeating the same language.
- Develop your points with reasons and explanations.
- Stick to the recommended number of words. If you try to write lots, you will rush and more errors will creep in.

Translation into Spanish

Foundation Question 4	Higher Question 1
• Five sentences with a minimum of 35 words.	• Five sentences with a minimum of 50 words.
• Grammar and vocabulary from the Foundation lists.	• Grammar and vocabulary from the Foundation and Higher lists.
• One verb will probably be a non-first person verb.	• At least one verb will be a non-first person verb.
• At least one sentence in a past or future tense.	• There will be verbs in the past, present and future (and probably at least one irregular verb).

- ✓ There will be a steady increase in the difficulty of the sentences from 1 to 5.
- ✓ Read through your work at the end, to ensure it makes sense and to spot any errors.

If you can't remember a word, such as **aprender** (to learn), try to get round it by using a similar word. 'I like **learning** languages' → 'I like **studying** languages'.

Writing paper tips

Of the 50 marks available for each paper, 25 marks are for communication and content, and 25 are for accuracy and knowledge of language.

- ✓ Complete the tasks (don't miss any out).
- ✓ Get the meaning across so what you write is understandable.
- ✓ Avoid leaving gaps.
- ✓ Read through to check you have considered all the words in the translation.
- ✓ Remember that word order in English may be different: un gato negro → a black cat.

Remember – there is often more than one possible correct translation.

93

Digital resources

Nouns and articles

Gender

Nouns are words that name things and people. Every Spanish noun has a gender – masculine (m) or feminine (f). If a word ends in -o or -a, it's easy to work out the gender.

ends in -o	masculine – el gato
ends in -a	feminine – la pera

Exceptions:

el día	day	la foto	photo
el turista	tourist	la radio	radio
el problema	problem	la mano	hand

Some nouns can be both feminine or masculine, depending on the gender of the person:

el / la estudiante	student
el / la modelo	model
el / la artista	artista

For words ending in any other letter, you need to learn the word with the article. If you don't know the gender, look it up in a dictionary.

cine nm cinema

noun masculine – so el cine

The definite article

The definite article ('the') changes to match the gender and number of the noun.

	Singular	Plural
Masculine	el libro	los libros
Feminine	la casa	las casas

The definite article is sometimes used in Spanish when we don't use it in English:

✓ with abstract nouns (things you can't see / touch)
  El fútbol es   Football is
  muy popular.   very popular.

✓ with likes and dislikes
  Me gusta el francés.   I like French.

✓ with days of the week to say 'on'
  el domingo   on Sunday
  los domingos   on Sundays

Remember that **a + el** combine to form **al** and **de + el** join to form **del**.
Voy **al** cine. I'm going **to the** cinema.
Salí **del** cine. I came out **of the** cinema.

The indefinite article

The indefinite article ('a / an') changes to match the gender and number of the noun. In the plural, the English is 'some' or 'any'.

	Singular	Plural
Masculine	un libro	unos libros
Feminine	una casa	unas casas

The indefinite article is NOT used when you talk about jobs.

Soy profesor.   I'm a teacher.

Plurals are easy to form in Spanish.

Singular	Plural
ends in a vowel un hombre	add -s unos hombres
ends in any consonant except -z el mes	add -es los meses
ends in -z la vez	drop z and add -ces las veces

Any noun that ends in -**ón** loses the accent in the plural: **región → regiones**, **millón → millones**.

Now try this

1 Make these nouns plural.

  (a) mercado _____

  (b) luz _____

  (c) tradición _____

  (d) café _____

  (e) actor _____

2 El or **la**? Use a dictionary to fill in the articles.

  (a) _____ ciudad

  (b) _____ tema

  (c) _____ nivel

  (d) _____ educación

  (e) _____ imagen

Adjectives

Adjective agreement

Adjectives describe nouns. They must agree with the noun in gender (masculine or feminine) and number (singular or plural).

Adjective	Singular	Plural
ending in -o		
Masculine	alto	altos
Feminine	alta	altas
ending in -e		
Masculine	importante	importantes
Feminine	importante	importantes
ending in a consonant		
Masculine	azul	azules
Feminine	azul	azules

A dictionary shows the masculine form of an adjective. Make sure you don't forget to make it agree when it's feminine and / or plural!

las faldas amarillas   the yellow skirts

Note the exceptions:

ending in -or		
Masculine	trabajador	trabajadores
Feminine	trabajadora	trabajadoras
adjectives of nationality ending in -s		
Masculine	inglés	ingleses
Feminine	inglesa	inglesas

Position of adjectives

Most Spanish adjectives come **after** the noun.
una falda azul   a blue skirt
These adjectives always come **before** the noun:

mucho	a lot	próximo	next
poco	a little	último	last
primero	first	alguno	some / any
segundo	second	ninguno	no
tercero	third		

Tengo muchos amigos.   I have a lot of friends.

grande comes **before** the noun when it means 'great' rather than 'big'. It changes to **gran** before both masculine and feminine singular nouns.
Fue una **gran** película. It was a great film.

Short forms of adjectives

Some adjectives are shortened when they come before a masculine singular noun.

bueno	good	buen
malo	bad	mal
primero	first	primer
alguno	some / any	algún
ninguno	no	ningún

Use **lo** + masculine singular adjective to say 'the ... thing':

lo bueno   the good thing
lo peor es que the worst thing is that

Now try this

1 Complete the text with the most appropriate adjective from the list. Then translate the text into **English**.

bonitas   divertidas   hermosos   internacionales   pequeñas   trabajadora   históricos   simpática

Las Islas Baleares* son un grupo de islas _____ . Tienen muchas playas _____ . Hay muchos turistas _____ en estas islas. La gente allí es muy _____ y _____ . Las islas tienen muchos museos _____ y muchas actividades _____ También, se puede visitar muchos pueblos _____ .
*The Balearic Islands

Possessives and pronouns

Possessive adjectives

Possessive adjectives agree with the noun they describe, **not** the owner, e.g. sus zapatos – his shoes.

	Singular	Plural
my	mi	mis
your	tu	tus
his / her / its	su	sus
our	nuestro/a	nuestros / as
your	vuestro/a	vuestros / as
their	su	sus

mis amigos
my friends

su colegio
their school

Possessive pronouns

These agree with the noun they replace, e.g. Su casa es más moderna que la nuestra. Their house is more modern than ours.

Singular		
mine	el mío	la mía
yours	el tuyo	la tuya
his / hers / its	el suyo	la suya
ours	el nuestro	la nuestra
yours	el vuestro	la vuestra
theirs	el suyo	la suya

Plural		
mine	los míos	las mías
yours	los tuyos	las tuyas
his / hers / its	los suyos	las suyas
ours	los nuestros	las nuestras
yours	los vuestros	las vuestras
theirs	los suyos	las suyas

Prepositional pronouns

These are used after prepositions.

para – for por – for sin – without a – to	mí – me	nosotros / as – us
	ti – you	vosotros / as – you
	él – him	ellos – them (m)
	ella – her	ellas – them (f)

Esta falda es para ti.
This skirt is for you.

 Note the accent on mí.

con + mí ➡ conmigo   with me
con + ti ➡ contigo   with you

The relative pronoun que

que ('which', 'that' or 'who') allows you to refer back to someone or something already mentioned. You must include it in Spanish, even when you might omit it in English.

El profesor que enseña francés.
The teacher who teaches French.
El libro que lee es español.
The book (that / which) he is reading is Spanish.

Now try this

Circle the correct form each time. Then translate the text into **English**.

Mis / Mi padrastro se llama Omar. **Su / Sus** hijas son muy simpáticas. **Mi / Mis** hermana, **que / por** se llama Sara, tiene un novio, Andrés. **Su / Sus** novio es mayor que **el mío / la mía**. Salgo con **él / ella** desde hace seis años. Sara sale con **el suyo / las suyas** desde hace un mes.

Comparisons

Digital resources

The comparative

The comparative is used to compare two things. It is formed as follows:

más + adjective + que = more ... than
menos + adjective + que = less ... than
tan + adjective + como = as ... as

The adjective agrees with the noun it describes.

La música es más interesante que el deporte.
Music is more interesting than sport.

Pablo es menos alto que su hermano.
Pablo is shorter (less tall) than his brother.

Mi habitación es tan pequeña como la tuya.
My bedroom is as small as yours.

The superlative

The superlative is used to compare more than two things. It is formed as follows:

el / la / los / las (+ noun) + más + adjective = the most ...
el / la / los / las (+ noun) + menos + adjective = the least ...

The definite article and the adjective agree with the noun described.

Buenos Aires es la ciudad más grande de Argentina.
Buenos Aires is the biggest city in Argentina.

Esta casa es la menos cara del pueblo.
This house is the least expensive in the village.

Irregulars

Learn these useful irregular forms:

Adjective	Comparative	Superlative
good	better	the best
bueno	mejor	el / la mejor los / las mejores
bad	worse	the worst
malo	peor	el / la peor los / las peores

Este hotel es el mejor de la región.
This hotel is the best in the region.

Los restaurantes de aquí son los peores.
The restaurants here are the worst.

Using -ísimo for emphasis

You can add -ísimo to the end of an adjective to make it stronger.

La excursión es carísima.
The trip is very expensive.
El libro es malísimo.
The book is very bad.

La comida es buenísima.
The food is really good.

Don't forget to make adjectives agree!

Now try this

Complete the sentences with the correct comparative or superlative.

1 Este libro es _____ de la serie. (*worst*)
2 Mis hermanos son _____ amigos que tengo. (*best*)
3 La falda es _____ de la tienda. (*prettiest*)
4 Este partido de fútbol es _____ . (*really boring*)
5 Carmen es _____ jugadora. (*best*)
6 Este piso es _____ que he visto hoy. (*ugliest*)
7 Lucas es _____ que Juan. (*more sporty*)
8 Mi hermana es _____ que mi hermano. (*funnier*)

Digital resources

Other adjectives

Demonstrative adjectives

Demonstrative adjectives ('this', 'that', 'these', 'those') agree with their noun in number and gender.

	Masculine	Feminine	
Singular	este	esta	this
Plural	estos	estas	these
Singular	ese	esa	that
Plural	esos	esas	those

este móvil	this mobile
esa regla	that ruler
esos chicos	those boys
estas chicas	these girls

When the gender is not known, the neutral forms esto (this) and eso (that) are used.

¿Qué es esto? What is this?

No quiero pensar en eso.
I don't want to think about that.

Using different words for 'that' and 'those'

In Spanish there are two words for 'that' / 'those': ese and aquel. You use aquel to refer to something further away.

esa chica y aquel chico that girl and that boy (over there)

H ONLY

	Masculine	Feminine	
Singular	aquel	aquella	that
Plural	aquellos	aquellas	those

Indefinite adjectives

Indefinite adjectives come up in a lot of contexts, so make sure you know how to use them.

cada	each
otro	another
todo	all
mismo	same
algún / alguna	some / any

As with all other adjectives, remember to make them agree. Exception: **cada** – it doesn't change.

Tengo otra entrevista.	I have another interview.
Todos los clientes estaban enojados.	All the customers were angry.
Llevamos la misma camiseta.	We're wearing the same T-shirt.
¿Tienes algún bolígrafo?	Do you have a pen?

Cada estudiante puede usar un ordenador.
Each student can use a computer.

Now try this

Translate these sentences into **Spanish**.

1 That boy is my cousin.
2 This apple is hard.
3 I want to buy those shoes.
4 That house over there is really big.
5 This film is boring.
6 I don't want this shirt. I prefer that T-shirt.

Pronouns

Digital resources

Subject, direct object and indirect object

- The **subject** is the person / thing doing the action (shown by the verb).
- The **object** is the person / thing having the action (shown by the verb) done to it. It can be **direct** or **indirect**.

Subject	Verb	Direct object	Indirect object
María	sends	the email	to David.
She	sends	it	to him.

Subject pronoun		Direct object pronoun		Indirect object pronoun	
I	yo	me	me	(to / for) me	me
you	tú	you	te	(to / for) you	te
he / it	él	him / it	lo	(to / for) him / it	le
she / it	ella	her / it	la	(to / for) her / it	le
we	nosotros / as	us	nos	(to / for) us	nos
you	vosotros / as	you	os	(to / for) you	os
they	ellos / ellas	them	los / las	(to / for) them	les

Subject pronouns aren't often used in Spanish because the verb ending is enough to show who is doing the action. They're sometimes used for **emphasis**.

A mí me gusta Perú, pero él quiere ir a México.   I like Peru but he wants to go to Mexico.

Position of object pronouns

In general, object pronouns come:
- **before** the verb
- **after** a negative

La compré en el supermercado.	I bought it in the supermarket.
No la tengo.	I don't have it.
Nadie les escribe.	No one writes to them.

The object pronoun can be added to the infinitive in the near future tense.

Voy a comprarlo por Internet.

or

Lo voy a comprar por Internet.
I'm going to buy it online.

Object pronouns are attached to the end of a positive imperative.

¡Hazlo!   Do it!

Now try this

Rewrite the sentences, replacing the words in bold with pronouns.
1 Voy a dar **el regalo** a mi padre.
2 Mando muchos mensajes **a mi hermana**.
3 Voy a comprar **un libro**.
4 Pon **los tomates** en la bolsa.
5 Voy a decir **a Raúl** la verdad.

 Digital resources

The present tense

This page covers all three types of regular verb and radical-changing verbs in the present tense.

Present tense (regular)

To form the present tense of regular verbs, replace the infinitive ending as follows:

	hablar – to speak	comer – to eat	vivir – to live
I	hablo	como	vivo
you	hablas	comes	vives
he / she / it	habla	come	vive
we	hablamos	comemos	vivimos
you	habláis	coméis	vivís
they	hablan	comen	viven

How to use the present tense

Use the present tense to talk about:
* what you are doing **now**
* what you do **regularly**
* what things are **like**.

You can also use the present tense to talk about planned future events.

Mañana voy a España.
Tomorrow I'm going to Spain.

Remember that **usted** (polite / formal form of 'you') takes the endings for 'he / she / it'.
¿Habla inglés?   Do you speak English?

Also use the present tense with desde hace.
Vivo aquí desde hace dos años.
I have been living here for two years.

Radical-changing verbs

In radical-changing verbs, the vowel in the syllable before the infinitive ending changes in the singular and third person plural. There are three common groups.

	o → ue	e → ie	e → i
	poder to be able	querer to want	pedir to ask
I	puedo	quiero	pido
you	puedes	quieres	pides
he / she / it	puede	quiere	pide
we	podemos	queremos	pedimos
you	podéis	queréis	pedís
they	pueden	quieren	piden

Other examples of radical-changing verbs:

u / o → ue	e → ie
jugar → juego to play	empezar → empiezo to start
dormir → duermo to sleep	entender → entiendo to understand
volver → vuelvo to return	pensar → pienso to think
encontrar → encuentro to meet	preferir → prefiero to prefer

¿Quieres salir esta noche?
Do you want to go out tonight?
Rafael juega al baloncesto los viernes.
Rafael plays basketball on Fridays.

Now try this

Complete the sentences using the present tense. Then translate the sentences into **English**.

1 No _____ música clásica. (*escuchar, I*)
2 Mis padres _____ inglés. (*hablar*)
3 Mi amigo _____ al baloncesto conmigo. (*jugar*)
4 ¿_____ ir al cine conmigo esta noche? (*querer, you singular informal*)
5 Siempre _____ fruta para estar sanos. (*comer, we*)
6 Siempre _____ dinero en la calle. (*encontrar, they*)
7 ¿_____ en el campo? (*vivir, you plural informal*)
8 Mi hermano _____ en su propio dormitorio. (*dormir*)

Reflexive verbs

Digital resources

Present tense (regular)

Reflexive verbs have the same endings as other present tense verbs but contain a reflexive pronoun. Some are also radical-changing verbs.

	lavarse to wash	vestirse to get dressed
I	me lavo	me visto
you	te lavas	te vistes
he / she / it / you (polite)	se lava	se viste

Plural forms (required for Higher tier only).

we	nos lavamos	nos vestimos
you	os laváis	os vestís
they	se lavan	se visten

In the infinitive form, the pronoun can be added to the end of the verb.

Voy a levantarme.   I'm going to get up.

> You can use the reflexive pronoun **se** to create an impersonal construction:
> Aquí no se puede nadar.
> You cannot swim here.
> Se necesita gente con experiencia.
> People with experience are needed.

Useful reflexive verbs

Infinitive	1st person singular	English
ponerse	me pongo	I put on
quedarse	me quedo	I stay
llamarse	me llamo	I am called
perderse	me pierdo	I get lost
sentirse	me siento	I feel
levantarse	me levanto	I get up
llevarse (con)	me llevo (con)	I get on (with)
dormirse	me duermo	I fall asleep
casarse	me caso	I get married
despertarse	me despierto	I wake up
parecerse a	me parezco a	I look like
acordarse (de)	me acuerdo	I remember
preocuparse	me preocupo	I worry
atreverse a	me atrevo a	I dare to
acostarse	me acuesto	I go to bed
quejarse	me quejo	I complain
pelearse con	me peleo con	I fight with
enamorarse	me enamoro	I fall in love
acostumbrarse	me acostumbro	I get used
divertirse	me divierto	I enjoy myself
negarse (a)	me niego a	I refuse to

The plural forms can often mean 'each other'.

Los novios se besaron. The bride and groom kissed each other.

Mis amigos y yo nos vemos los fines de semana. My friends and I see each other at the weekend

Now try this

Complete the sentences with the correct reflexive pronouns.
1 Normalmente _____ despierto temprano.
2 Mi hermano _____ levanta a las seis.
3 Mis amigos y yo _____ divertimos mucho en la fiesta.
4 ¿A qué hora _____ acuestas durante la semana?
5 Los perros siempre _____ duermen al sol.
6 Siempre _____ lleváis bien cuando estamos de vacaciones.

Digital resources

Irregular verbs

The verbs ir and tener

These key verbs are irregular in the present tense.

	ir – to go
I	voy
you	vas
he / she / it / you (polite)	va
we	vamos
you	vais
they	van

	tener – to have
I	tengo
you	tienes
he / she / it / you (polite)	tiene
we	tenemos
you	tenéis
they	tienen

Tengo que hacer los deberes y luego voy al cine.
I have to do my homework and then I'm going to the cinema.

Other irregular verbs

Some other useful verbs are also irregular in the present tense.

decir – to say	digo, dices, dice, decimos, decís, dicen
oír – to hear	oigo, oyes, oye, oímos, oís, oyen
venir – to come	vengo, vienes, viene, venimos, venís, vienen

Irregular 'I' forms

Some verbs are irregular in the 'I' form only.

conocer	to know / meet	➡	conozco
dar	to give	➡	doy
hacer	to make / do	➡	hago
poner	to put	➡	pongo
saber	to know	➡	sé
salir	to go out	➡	salgo
traer	to bring	➡	traigo

H ONLY

Some verbs are irregular to keep the pronunciation correct.
proteger – to protect ➡ protejo – I protect
coger – to take ➡ cojo – I take

Now try this

Complete these sentences with the correct form of the verb in brackets. Then translate them into **English**.

1 Yo _____ a las siete y media para ir al concierto. (*salir*)
2 Mis primos _____ los ojos azules y son rubios. (*tener*)
3 Me gusta mucho ir a la playa pero no _____ nadar. (*saber*)
4 Siempre _____ el autobús cuando voy al instituto. (*coger*)
5 Mis amigos _____ los deberes en la biblioteca pero yo los _____ en casa. (*hacer*)

Ser and *estar*

Digital resources

Spanish has two verbs meaning 'to be': ser and estar. Both are irregular – you need to know them well.

The present tense of ser

	ser – to be
I am	soy
you are	eres
he / she / it is	es
we are	somos
you are	sois
they are	son

Roberto es un chico feliz.
Roberto is a happy boy.

When to use ser

Use ser for **permanent** things.
- nationality

| Soy británico. | I'm British. |

- occupation

| Es profesor. | He's a teacher. |

- colour and size

| Es rojo. Es pequeño. | It's red. It's small. |

- personality

| Son trabajadoras. | They're hard-working. |

- telling the time

| Son las tres. | It's three o'clock. |

Always use ser with joven (young), viejo (old), barato (cheap) and caro (expensive).

The present tense of estar

	estar – to be
I am	estoy
you are	estás
he / she / it is	está
we are	estamos
you are	estáis
they are	están

Hoy Andrea está muy aburrida.
Andrea is very bored today.

When to use estar

Use estar for **temporary** things and **locations**.

- illness

| Estoy enfermo. | I'm unwell. |

- appearance (temporary)

| Estás guapo. | You look handsome. |

- feelings (temporary)

Estoy contento porque gané un premio.
I'm happy because I won a prize.

- location

Mi madre está en el jardín.
My mother is in the garden.

Watch out for this one!
| ser listo | to be clever |
| estar listo | to be ready |

Now try this

Complete the sentences with **ser** or **estar** in the present tense.

1 ¿Dónde _____ la estación de autobuses?
2 Barcelona _____ grande e interesante.
3 Mi hermana _____ policía.
4 Yo _____ cansado.
5 Los zapatos _____ negros.

6 Mi mejor amiga _____ chilena.
7 Hoy mis amigos no _____ contentos porque tienen una prueba.
8 Natalia _____ muy bonita esta noche con su vestido nuevo.

 Digital resources

The gerund / present participle

The gerund, also known as the present participle, is the equivalent of the English '-ing'.

The gerund

To form the gerund of regular verbs, replace the infinitive ending as follows:

hablar – hablando

comer – comiendo

vivir – viviendo

Common irregular gerunds:

caer	cayendo	falling
leer	leyendo	reading
construir	construyendo	building
pedir	pidiendo	asking for
decir	diciendo	saying, telling
servir	sirviendo	serving

Está jugando al fútbol.
She's playing football.

Uses of the gerund

You use the gerund:

- to give more information about how something was or is being done
  Voy andando al instituto.
  I go to school on foot.
- to form the present continuous and imperfect continuous tenses (see below).
- in Higher tier, after seguir to form the construction 'to keep on / carry on -ing'.
  Sigo estudiando dibujo porque me gusta.
  I keep studying Art because I like it.

You can't always translate an '-ing' verb in English by the gerund in Spanish, e.g.
Aprender español es emocionante.
Learning Spanish is exciting.
Vamos a salir mañana.
We're leaving tomorrow.

Present continuous tense

The present continuous describes what is happening at this moment:

present tense of estar + the gerund

	estar – to be	gerund
I	estoy	
you	estás	viajando
he / she / it	está	saliendo
we	estamos	pidiendo
you	estáis	diciendo
they	están	

Estoy viendo la televisión. I'm watching TV.

Imperfect continuous tense

This tense describes what was happening at a certain moment in the past:

imperfect tense of estar + the gerund

	estar – to be	gerund
I	estaba	
you	estabas	visitando
he / she / it	estaba	estudiando
we	estábamos	escribiendo
you	estabais	buscando
they	estaban	

Estaba leyendo. I was reading.

Now try this

Rewrite the sentences using the present continuous tense. Write them again using the imperfect continuous.

1 Juego al fútbol.
2 Escribo un correo electrónico.
3 Habla con mi amigo Juan.
4 Duerme en la cama.
5 Como tapas.
6 Tomo el sol en la playa.
7 Navega por Internet.
8 ¿Cantas en tu habitación?

The preterite tense

Digital resources

The preterite tense is used to talk about completed actions in the past.

Preterite tense (regular)

To form the preterite tense of regular verbs, replace the infinitive ending as follows:

	hablar – to speak	comer – to eat	vivir – to live
I	hablé	comí	viví
you	hablaste	comiste	viviste
he / she / it	habló	comió	vivió
we	hablamos	comimos	vivimos
you	hablasteis	comisteis	vivisteis
they	hablaron	comieron	vivieron

> Be careful – accents can be significant.
> Hablo. I speak.
> Habló. He / She spoke.

How to use the preterite tense

You use the preterite to describe completed actions in the past.

El año pasado viajé a Estados Unidos.
Last year I travelled to the United States.

 Some verbs have a spelling change in the third persons singular and plural:

	pedir	dormir	leer
I	pedí	dormí	leí
you	pediste	dormiste	leíste
he / she / it	pidió	durmió	leyó
we	pedimos	dormimos	leímos
you	pedisteis	dormisteis	leísteis
they	pidieron	durmieron	leyeron

Preterite tense (irregular)

	ir – to go ser – to be	hacer – to do
I	fui	hice
you	fuiste	hiciste
he / she / it	fue	hizo
we	fuimos	hicimos
you	fuisteis	hicisteis
they	fueron	hicieron

> The verbs **ir** and **ser** have the same forms in the preterite. Use context to work out which is meant.

Irregular preterite stems of common verbs:

dar	di	I gave
decir	dije	I said, told
estar	estuve	I was
poder	pude	I could
poner	puse	I put
querer	quise	I wanted
tener	tuve	I had
traer	traje	I brought
venir	vine	I came

verbs with an irregular 1st person singular

cruzar	crucé	I crossed
empezar	empecé	I started
jugar	jugué	I played
llegar	llegué	I arrived
tocar	toqué	I played

Now try this

Identify the tense in each sentence (present or preterite). Then translate the sentences into **English**.

1 Voy a España.
2 Llegué a las seis.
3 Navego por Internet.
4 Escuchó música.
5 Fue a una fiesta que fue guay.
6 Hizo frío y llovió un poco.
7 Vimos a Pablo en el mercado.
8 Jugué al baloncesto en la playa.

Digital resources

The imperfect tense

Foundation students only need to know the singular forms. (I, you, he / she / it)

Imperfect tense (regular)

To form the imperfect tense of regular verbs, replace the infinitive ending as follows:

	hablar – to speak	comer – to eat	vivir – to live
I	hablaba	comía	vivía
you	hablabas	comías	vivías
he / she / it	hablaba	comía	vivía
we	hablábamos	comíamos	vivíamos
you	hablabais	comíais	vivíais
they	hablaban	comían	vivían

-er and -ir verbs have the same endings.

Try to use both the **imperfect** and the **preterite** in your work to aim for a higher grade.

How to use the imperfect tense

You use the imperfect to talk about:

- what people used to do / how things used to be
  Antes no separaba la basura.
  I didn't use to sort the rubbish before.

- repeated actions in the past
  Jugaba al tenis todos los días.
  I played tennis every day.

- descriptions in the past.
  El hotel era caro.
  The hotel was expensive.

Antes, trabajaba en un café.
Ahora ayudo en una tienda.
I used to work in a café.
Now I help in a shop.

Imperfect tense (irregular)

Only three verbs are irregular:

	ir – to go	ser – to be	ver – to see
I	iba	era	veía
you	ibas	eras	veías
he / she / it	iba	era	veía
we	íbamos	éramos	veíamos
you	ibais	erais	veíais
they	iban	eran	veían

Preterite or imperfect?

- Use the preterite tense for a **single / completed** event in the past.
- Use the imperfect tense for **repeated / continuous** events in the past.
  Cerca de aquí había un castillo.
  There used to be a castle near here.
  Ayer fui a visitar el castillo.
  Yesterday I went to visit the castle.

Now try this

Complete the sentences with the imperfect or preterite tense, as appropriate.

1 Mi hermano _____ en la piscina todos los veranos. trabajar
2 Ayer _____ muchos caramelos. comer (*I*)
3 Antes _____ a la costa con mis padres. ir (*I*)
4 Cuando yo era joven, _____ un mercado aquí los viernes. haber
5 El verano pasado _____ Buenos Aires por primera vez. visitar (*I*)
6 De pequeño, mi hermanita siempre _____. llorar

The future tense

Digital resources

Future tense

To form the future tense of most verbs, add the following endings to the infinitive:
(The plural forms 'we', 'you' and 'they' are only required at Higher level.)

ir – to go			
I	iré	we	iremos
you	irás	you	iréis
he / she / it	irá	they	irán

Some verbs use a different stem. You need to memorise these:

decir to say   ➡   diré I will say
haber there is / are   ➡   habrá there will be
hacer to make / do   ➡   haré I will make / do
poder to be able to   ➡   podré I will be able to
querer to want   ➡   querré I will want
saber to know   ➡   sabré I will know
salir to leave   ➡   saldré I will leave
tener to have   ➡   tendré I will have
venir to come   ➡   vendré I will come
poner to put   ➡   pondré I will put

Immediate future tense

You form the immediate future tense as follows:
present tense of ir + a + infinitive

	ir – to go		infinitive
I	voy		
you	vas		mandar
he / she / it	va	a	bailar
we	vamos		salir
you	vais		venir
they	van		

¿Vas a comer algo?
Are you going to have something to eat?

Vamos a ir a la fiesta.
We're going to go to the festival.

Recognise and use a range of time expressions that indicate the future, for example:

mañana   tomorrow   mañana por la mañana   tomorrow morning
esta noche   tonight   el próximo viernes   next Friday.

Using the future tense

Use the future tense to talk about what **will** happen in the future.

El año que viene será difícil encontrar un buen trabajo.
Next year it will be difficult to find a good job.
Si llueve, iremos al cine.
If it rains, we will go to the cinema.

Using the immediate future tense

You use the immediate future tense to say what is going to happen. It is used to talk about future plans.
En Barcelona va a comprar recuerdos.
He's going to buy souvenirs in Barcelona.
Voy a salir esta tarde.
I'm going to go out this afternoon.

Now try this

1 Rewrite the sentences using the future tense.
  (a) Nunca fumo.
  (b) Ayudo a otras personas.
  (c) Cambiamos el mundo.
  (d) Trabajo en un aeropuerto.

2 Rewrite the sentences using the immediate future tense.
  (a) Salgo a las seis.
  (b) Soy médico.
  (c) Va a Ecuador.
  (d) Mañana juego al tenis.

Digital resources

The conditional tense

The conditional

To form the conditional, you add the following endings to the infinitive:

	hablar – to speak
I	hablaría
you	hablarías
he / she / it	hablaría
we	hablaríamos
you	hablaríais
they	hablarían

The endings are the same for ALL verbs.

Some verbs use a different stem.

haber there is / are	➡	habría
hacer to do	➡	haría
poder to be able to	➡	podría
tener to have	➡	tendría
poner to put	➡	pondría
decir to say	➡	diría
querer to want	➡	querría
saber to know	➡	sabría
salir to leave	➡	saldría
venir to come	➡	vendría

Construir un parque infantil **sería** una idea muy buena.
Building a children's playground would be a really good idea.

Use **poder** in the conditional + the infinitive to say what you **could** do.
Podríamos ir a Ibiza.   We could go to Ibiza.

Use **deber** in the conditional + the infinitive to say what you **should** do.
Nunca deberías fumar.
You should never smoke.

Expressing future intent

The conditional can be used to express future intent. Use gustar in the conditional + the infinitive.
En el futuro ...   In the future ...

... me gustaría ir a Sudamérica.
... I'd like to go to South America.

... me gustaría ser escritora.
... I'd like to be a writer.

... me gustaría comprarme un coche nuevo.
... I'd like to buy a new car.

You can also use me encantaría:
Me encantaría tener una casa al lado del mar.
I'd love to have a house by the sea.

Now try this

Rewrite the text, changing the verbs in bold to the conditional.

> Para mantenerme en forma **bebo** mucha agua. **Hago** mucho ejercicio y **practico** mucho deporte. Nunca **tomo** drogas y no **bebo** alcohol. **Como** mucha fruta y **me acuesto** temprano – siempre **duermo** ocho horas, gracias a eso **llevo** una vida sana.

The perfect tense

The perfect tense

The perfect tense describes what someone has done or something that has happened.

He ido a la piscina.

I have been to the swimming pool.

To form the perfect tense, use the present tense of haber + past participle:

	haber – to have
I	he
you	has
he / she / it	ha
we	hemos
you	habéis
they	han

The past participle

To form the past participle, replace the infinitive ending as follows:

hablar ➡ hablado

comer ➡ comido

vivir ➡ vivido

Ha bajado una película.

He has downloaded a film.

¿Has visto a María?   Have you seen María?

The past participle does not change or agree when it forms part of the perfect tense.

Word order

The two parts of the verb are never split.

- Negatives go in front or around the verb:
  Nunca he estado en Madrid.
  I have never been in Madrid.
  No he hablado con nadie hoy.
  I have not spoken to anyone today.
- Object / reflexive pronouns go before the verb:
  Se las he mandado a mi madre.
  I have sent them to my mother.

Some past participles are irregular. These are needed at **Higher** level:

abrir	➡ abierto	opened
decir	➡ dicho	said
escribir	➡ escrito	written
hacer	➡ hecho	done, made
poner	➡ puesto	put
romper	➡ roto	broken
ver	➡ visto	seen
volver	➡ vuelto	returned

Mi hermanito se ha quemado al sol.

My little brother has got burnt in the sun.

Las chicas han vuelto de sus vacaciones.

The girls have returned from their holidays.

Now try this

Complete the sentences with the correct perfect tense form of the verb in brackets.

1 Miguel _____ (*recomendar*) esta película porque yo no la _____ (*ver*).

2 Mis hermanos _____ (*perder*) el plano y yo no _____ (*poder*) encontrar el restaurante.

3 ¿Tú _____ (*probar*) la tortilla que Andrea y yo _____ (*hacer*) esta mañana?

4 Los niños _____ (*pedir*) perdón, pero no sé si nos _____ (*decir*) la verdad.

Digital resources

Giving instructions

The imperative

The construction used for giving instructions or commands is called the imperative.

The ending of the verb in the imperative depends on whether you are talking to one person (tú) or more than one person (vosotros/as).

Toma la primera calle a la derecha.　Take the first street on the right. (Talking to tú)

Tomad la primera calle a la derecha.　Take the first street on the right. (Talking to vosotros/as)

> At Foundation tier, you need to know the **tú** commands only. For Higher tier, you need to know both the **tú** and the **vosotros/as** commands.

Forming the imperative (Foundation – tú form only; Higher – both forms)

The tú command is formed by removing the -s from the tú form of the present tense.

Infinitive	Tú (present)	Tú (imperative)
hablar	hablas	habla
comer	comes	come
escribir	escribes	escribe

This means that the radical change that occurs in the present tense also affects this form of the imperative:

¡Vuelve pronto!　　　Come back soon!

Despierta a los niños.　Wake the children up.

Object / reflexive pronouns go on the end of the verb in the imperative form:

¡Levántate, Carmen!　Get up, Carmen!

Mándalos a tu amiga.　Send them to your friend.

The vosotros/as command is formed by taking the infinitive, removing the -r and adding -d.

Infinitive	Vosotros / as form
hablar	hablad
comer	comed
escribir	escribid

Irregular imperatives in the tú form:

ser	➡	¡Sé!	Be!
hacer	➡	¡Haz!	Do! Make!
ir	➡	¡Ve!	Go!
salir	➡	¡Sal!	Go out! Leave!
tener	➡	¡Ten!	Have!
poner	➡	¡Pon!	Put!
venir	➡	¡Ven!	Come!

> There are no radical changes or irregular in the **vosotros/as** forms.

Now try this

Translate the instructions into **English**.

Foundation and Higher		Higher only	
1	Escribe a tu primo.	1	Comed las verduras, niños.
2	Pon las flores en la mesa.	2	Hablad con la directora.
3	Coge el autobús número diez.	3	Subid las fotos a Internet.
4	Haz tus deberes ahora.	4	Venid a jugar al parque.
5	Prepara la cena para la familia.	5	Esperad el autobús en la esquina.
6	Ven aquí, Paula.	6	Coged el tren de las ocho.
7	Lee esta novela. Te encantará.	7	Poned los libros en la mesa.
8	Baila conmigo. Es mi canción favorita.	8	Mandadme unas fotos.
9	Cómprame una revista.	9	Bebed más agua, hijos.
10	¡Despiértate, Miguel!	10	Compartid los caramelos.

The present subjunctive

Digital resources

Formation of the present subjunctive

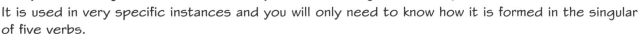

The present subjunctive tense is a requirement at Higher tier only.

It is used in very specific instances and you will only need to know how it is formed in the singular of five verbs.

hacer – to do, make	**ir** – to go	**ser** – to be	**venir** – to come	**tener** – to have
haga	vaya	sea	venga	tenga
hagas	vayas	seas	vengas	tengas
haga	vaya	sea	venga	tenga

The subjunctive is used:

• after cuando when the action of the verb has not yet taken place:
Te mostraré el libro **cuando** vengas a mi casa.
I will show you the book when you come to my house.

Cuando vayas a la universidad, tendrás que cuidar tu dinero.
When you go to university you will have to look after your money.

• after para que (so that ...)
Te doy esto **para que** tengas toda la información importante.
I'm giving you this so that you have all the important information.
Deberías ver este programa **para que** seas consciente de la situación.
You should watch this programme so that you are aware of the situation.

• after verbs of wishing, commanding requesting + que
Mi madre **quiere que** haga la cama.
My mother wants me to make the bed.
Le **pediré que** venga a las nueve.
I will ask him to come at nine.

Me **sorprende** que Lola sea tu hermana; sois muy diferentes.
I am surprised that Lola is your sister; you are very different.

• after verbs of emotion + que
Me **molesta** que hagas tanto ruido cuando estoy trabajando.
It annoys me that you make so much noise when I am working.

Now try this

Translate the sentences into **English**.

1 Cuando vaya a la universidad, estudiaré ciencias.
2 Quiero que tengas estas entradas para el concierto el sábado.
3 Diego, quiero que seas más responsable en el futuro.
4 Le pediré a Sofía que nos espere en el café.
5 Me molesta que mi hija haga los deberes a esta hora de la noche.
6 Voy a ayudarte para que tengas tiempo para salir con tu amiga.

Digital
resources

Negatives

Negatives

no	not
no … nada	nothing / not anything
no … nadie	no one, nobody
no … ningún / ninguna	no / not any
ni … ni	neither … nor
no … ni	not … or
no … tampoco	not … either
ya no	no longer, not any more

Notice that when **nadie** comes after a verb, the personal 'a' is used before the word.

How to use negatives

The simplest way to make a verb negative in Spanish is to use no before the verb:

No vi la tele ayer.
I didn't watch TV yesterday.

Nunca also goes before the verb:

Nunca van al extranjero.
They never go abroad.

Nadie can go before or after the verb, but if it comes after the verb, the negative no must go before the verb:

Nadie está aquí.
No one is here.

No vi a nadie en la calle.
I didn't see anyone in the street.

Using negatives

Ya no estudio educación física.
I don't study PE any more.

No me gusta cantar ni bailar.
I don't like singing or dancing.

Ni María ni Jorge me ayudaron.
Neither María nor Jorge helped me.

Si tú no vas, yo no voy tampoco.
If you don't go, I'm not going either.

Useful expressions:

Espero que no.	I hope not.
Creo que no.	I don't think so.
Claro que no.	Of course not.
Nunca se sabe.	You never know.

Hoy, no quiero hacer nada.
Today, I don't want to do anything.

Now try this

Make the sentences negative, giving the opposite meanings. Then translate the original sentences into **English**.
1 Siempre como verduras.
2 Tengo un libro.
3 Conozco a todos.
4 Todo el mundo juega al baloncesto.
5 Siempre hago mis deberes.
6 Me gusta navegar por Internet y bajar música.
7 Tiene todo.
8 Tengo muchos amigos en Madrid.

Special verbs

Digital resources

Present tense of gustar

Me gusta ('I like') literally translates as 'it pleases me'. The thing that does the pleasing (i.e. the thing I like) is the subject.

Me gusta este libro.   I like this book.

If the subject is plural, use me gustan.

Me gustan estos libros.

I like these books.

The pronoun changes as follows:

me	gusta(n)	I like
te	gusta(n)	you like
le	gusta(n)	he / she / it likes
nos	gusta(n)	we like
os	gusta(n)	you like
les	gusta(n)	they like

encantar behaves in the same way as gustar:
Le encanta la música rock. He loves rock music.

Preterite tense of gustar

In the preterite:

me gusta ➡ me gustó

me gustan ➡ me gustaron

The pronouns in the other forms are the same as for the present tense.

Nos gustó la comida china.
We liked Chinese food.

Le gustaron las tiendas.
He liked the shops.

To talk about other people's likes / dislikes, you need **a** before their name:
A Ignacio le gusta el deporte.
Ignacio likes sport.

If you're aiming for higher grades, use **gustar** in the preterite to extend your language range.

Other verbs like gustar

Other verbs follow the same pattern as gustar:
pronoun + 3rd person singular of the verb

doler	Me duele(n) ...	My ... hurts / aches
importar	No me importa(n) ...	I don't mind ...
interesar	Me interesa(n) ...	I'm interested in ...
hacer falta	Me hace(n) falta ...	I need ...

Me duele la cabeza.
My head aches.

¿Te interesa la música?
Are you interested in music?
Les hace falta un vaso. They need a glass.

Other special verbs

- acabar de + infinitive ➔ to have just ...
  Use the present tense of acabar + de + infinitive
  Acabo de llegar.   I have just arrived.
  El tren acaba de salir.   The train has just left.

  (See page 62 for more about acabar.)

- falta + infinitive ➔ it is still to be + past participle
  Solo falta pintar la puerta.
  It's just the door that is still to be painted.

- llevar + time + present participle ➔ to have been ... ing for + time
  Use the present tense of llevar + time + gerund / present participle.
  Llevo tres meses trabajando en Madrid.
  I've been working in Madrid for three months.

  (See page 34 for more about llevar.)

Now try this

Complete the sentences.

1 _____ el brazo. (*doler, I*)

2 _____ el jamón. (*gustar, she*)

3 ¿_____ las naranjas? (*gustar, you singular*)

4 _____ los pies. (*doler, he*)

5 No _____ el frío. (*importar, I*)

6 _____ mucho los idiomas. (*interesar, they*)

7 _____ dos meses viviendo en Barcelona. (*llevar, I*)

8 _____ platos. (*hacer falta, they*)

Digital resources

Por and *para*

Using por

You use por for:

- exchange
  Pagué cien euros por el vuelo.
  I paid €100 for the flight.

- cause
  El avión salió tarde por la lluvia.
  The plane set off late because of the rain.

- action **on behalf of** someone
  Lo hizo por mí.   She did it for me.

- **rates**
  Gano seis euros por hora.
  I earn €6 per hour.

- means of **communication**
  Me llamó por teléfono.
  He called me on the phone.

- unspecified periods of **time**
  Me quedaré en Buenos Aires por poco tiempo.
  I will stay in Buenos Aires for a short time.

Me llamó por teléfono.
He called me on the phone.

Set phrases with por

por favor	please
por primera vez	for the first time
por aquí	over here, around here
por todas partes	everywhere
por la mañana	in the morning
por ciento	per cent

Using para

You use para for:

- **purpose** (it can often be translated by 'in order to')
  Llevamos una botella de agua fría para el viaje.
  We're taking a bottle of cold water for the journey.
  Voy a utilizar mi tarjeta de crédito para pagar el hotel.
  I'm going to use my credit card to pay for the hotel.

- **destination (place or people)**
  Ha salido para Madrid.
  He has left for Madrid.

- specific **time** periods or **deadlines** in the future
  Quisiera una habitación para quince días.
  I would like a room for a fortnight.

Voy a comprar unos regalos para mi familia.
I'm going to buy some presents for my family.

Try writing out phrases with **por** and **para**, using one colour for **por** each time and another colour for **para**. Then when you're trying to remember which one to use, try to visualise the colour.

Now try this

1 Choose **por** or **para** to complete these sentences.
   (a) Voy a ir a la ciudad _____ hacer compras.
   (b) El tren _____ Madrid sale a las seis.
   (c) Gracias _____ el regalo.
   (d) Los deberes son _____ mañana.
   (e) Este regalo es _____ mi profesor.
   (f) Voy a llamarle _____ teléfono.
   (g) Mi hermana gana veinte euros _____ hora.

2 Tick the sentences which are correct. Correct those that are wrong.
   (a) Salimos por Nueva York.
   (b) Solo estudio para la mañana.
   (c) Por ganar hay que trabajar duro.
   (d) Voy a hacerlo para ti.
   (e) Juego al fútbol para divertirme.
   (f) Estas flores son por mi novia.
   (g) Gano dinero para comprar un móvil nuevo.
   (h) Un gran porcentaje de jóvenes escucha música cuando hace los deberes.

Asking questions

Being able to ask and understand questions is an important part of learning the language. You will need to ask a question during the role play in the speaking exam.

How to ask questions

To ask yes / no questions, use the same language as you would to say the sentence and:

- if you're writing, add question marks
- if you're speaking, use a rising intonation at the end.

¿Estudias español?
Do you study Spanish?
¿Quieres ir al polideportivo?
Do you want to go to the leisure centre?

> Remember the ¿ at the start.

To ask open questions, use a question word.

¿Cuándo?	When?
¿Dónde?	Where?
¿Adónde?	Where to?
¿Cuánto/a?	How much?
¿Cuántos/as?	How many?
¿Qué?	What?
¿Por qué?	Why?
¿Cómo?	How?
¿Cuál(es)?	Which (ones)?
¿Quién(es)?	Who?
¿Cuál (de estos libros) te gusta más?	Which (one of these books) do you like more?
¿De dónde?	From where?

> Don't forget the accents on question words.

H ONLY · Using quién / quiénes

¿De quién(es) … ?	Whose … ?
¿A quién(es) … ?	To whom … ? / Who … to?
¿Con quién(es) … ?	With whom … ? / Who … with?
¿Para quién(es) … ?	For whom … ? Who … for?

¿De quién es este cuaderno?
Whose is this exercise book?

Note the word order:
¿A quién escribes?
Who are you writing to?

¿Para quién son estas flores?
Who are these flowers for?

¿Con quiénes vas de vacaciones?
Who are you going on holiday with?

Question tag

English has a lot of different ways of asking for confirmation, e.g. 'doesn't he?', 'haven't they?', 'can't you?'. In Spanish it's much easier. You just put verdad at the end of a question.

¿Pablo es tu novio, verdad?
Pablo is your boyfriend, isn't he?

Now try this

Match the sentence halves.

1 ¿Cuál   **a** cuesta?
2 ¿Adónde   **b** personas hay en tu clase?
3 ¿Quién   **c** te llamas?
4 ¿Dónde   **d** es tu asignatura preferida?
5 ¿Cuánto   **e** está Benidorm?
6 ¿Cuántas   **f** fuiste de vacaciones el año pasado?
7 ¿Cómo   **g** es tu cumpleaños?
8 ¿Cuándo   **h** es tu cantante preferido?

Digital resources

The passive (H)

The passive is a construction which, in English, consists of an action being conveyed by any tense of the verb **to be** + *past participle*.

For example: Spanish **is** *spoken* in Costa Rica.

The results **will be** *published* next week.

Using ser + past participle

This works very much like the English passive. For **to be**, use the appropriate tense of **ser** and then add the past participle.

> The regular past participle is formed by removing the infinitive ending and adding -**ado** to -**ar** verbs and -**ido** to -**er** / -**ir** verbs.

The car **was** *sold* last week. ➡
El coche **fue** *vendido* la semana pasada.

The website **is** mainly *used* by young people. ➡
El sitio web **es** *usado* principalmente por los jóvenes.

The programme **will be** *watched* by millions of people. ➡ El programa **será** *visto* por millones de personas.

> Be careful to make the past participle agree with the noun it refers to:
>
> The computers **are** *turned off* at the end of the lesson. ➡ Los ordenadores **son** *apagados* al final de la clase.
>
> The room **was** *cleaned* this morning. ➡ La habitación **fue** *limpiada* esta mañana.

Using the reflexive se

Another way of producing the passive in Spanish is to make the verb reflexive. This sounds very odd to English people, as it sounds as if the verb 'does itself'! However, it is very common in Spanish.

The website **is** mainly *used* for downloading music. ➡
El sitio web **se** usa principalmente para bajar música.

The results **will be** *published* next week. ➡
Se publicarán los resultados la semana próxima.

To decide which tense to use, look at the verb 'to be' in English: **is / are** ➡ present, **was / were** ➡ preterite, **will be** ➡ future

The car **was** *sold* last week. ➡
El coche **se** *vendió* la semana pasada.

Now try this

Translate these sentences into **English**.

1 La novela fue escrita en dos mil diecinueve.
2 Los ejercicios se hacen online.
3 Los resultados serán publicados el viernes.
4 Se invita a mucha gente a la fiesta.
5 Las instalaciones fueron mejoradas antes de la visita.
6 El clima es afectado por las acciones que tomamos.
7 Las consecuencias todavía no se saben.
8 No se venden juguetes en el mercado.
9 Se construirán unos pisos nuevos en las afueras.
10 El dinero fue encontrado en la calle.

Numbers

Digital resources

Numbers 1–1000

1	uno	11	once	21	veintiuno	100	cien
2	dos	12	doce	22	veintidós	101	ciento uno
3	tres	13	trece	30	treinta	200	doscientos/as
4	cuatro	14	catorce	31	treinta y uno	333	trescientos/as
5	cinco	15	quince	32	treinta y dos		treinta y tres
6	seis	16	dieciséis	40	cuarenta	1000	mil
7	siete	17	diecisiete	50	cincuenta		
8	ocho	18	dieciocho	60	sesenta		
9	nueve	19	diecinueve	70	setenta		
10	diez	20	veinte	80	ochenta		
				90	noventa		

The hundreds need to agree. Note: there are some irregular forms:
500 – **quinientos**,
700 – **setecientos**,
900 – **novecientos**.

Numbers ending in **uno** need to agree. They drop the -o before a masculine noun:
veintiún años

The pattern for 31, 32, etc., is the same for 41, 42, etc.

Dates

Dates follow this pattern:
13 December 1978 =
el trece de diciembre de mil novecientos setenta y ocho
21 July 2016
el veintiuno de julio del dos mil dieciséis
The first of the month can be either:
el primero de abril or el uno de abril.

You don't use a capital letter for the months.

Telling the time

Son las cinco.	It's five o'clock.
A las diez.	At ten o'clock.

One o'clock is different:
Es la una.

3.05	las tres y cinco
3.15	las tres y cuarto
3.30	las tres y media
3.45	las cuatro menos cuarto
3.55	las cuatro menos cinco

Ordinal numbers

When used with nouns, ordinal numbers agree: la segunda calle – the second street

Ordinals are NOT used for dates except for the 1st.

primero	first
segundo	second
tercero	third

Primero and tercero change to primer and tercer before a masculine singular noun, e.g. el tercer día.

Now try this

Write the numbers, dates and times in **Spanish**.
1 8.40   **2** 465   **3** 12 June 2014   **4** 543   **5** 11.30   **6** 76   **7** 1 January 1997   **8** 3rd

Vocabulary

This vocabulary section contains a comprehensive list of words that are in the AQA GCSE Spanish vocabulary list. Verbs are included in their infinitive form only; please refer to the specification for more on the forms and tenses required. To help you learn the words, they have been divided into subjects. However, words are flexible and you can use them for a variety of subjects. Remember words may appear in various contexts in the exam. Words that are shaded purple are Higher tier only.

1 Basic vocabulary

Numbers

cero	zero
uno	one
dos	two
tres	three
cuatro	four
cinco	five
seis	six
siete	seven
ocho	eight
nueve	nine
diez	ten
once	eleven
doce	twelve
trece	thirteen
catorce	fourteen
quince	fifteen
dieciséis	sixteen
diecisiete	seventeen
dieciocho	eighteen
diecinueve	nineteen
veinte, veinti-	twenty
treinta	thirty
cuarenta	forty
cincuenta	fifty
sesenta	sixty
setenta	seventy
ochenta	eighty
noventa	ninety
ciento	one hundred (and)
quinientos	five hundred (and)
mil	thousand
millón	million

Question words

¿quién(es)?	who? (m,f) (pl)
¿cuál(es)?	which? (m,f) (pl)
¿por qué?	why?
¿cuándo?	when?
¿cómo?	how?
¿dónde?	where?
¿cuánto(s)?, ¿cuánta(s)?	how much, how many? (m), how much, how many? (f)

Short phrases

lo bueno	the good thing
gracias	thanks, thank you
vale	ok
hola	hello, hi
¡Vamos!	Come on! Let's go!
¡Perdón!	Sorry!
por favor	please, excuse me
adiós	goodbye
¡Enhorabuena!	Congratulations!
buenos días	good morning!
hay que	you must (general)
tener que	(to) have to, must
hace (+noun)	it is (+ weather)
se puede	you can (general)
se necesita	you need (to) (general),
¿Qué tal?	How are you? (informal)
¿Cómo es?	What is it like?
lo siento	I'm sorry
de acuerdo	ok, in agreement
sin embargo	however
por eso	so, therefore
fin de semana	weekend
tan ... como	as ... as
¡Ojalá!	I hope so! I wish!
ya no	no longer, no more
desde hace + present tense	(to) have been + -ing + for + time
acabar de (+ infinitive)	(to) have just + pp
hace falta (+ infinitive)	it's necessary (+ verb)
vale la pena + infinitive	it's worth -ing

Negatives

ninguno	no, not ... any (m)
ningún	no, not ... any (m, before a noun)
nadie, (no) nadie	nobody, no one, anybody (after negative verb)
ninguno, (no) ninguno	no-one, none, (a single) anyone (after negative verb)
nada, (no) nada	nothing, anything (after negative verb)

Prepositions

a	to, at
en	in, on
entre	between, among
de	of, from
del	of the (m, sing)
al	to the (m, sing)
con	with
por	around, because of, by, for, through
para, para (+ infinitive)	for, in order to (+ verb)
sin (+ infinitive)	without (+ -ing)
hacia	towards
hasta	up to, as far as, until
sobre	on top of, over, about
desde	from, since
durante	during
contra; en contra	against, opposite; in opposition, against
según	according to
debajo	underneath, below

Conjunctions

si	if, whether
que	that
y	and
como	like, as
o	or
pero	but
porque	because
mientras	while, whilst
aunque	although
para que	so that, in order that
(no) ni ... (ni) ...	nor, or (after negative verb) neither ... nor ...
sino	but (rather), except

② General vocabulary – verbs

abrir; abrirse	(to) open, unwrap	encantar	(to) love,	practicar	(to) practise
aceptar	(to) accept	encontrar	(to) find	preferir	(to) prefer
acercarse	(to) come closer	entender; entenderse	(to) understand; (to) get on	preguntar	(to) ask
acordar; acordarse	(to) agree on, remind; (to) remember	entrar	(to) enter	preocupar; preocuparse por	(to) worry; (to) worry about
afectar; afectarse	(to) affect	escoger	(to) choose	preparar	(to) prepare
		escuchar	(to) listen (to)	presentar	(to) introduce, present
aguantar	(to) put up with	esperar	(to) wait, hope (for)	producir	(to) produce
ahorrar	(to) save (time, money)	estar	(to) be (state, location)	prohibir	(to) prohibit
		evitar	(to) avoid	quedar; quedar(se)	(to) arrange to meet; (to) stay
andar	(to) walk	explicar	(to) explain	querer	(to) want (to), love
aumentar	(to) increase	guardar	(to) keep, save		
ayudar	(to) help	gustar	(to) please	quitar; quitarse	(to) remove, take away; (to) take off (clothes)
bajar	(to) go down, get off, download	hablar	(to) speak, talk		
		hacer	(to) do, make		
		importar	(to) matter, be important	recibir	(to) receive
caer; caerse	(to) fall			recomendar	(to) recommend
cambiar; cambiarse	(to) change; (to) get changed	intentar	(to) try	recordar	(to) remember, remind
		interesar	(to) interest		
		ir	(to) go		
causar	(to) cause	llegar; llegar a (+ infinitive)	(to) arrive; (to) manage to / succeed in	reducir	(to) reduce
cerrar	(to) close			repetir	(to) repeat
coger	(to) take, catch			resolver	(to) solve, resolve
		llevar	(to) take, carry, wear, lead		
comenzar	(to) start			responder	(to) reply
comparar	(to) compare	mantener	(to) keep	saber	(to) know (how to)
compartir	(to) share	mejorar	(to) improve		
conocer	(to) know, meet	mirar	(to) look, watch	sacar	(to) take out, get, obtain
contestar	(to) answer	molestar; molestarse	(to) bother, annoy; (to) be offended	salir	(to) go out, leave
continuar	(to) continue				
crear	(to) create			seguir	(to) follow
creer	(to) believe, think	mostrar	(to) show	sentir; sentirse	(to) feel, sense
		necesitar	(to) need	sonreír	(to) smile
criticar	(to) criticise	odiar	(to) hate	subir	(to) go up, upload
dar	(to) give	oír	(to) hear		
deber	(to) have to	olvidar	(to) forget	tardar	(to) take (time)
decidir	(to) decide	organizar	(to) organise	tener	(to) have
decir	(to) say, tell	parar	(to) stop	terminar	(to) finish
dejar; dejar de (+ infinitive)	(to) let, leave; (to) stop (+ing)	parecer; parecerse a	(to) seem, look like	tirar	(to) throw, pull
				tomar	(to) take, have, drink
		pasar	(to) spend (time), happen	traer	(to) bring
depender	(to) depend			usar	(to) use
describir	(to) describe	pedir	(to) ask for	ver	(to) see, watch
descubrir	(to) discover	pensar	(to) think	vestir; vestirse	(to) dress; (to) get dressed
despertar; despertarse	(to) wake (someone); (to) wake (up)	permitir; permitirse	(to) allow		
		poder	(to) be able to	visitar	(to) visit
disfrutar	(to) enjoy	poner; ponerse	(to) put (on); (to) get, become	vivir	(to) live
durar	(to) last			volver; volver a	(to) return; (to) do again
empezar	(to) begin, start				
empujar	(to) push				

Now try this

Choose five verbs from this page. Write out the full conjugation for the present, preterite and future tenses.

③ General vocabulary – nouns

abril (m)	April
acción (f)	action, act
actitud (f)	attitude
actividad (f)	activity
agosto (m)	August
alegría (f)	joy, happiness
ambiente (m)	atmosphere, environment
año (m)	year
aspecto (m)	aspect
ayuda (f)	help
cambio (m); en cambio	change; on the other hand
camisa (f)	shirt
camiseta (f)	t-shirt
causa (f)	cause
centro (m)	centre, middle
chica (f)	girl
chico (m)	boy
cifra (f)	number, amount
clase (f)	class, type, lesson
color (m)	colour
conversación (f)	conversation
cosa (f)	thing
cuarto (m)	quarter, room
decisión (f)	decision
derecha (f)	right
desventaja (f)	disadvantage
detalle (m)	detail
día (m)	day
diciembre (m)	December
diferencia (f)	difference
dinero (m)	money
domingo (m)	Sunday
edad (f)	age
efecto (m)	effect
ejemplo (m)	example
enero (m)	January
éxito (m)	success
experiencia (f)	experience
falda (f)	skirt
falta (f)	lack, mistake
febrero (m)	February
fecha (f)	date, day
felicidad (f)	happiness
fin (m); por fin	end; finally
final (m)	end, ending
foto (f)	photo, picture
futuro (m)	future
ganas (fpl)	desire
gente (f)	people
grupo (m)	group
hombre (m)	man
hora (f)	hour, time (specific)
idea (f)	idea
imagen (f)	image, picture
importancia (f)	importance
información (f)	information
intención (f)	intention
interés (m)	interest
izquierda (f)	left
joven (m/f)	young person
jueves (m)	Thursday
julio (m)	July
junio (m)	June
juventud (f)	youth
lado (m)	side
letra (f)	letter, lyrics
lugar (m)	place, position
lunes (m)	Monday
mañana (f)	morning
martes (m)	Tuesday
marzo (m)	March
mayo (m)	May
mayoría (f)	majority
mentira (f)	lie
mes (m)	month
miedo (m)	fear
miércoles (m)	Wednesday
minuto (m)	minute
mitad (f)	half, middle
momento (m); de momento	moment; at the moment
(un) montón (m)	(a) lot of, pile
mujer (f)	woman, wife
noche (f); por la noche; esta noche	night, evening; at night, in the evening; tonight
noticia (f)	news
noviembre (m)	November
número (m)	number
octubre (m)	October
opinión (f)	opinion, view
oportunidad (f)	opportunity
organización (f)	organisation
pantalón (m)	trousers
pasado (m)	past
pena (f)	sadness, trouble
persona (f)	person
plan (m)	plan
plástico (m)	plastic
pregunta (f)	question
principio (m)	beginning, start
problema (m)	problem
rato (m)	moment, while
razón (f)	reason
reloj (m)	clock, watch
resto (m)	rest, remainder
risa (f)	laugh
sábado (m)	Saturday
santo (m)	saint, saint's day
segundo (m)	second
semana (f)	week
señor (m)	Mr, man, Sir
señora (f)	Mrs, lady, Madam
sentido (m)	sense, meaning
septiembre (m)	September
sitio (web) (m)	place (website)
situación (f)	situation
sonrisa (f)	smile
sorpresa (f)	surprise
suerte (f)	luck, fortune
tarde (f); por la tarde	afternoon, evening; in the afternoon, in the evening
tema (m)	issue, subject
tiempo (m)	time (general), weather
tipo (m)	type, kind
trabajo (m)	work, job, effort
uso (m)	use
variedad (f)	variety
ventaja (f)	advantage
verdad (f)	truth
vestido (m)	dress
vez (f); a veces	time (specific occurrence); sometimes
vida (f)	life
viernes (m)	Friday
violencia (f)	violence
zapato (m)	shoe

Now try this

Choose five nouns from this page that you find difficult to remember. Write a sentence using each one.

4 General vocabulary – adjectives and adverbs

Adjectives

libre	free, vacant
abierto/a	open, unlocked
aburrido/a	bored, boring
actual	current
agradable	pleasant, nice
alegre	cheerful, happy
alto/a	tall, high, loud
amarillo/a	yellow
animado/a	lively
antiguo/a	former; old, ancient
azul	blue
bajo/a	short, low
barato/a	cheap
blanco/a	white
bonito/a	nice, beautiful
bueno/a	good
caro/a	expensive
cerrado/a	closed
cierto/a	certain, true
cómodo/a	comfortable
común	common
contento/a	happy, pleased
correcto/a	correct, suitable
corto/a	short, brief
debido (a)	due (to)
diferente	different
difícil	difficult, hard
directo/a	direct, straight
divertido/a	fun, enjoyable
duro/a	hard, resilient
emocionante	exciting
enojado/a	angry
especial	special
estupendo/a	wonderful
exacto/a	exact, true
excelente	excellent
falso/a	false
favorito/a	favourite
feliz	happy, glad
físico/a	physical
general	general
genial	great
grande	big, large (m, f)
gris	grey
guay	cool
horrible	horrible
ideal	ideal
importante	important
imposible	impossible
increíble	incredible

interesante	interesting
justo/a	fair, just
largo/a	long
lento/a	slow
ligero/a	light (in weight)
lleno/a	full
malo/a	bad
marrón	brown
mayor	larger, older, main
medio/a	half, middle, average
mejor	better, best
moderno/a	modern
necesario/a	necessary
negativo/a	negative
negro/a	black
nuevo/a	new, another
peor	worse, worst
pequeño/a	little, young
perfecto/a	perfect
posible	possible
positivo/a	positive
primero/a	first (m)
principal	main, principal
próximo/a	next
público/a	public
raro/a	strange, rare
real	royal, real
reciente	recent
rojo/a	red
roto/a	broken, torn
seguro/a	safe, secure
semejante	similar
sencillo/a	simple, easy
siguiente	following, next
suficiente	sufficient
temprano/a	early
tercero/a	third (m)
típico/a	typical
tradicional	traditional
tranquilo/a	calm, tranquil
triste	sad, unhappy
último/a	last, final
único/a	only, unique
útil	useful
vacío/a	empty, vacant
varios/a	several, various
verde	green
viejo/a	old

Adverbs

además	also, as well, besides
ahora	now, these days
allí	there, over there
anoche	last night
antes	before
aparte (de)	apart (from)
aquí	here
así	like this, like that
aun	even, still
ayer	yesterday
bastante	quite
bien	well
casi	almost, nearly
cerca	close, near, nearby
claro	of course, clearly
delante	in front, ahead
demasiado(s)	too much (many)
después	after, afterwards
detrás	behind
encima	on top
entonces	then, so
finalmente	finally, at last
hoy	today, nowadays
lejos	far (away)
luego	then, later
mal	badly
mañana	tomorrow
más (que)	adv + -er (... than), more (... than)
menos (que)	less (... than)
mucho(s)	much a lot (many)
muy	very, really
no	no, not
normalmente	normally
poco(s)	little, not much
probablemente	probably
quizás	perhaps, maybe
rápidamente	quickly
sí	yes
siempre	always, forever
también	also, too, as well
tan	so (+ adjective)
tanto(s)	so much (many)
tarde	late
ya	already

Now try this

Find some of the adjectives on this page. Think of something that each one describes.

121

⑤ General vocabulary – higher only – Verbs and adverbs

Verbs

abandonar	(to) abandon
acompañar	(to) accompany
acostumbrarse	(to) get used
advertir	(to) warn
agradecer	(to) be grateful for
alcanzar	(to) reach
alegrar	(to) make happy
añadir	(to) add
animar	(to) encourage, cheer up
aparecer	(to) appear
apreciar	(to) appreciate
arreglar; arreglarse	(to) repair, tidy; (to) get ready
asegurar; asegurarse (de que)	(to) assure; (to) ensure (that)
atreverse	(to) dare
¡Basta!, basta + infinitive	enough!, you only have to + verb
comentar	(to) comment
comprender	(to) understand
conseguir	(to) get, obtain
considerar	(to) consider
consistir (en)	(to) consist (of)
contar	(to) tell, count
contribuir	(to) contribute
controlar	(to) control
convertirse	(to) transform
crecer	(to) grow, increase
cubrir	(to) cover
dedicar	(to) dedicate
desaparecer	(to) disappear
desarrollar	(to) develop
despedir: despedirse (de)	(to) sack, dismiss; (to) say goodbye (to)
destacar	(to) emphasise, highlight
dirigir	(to) manage
echar; echarse	(to) throw, cast; (to) lie down
elegir	(to) choose, elect

equivocarse	(to) be wrong, make a mistake
escapar; escaparse	(to) escape; (to) run away
esconder	(to) hide
exigir	(to) demand
existir	(to) exist
falta (+ infinitive)	it's / is still to be (+ pp)
formar	(to) form, set up
identificar	(to) identify
imaginar	(to) imagine
impedir	(to) prevent
incluir	(to) include
indicar	(to) point (out), indicate
influir	(to) influence
insistir	(to) insist
introducir	(to) introduce, bring in
luchar	(to) fight, struggle
mencionar	(to) mention
merecer	(to) deserve
meter	(to) put, place
mezclar	(to) mix
mover	(to) move
negar	(to) refuse
notar	(to) notice
obtener	(to) obtain, get
ocurrir	(to) occur
ofrecer	(to) offer, present
ordenar	(to) tidy, organise
parece	it seems
pegar	(to) hit, stick on
prestar	(to) lend, pay (attention)
prometer; prometerse	(to) promise; (to) get engaged
proponer	(to) propose, suggest
quejarse	(to) complain
rechazar	(to) reject
reconocer	(to) recognise, admit
referir	(to) refer
reflejar	(to) reflect
regresar	(to) return
resultar	(to) be, turn out

reunir; reunirse	(to) gather
significar	(to) mean
soler	(to) normally (+ verb)
sorprender	(to) surprise
sugerir	(to) suggest
temer	(to) fear
tratar; tratar de	(to) treat, deal with; (to) try to
utilizar	(to) use

Adverbs

todavía	still, yet
fuera	outside, out
incluso	even, including
(no) tampoco	neither, either (after negative verb)
pronto	soon, early, quick
apenas	hardly, barely
dentro	inside, within
jamás	never
arriba	upstairs, above
abajo	down, below, downstairs
actualmente	now, at present, currently
completamente	completely
enseguida	straight away
despacio	slow
afortunadamente	fortunately
desafortunadamente	unfortunately

❻ General vocabulary – higher only – nouns and adjectives

Nouns

adulto (m)	adult
asunto (m)	matter, issue,
atención (f)	attention
aumento (m)	increase, rise
belleza (f)	beauty
beneficio (m)	benefit
calidad (f)	quality
cantidad (f)	quantity, amount
caso (m)	case, occasion
clave (f)	key, crucial thing
comienzo (m)	start, beginning
conocimiento (m)	knowledge
consecuencia (f); como consecuencia	consequence; as a result
creación (f)	creation
cuestión (f)	issue, question
dato (m)	data, information, fact
desarrollo (m)	development
deseo (m)	desire, wish
dificultad (f)	difficulty
distancia (f)	distance
duda (f)	doubt
emoción (f)	emotion
época (f)	time, age, period
esperanza (f)	hope
estado (m)	state, condition
estilo (m)	style
evento (m)	event
expresión (f)	expression
factor (m)	factor
fondo (m)	bottom, back, background
forma (f)	form, shape, way
frecuencia (f)	frequency
impacto (m)	impact
impresión (f)	impression
independencia (f)	independence
influencia (f)	influence
iniciativa (f)	initiative
libertad (f)	freedom
límite (m)	limit
línea (f)	line, course
manera (f)	way, manner
medida (f)	measure

motivo (m)	reason, motive
objeto (m)	object, thing
ocasión (f)	occasion, opportunity
orden (m)	order
parte (f)	part
permiso (m)	permission
posibilidad (f)	possibility
preocupación (f)	worry, concern
punto (m)	point, full stop, dot
reacción (f)	reaction
realidad (f)	reality
responsabilidad (f)	responsibility
sección (f)	section, department
sensación (f)	feeling, sensation
solución (f)	solution, answer

Adjectives

ambos, ambas	both
anterior	previous
asqueroso/a	disgusting
capaz	capable, able
complicado/a	complicated
comprensivo/a	understanding
consciente	conscious, aware
decepcionante	disappointing
diario/a	daily
dispuesto/a	ready, willing
distinto/a	distinct, different
económico/a	cheap, economic
efectivo/a	effective
emocionado/a	excited
enorme	enormous,
entero/a	entire, whole
evidente	obvious
extraño/a	strange
fatal	terrible, awful
igual	equal, alike
inútil	useless
junto/a	together
maravilloso/a	marvellous
máximo/a	maximum
mínimo/a	minimum
numeroso/a	numerous, large, big
ocupado/a	busy, taken, occupied
oscuro/a	dark, obscure
pesado/a	heavy, boring
precioso/a	beautiful, precious
preferible	preferable
privado/a	private
propio/a	own (pre-noun)
solo/a	only, single, lonely, alone
suave	soft, gentle,
total	total, entire
verdadero/a	true, real
vivo; en vivo	alive, bright, live (TV)

Identity and relationships

Spanish	English	Spanish	English
abuela (f)	grandmother	gay	gay
abuelo (m)	grandfather	gordo/a	fat
alegre	cheerful, happy,	gracioso/a	funny
alemán	German	gritar	(to) shout
amigo (m)	friend	guapo/a	good-looking
amistad (f)	friendship	hermana (f)	sister
amor (m)	love	hermano (m)	brother
animal (m)	animal	hermoso/a	beautiful, handsome
apellido (m)	surname		
argentino/a	Argentinian	hetero(sexual)	heterosexual
artístico/a	artistic	hija (f)	daughter
bebé (m)	baby	hijo (m)	son
besar	(to) kiss	hombre (m)	man
bi(sexual)	bi(sexual)	humor (m)	humour, mood
boda (f)	wedding	identidad (f)	identity
británico/a	British	independiente	independent
caballo (m)	horse	inglés/inglesa	English
carácter (m)	character	italiano/a	Italian
casado/a	married	joven (m/f)	young
casarse	(to) get married	judío/a	Jewish
castellano/a	(Castilian) Spanish	llamar; llamarse	(to) call, name, (to) be called
		madrastra (f)	stepmother
católico/a	Catholic	madre (f)	mother
chileno/a	Chilean	marido (m)	husband
chino/a	Chinese	menor	younger
civil	civil	mexicano/a	Mexican
colombiano/a	Colombian	miembro (m)	member
confianza (f)	confidence, trust	moreno/a	brown (hair), dark (skin)
consejo (m)	advice	morir	(to) die
contacto (m)	contact	muerto/a	dead
cristiano/a	Christian	mujer (f)	woman, wife
cubano/a	Cuban	musulmán	Muslim
cuidar	(to) take care of	nacer	(to) be born
		nervioso/a	nervous, uptight
cuidado (m)	care, carefulness	niña (f)	child, young girl
débil	weak		
delgado/a	thin, slim	niño (m)	child, young boy
deportivo/a	sporty, sports	nombre (m)	name
discusión (f)	discussion, argument	novia (f)	girlfriend, bride
		novio (m)	boyfriend, groom
discutir	(to) argue, discuss	ojo (m)	eye
divorciarse	(to) get divorced	optimista	optimistic
		padrastro (m)	stepfather
duro/a	hard, resilient	padre (m); padres	father; parents
enojado/a	angry		
entenderse	(to) get on	pareja (f)	couple, partner
español/a	Spanish	pelearse	(to) fight
europeo/a	European	pelo (m)	hair
familia (f)	family	pequeño/a	little, young
feo/a	ugly	perezoso/a	lazy
físico/a	physical	perro (m)	dog
francés/francesa	French		
fuerte	strong		
gafas (fpl)	glasses		
gato (m)	cat		

Spanish	English
pobre	poor
primo (m)	cousin
relación (f)	relationship
religioso/a	religious
respetar	(to) respect
romper	(to) break
rubio/a	blond, fair
sentimiento (m)	feeling, sentiment
separarse	(to) separate
serio/a	serious
sexo (m)	sex
simpático/a	nice, friendly
soltero/a	single, unmarried
tatuaje (m)	tattoo
tía (f)	aunt
tío (m)	uncle
tonto/a	silly
trabajador/a	hardworking
transgénero	transgender
vecino (m/f)	neighbour
abrazar	(to) hug
ambicioso/a	ambitious
anciano/a (m/f)	elderly person
atraer	(to) attract
cara (f)	face, expression
cariño (m)	affection, love
cita (f)	(romantic) date
confiar	(to) trust,
conflicto (m)	conflict
culpa (f)	blame, fault
enamorarse	(to) fall in love
estricto/a	strict
familiar (m)	relative
fiel	faithful, loyal
género (m)	gender, genre
infantil	children's
latino/a	Latin American
loco/a	crazy, insane
mamá (f)	mum
mascota (f)	pet
nacimiento (m)	birth, origin
orgulloso/a	proud
papá (m)	dad
perdonar	(to) forgive
reírse	(to) laugh
relacionarse con	(to) relate to
romántico/a	romantic
tolerante	tolerant
vago/a	lazy

8 Healthy living and lifestyle

accidente (m)	accident
agua (f)	water
aire (m)	air
apoyar	(to) support
azúcar (m)	sugar
beber	(to) drink
bebida (f)	drink
bicicleta, bici (f)	bicycle, bike
bocadillo (m)	sandwich
botella (f)	bottle
cabeza (f)	head
caer; caerse	(to) fall
café (m)	coffee, café
cambiar; cambiarse	(to) change; (to) get changed
cansado/a	tired, tiring
caramelo (m)	sweet (noun)
carne (f)	meat
carta (f)	letter, menu
cena (f)	evening meal
cenar	(to) have dinner
comer	(to) eat
comida (f)	food, meal, lunch
copa (f)	cup, glass
corazón (m)	heart
correr	(to) run
costumbre (f)	custom, habit
cuerpo (m)	body
dar un paseo	(to) go for a walk
débil	weak
desayuno (m)	breakfast
descansar	(to) rest, relax
diente (m)	tooth
dieta (f)	diet
doler	(to) hurt
dormirse	(to) fall asleep
droga (f)	drug
dulce	sweet (adj)
ejercicio (m)	exercise
energía (f)	energy, power
enfermedad (f)	illness, disease
enfermo/a	ill, sick
ensalada (f)	salad
entrenarse	(to) train
equilibrado/a	balanced
equipo (m)	team, equipment
estar en forma	to be fit
estrés (m)	stress
físico/a	physical
fruta (f)	fruit
fuerte	strong

Spanish	English
fumar	(to) smoke
gimnasio (m)	gym
grasa (f)	fat, grease
grave	serious
hambre (f)	hunger
hamburguesa (f)	burger
hospital (m)	hospital
huevo (m)	egg
jamón (m)	ham
lavarse	(to) have a wash
leche (f)	milk
levantarse	(to) get up
mano (f)	hand
manzana (f)	apple
medicina (f)	medicine
médico (m/f)	doctor
morir	(to) die
muerto/a	dead
nadar	(to) swim
naranja (f)	orange (fruit)
ojo (m)	eye
paciente (m/f)	patient
paella (f)	paella
pan (m)	bread
patatas fritas	chips, fries
peligro (m)	danger
peligroso/a	dangerous
pelo (m)	hair
pescado (m)	fish
peso (m)	weight, peso
pie (m); a pie	foot; on foot
piel (f)	skin
pollo (m)	chicken
probar	(to) taste, try
producto (m)	product
régimen (m)	diet
respirar	(to) breathe
responsable	responsible
riesgo (m)	risk
sal (f)	salt
salud (f)	health
sano/a	healthy
sed (f)	thirst
sociedad (f)	society
sueño (m)	dream, sleep
tapas (fpl)	bar snacks
tomate (m)	tomato
uva (f)	grape
vaso (m)	(drinking) glass

Spanish	English
vegano/a	vegan
vegetariano/a	vegetarian
verdura (f)	vegetable
vida (f)	life
vino (m)	wine
aceite (m)	oil
acostar; acostarse	(to) put to bed; (to) go to bed
alcohol (m)	alcohol
alimento (m)	food
arroz (m)	rice
asistir	(to) attend
boca (f)	mouth
brazo (m)	arm
caminar	(to) walk
cáncer (m)	cancer
cerebro (m)	brain
cigarrillo (m)	cigarette
cocinar	(to) cook
consumo (m)	consumption
dolor (m)	pain, ache
gobierno (m)	government
herida (f)	wound, injury
matar	(to) kill
mental	mental
mente (f)	mind
muerte (f)	death
natación (f)	swimming
nivel (m)	level
pasear	(to) go for a walk
paz (f)	peace
pierna (f)	leg
promover	(to) promote
puro/a	pure, clean
relajante	relaxing
saludable	healthy
sangre (f)	blood
secreto (m)	secret
sensible	sensitive
silencio (m)	silence
sobrepeso (m)	obesity
soledad (f)	loneliness
sufrir	(to) suffer
vergüenza (f)	embarrassment

Now try this

Use some of the words on this page to describe your lifestyle.

⑨ Education and work

Spanish	English
alumno (m)	student, pupil
abogado (m/f)	lawyer
acoso (m)	bullying
apoyo (m)	support
aprender	(to) learn
aprobar	(to) pass (a test)
arte (m)	art
asignatura (f)	school subject
autor (m)	writer, author
Bachillerato (m)	Baccalaureate (like A levels)
biblioteca (f)	library
bolígrafo (m)	pen
bolsa (f)	bag
callarse	(to) be quiet
camarero/a (m/f)	waiter / waitress
carrera (f)	career, degree course, race
ciencias (f)	science(s)
científico (m/f)	scientist
clase (f)	class, type, lesson
cliente (m/f)	client, customer
colegio (m)	(secondary) school
compañero (m/f)	classmate, companion, colleague
compañía (f)	company
comportamiento (m)	behaviour
construir	(to) build
cuidador (m)	carer
deberes (m)	homework
director (m/f)	headteacher, director
diseñar	(to) design
economía (f)	economics
educación (f)	education
educativo/a	educational
ejército (m)	army
empleado (m)	employee
empleo (m)	work, job
empresa (f)	company, business
enfermero (m)	nurse
enseñar	(to) teach, show
entrevista (f)	interview
escribir	(to) write
escuela (f)	(primary) school
esfuerzo (m)	effort
espectáculo (m)	show, spectacle
estudiante (m/f)	student
estudiar	(to) study
estudio (m)	study, studio
examen (m)	exam
excursión (f)	trip, excursion
éxito	success
experiencia (f)	experience
extranjero (m)	abroad, foreigner
fábrica (f)	factory
frase (f)	phrase, sentence
geografía (f)	geography
grabar	(to) record
gritar	(to) shout
historia (f)	history, story
horario (m)	timetable, schedule
industria (f)	industry
industrial	industrial
informática (f)	ICT
ingeniero (m/f)	engineer
inglés/inglesa	English
instalación (f)	facility
instituto (m)	secondary school
jefe (m/f)	boss, leader
laboral	(of) work
libro (m)	book
lista (f)	list, register
listo/a	ready (after estar), clever (after ser)
matemáticas (fpl)	maths
medicina (f)	medicine
mesa (f)	table
mochila (f)	rucksack, school bag
mundo (m)	world
músico (m/f)	musician
negocio (m)	business
nota (f)	grade, note, mark
novela (f)	novel
oferta (f)	offer
oficina (f)	office
opción (f)	option, choice
pagar	(to) pay (for)
palabra (f)	word
paro (m)	unemployment, strike
patio (m)	yard, playground
peluquero (m)	hairdresser
perezoso/a	lazy
periodista (m/f)	journalist
pintor (m/f)	painter
policía (m/f)	police, police officer
presión (f)	pressure
profesión (f)	profession
profesor (m/f)	teacher
proyecto (m)	project, plan
prueba (f)	test, trial, proof
recreo (m)	break (at school)
regla (f)	rule, ruler
repasar	(to) revise, review
ropa (f)	clothes
salario (m)	salary
secretario (m/f)	secretary
señor (m)	Mr., man, Sir
servicios (mpl)	toilets
servir	(to) serve
silla (f)	chair, seat
tarea (f)	task, homework
teatro (m)	theatre, drama
trabajar	(to) work
uniforme (m)	uniform
universidad (f)	university
vender	(to) sell
ventana (f)	window
atender (to)	serve
aula (f)	classroom
autoridad (f)	authority
campaña (f)	campaign
castigar (to)	punish
comercio (m)	business person
derecho (m)	law (subject)
emplear (to)	employ
empresario (m/f)	business
enseñanza (f)	education
entregar (to)	deliver, hand in
expresar (to)	express
formación (f)	training
fundar (to)	set up
huelga (m)	strike
igualdad (f)	equality
instalar (to)	install
inteligencia (f)	intelligence
investigar (to)	investigate
laboratorio (m)	laboratory
lenguaje (m)	language, speech
ley (f)	law, rule
lograr (to)	achieve,
obligatorio/a	compulsory
obrero (m)	worker, labourer
profesional	professional
respuesta (f)	answer, reply
reunión (f)	meeting
soldado (m/f)	soldier
solicitar (to)	request
superar (to)	overcome
suspender (to)	fail
tasa (f)	rate
título (m)	(uni) degree
universitario/a	university

10 Free-time activities

actividad (f)	activity
activo/a	active
agua (f)	water
arte (m)	art
artículo (m)	article, product, item
bailar	(to) dance
baile (m)	dance
baloncesto (m)	basketball
beber	(to) drink
bicicleta, bici (f)	bicycle, bike
bienvenido/a	welcome
café (m)	coffee, café
caja (f)	box, till (in shop)
cámara (f)	camera
cantar	(to) sing
centro (m) comercial	shopping centre
cine (m)	cinema
clásico/a	classic, classical
club (m)	club
cocina (f)	cooking, kitchen
compra(s)(f/fpl)	shopping
concierto (m)	concert
concurso (m)	competition, quiz
correr	(to) run
cultura (f)	culture
deporte (m)	sport
descansar	(to) rest, relax
dibujo (m)	drawing, art
entrada (f)	entrance, admission ticket
entrenar; entrenarse	(to) train; (to) train
equipo (m)	team, equipment
escena (f)	scene (of film), stage
escribir	(to) write
estadio (m)	stadium
excursión (f)	trip, excursion
ficción (f)	fiction
fiesta (f)	party, festival
físico/a	physical
flamenco (m)	flamenco
fútbol (m)	football
ganar	(to) win, earn

gastar	(to) spend (money)
grabar	(to) record
gracioso/a	funny
guitarra (f)	guitar
influencer (m/f)	influencer
instrumento (m)	instrument
invitar	(to) invite
juego (m)	game
jugador (m/f)	player
jugar	(to) play
leer	(to) read
letra (f)	letter, lyrics
libro (m)	book
miembro (m)	member
moda (f); de moda	fashion; fashionable
música (f)	music
musical	musical
nadar	(to) swim
novela (f)	novel
organizar	(to) organise
parque (m) temático	theme park
participar	(to) participate
partido (m)	(sports) match
pasarlo bien / mal	to have a good / bad time
película (f)	film, movie
pintar; pintarse	(to) paint; (to) put on makeup
piscina (f)	swimming pool
premio (m)	prize, award
risa (f)	laugh
tamaño (m)	size, dimension
tarjeta (f)	written card, bank card
teatro (m)	theatre, drama
tele, televisión (f)	TV, television
telerrealidad (f)	reality TV
temporada (f)	season (of sports, music)
tocar	(to) touch, play (an instrument)
tomar el sol	(to) sunbathe / sunbathing
uva (f)	grape
ver	(to) see, watch
vídeo	video

actuación (f)	performance, acting
actuar	(to) act
acuático/a	water, aquatic
asistir	(to) attend
aventura (f)	adventure
banda (f)	(musical) band
caminar	(to) walk
canal (m)	channel
charlar	(to) chat
cocinar	(to) cook
cola (f)	queue, tail
divertir; divertirse	(to) amuse, entertain
exposición (f)	exhibition, display
firmar	(to) sign
género (m)	gender, genre
guía (m/f)	guide, guide book
imaginación (f)	imagination
influencia (f)	influence
influir	(to) influence
juguete (m)	toy
lectura (f)	reading
literatura (f)	literature
nacional	national
natación (f)	swimming
obra (f)	work, book, play
orquesta (f)	orchestra
pintura (f)	painting, paint
protagonista (m/f)	protagonist / main character
radio (f)	radio
realidad (f)	reality
regalar	(to) give (as a gift)
relajante	relaxing
selección (f)	choice, selection, national sports team
sentarse	(to) sit (down)
sombra (f)	shade, shadow
telenovela (f)	soap (opera), TV serial
torneo (m)	tournament
venta (f)	sale
visita (f)	visit, visitor

Now try this

Make a list of your five favourite and five least favourite free-time activities.

Customs, festivals and celebrations

alegría (f)	joy, happiness	Las Fallas (fpl)	Valencian celebration involving burning of wood and papier mâché models	asistir	(to) attend
animado/a	lively			atraer	(to) attract
animal (m)	animal			banda (f)	(musical) band
artista (m/f)	artist, performer			caminar	(to) walk
ayuntamiento (m)	Spanish town council			camino (m)	way, route, path
baile (m)	dance	luz (f)	light, electricity	cola (f)	queue, tail
boda (f)	wedding	matrimonio (m)	marriage	divertir; divertirse	(to) amuse, entertain; (to) enjoy oneself, have a good time
caballo (m)	horse	mezquita (f)	mosque		
cantar	(to) sing	música (f)	music		
capital (f)	capital (city)	musical	musical		
celebración (f)	celebration	Navidad (f)	Christmas	hispanohablante	Spanish-speaking
celebrar; celebrarse	(to) celebrate; (to) hold (an event)	Nochebuena (f)	Christmas Eve	internacional	international
		Nochevieja (f)	New Year's Eve	latino/a	Latin American, Latin
		paso (m)	step, pace, religious image carried in Holy Week processions		
colombiano/a	Colombian			literatura (f)	literature
comer	(to) eat			muerte (f)	death
comida (f)	food, meal, lunch			nacional	national
compartir	(to) share	película (f)	film, movie	publicar	(to) publish, post (online)
corrida (f)	bullfight	plato (m)	plate, dish		
costumbre (f)	custom, habit, tradition	plaza (f)	square	quemar; quemarse	(to) burn; (to) get sunburnt
		plaza (f) de toros	bullring		
cultura (f)	culture			siglo (m)	century
cultural	cultural	recibir	(to) receive	sombra (f)	shade, shadow
cumpleaños (m)	birthday	regalo (m)	present, gift	sorprender	(to) surprise
descubrir	(to) discover	reina (f)	queen	visita (f)	visit, visitor
desfile (m)	procession, parade	religión (f)	religion		
		religioso/a	religious		
Día de Muertos	Day of the Dead (Mexican celebration)	rey (m)	king		
		Reyes Magos	the Three Kings / Three Wise Men		
Día de Reyes	Epiphany, 6th January	ropa (f)	clothes, clothing		
disfraz (m)	costume, fancy dress	Sanfermines (mpl)	festival in Pamplona involving running of the bulls		
divertido/a	fun, enjoyable				
especial	special				
fiesta (f)	party, festival				
flamenco (m)	flamenco (dance / music from the south of Spain)	santo (m)	saint, saint's day		
		Semana Santa	Easter Week, Holy Week		
fuegos artificiales (mpl)	fireworks	sinagoga (f)	synagogue		
habitante (m)	local (person), inhabitant	teatro (m)	theatre, drama		
		templo (m)	temple		
historia (f)	history, story	tirar	(to) throw, pull		
histórico/a	historic, historical	Tomatina (f)	Spanish tomato festival		
iglesia (f)	church	toro (m)	bull		
interés (m)	interest	tradición (f)	tradition		
invitar	(to) invite	traje (m)	suit, costume		
juego (m)	game	vestirse	(to) get dressed		
		vista (f)	view, sight		

12 Celebrity culture

actor / actriz (m/f)	actor
bailar	(to) dance
canción (f)	song
cantante (m/f)	singer
club (m)	club
comportamiento (m)	behaviour
conocido/a	known, well-known
dinero (m)	money
divorciarse	(to) get divorced
droga (f)	drug
entrevista (f)	interview
escritor (m/f)	writer
escuchar	(to) listen (to)
especial	special
estrella (f)	star
éxito (m)	success
familia (f)	family
famoso/a	famous, well-known
famoso (m)	celebrity, famous person
foto (f)	photo, picture
ganar	(to) win, earn
grabar	(to) record
gracioso/a	funny
grupo (m)	group
guapo/a	good-looking
guitarra (f)	guitar
identidad (f)	identity
imagen (f)	image, picture
industria (f)	industry
letra (f)	letter, lyrics
libro (m)	book
marca (f)	make, brand
medios (mpl) de comunicación	media
moda (f); de moda	fashion; in fashion, fashionable
modelo (m/f)	model
mundo (m)	world

Spanish	English
música (f)	music
musical	musical
nacer	(to) be born
pareja (f)	couple, partner
pasarlo bien / mal	to have a good / bad time
película (f)	film, movie
peligro (m)	danger
peligroso/a	dangerous
periódico (m)	newspaper
personaje (m)	character (in book, film)
personalidad (f)	personality, celebrity
popular	popular
presentar	(to) introduce, present
programa (m)	programme
proyecto (m)	project, plan
público (m)	public, audience
relación (f)	relationship
respetar	(to) respect
respeto (m)	respect, regard
revista (f)	magazine
rico/a	rich, wealthy, tasty
seguir	(to) follow
separar; separarse	(to) separate
serie (f)	series
sociedad (f)	society
soltero/a	single, unmarried
teatro (m)	theatre, drama
tele, televisión (f)	TV, television
telerrealidad (f)	reality TV
vestir; vestirse	(to) dress; (to) get dressed
viajar	(to) travel
vídeo (m)	video
votar	(to) vote
voz (f)	voice

Spanish	English
actuación (f)	acting
actuar	(to) act
aficionado/a (m/f)	fan
apropiado/a	appropriate,
banda (f)	(musical) band
comentario (m)	comment
deportista (m/f)	sportsperson
diario (m)	newspaper, diary
digital	digital
discriminación (f)	discrimination
engañar	(to) trick, deceive
estilo (m)	style
generación (f)	generation
imaginación (f)	imagination
impuesto (m)	tax
influencia (f)	influence
influir	(to) influence
internacional	international
llorar	(to) cry
lujo (m)	luxury
mundial	world(wide)
nacional	national
nacionalidad (f)	nationality
obra (f)	work, book, play
oro (m)	gold
orgulloso/a	proud
política (f)	politics, policy
prensa (f)	press
promover	(to) promote
radio (f)	radio
realidad (f)	reality
reconocer	(to) recognise, admit
relacionarse con	(to) relate to, get on with
riqueza (f)	wealth, riches
talento (m)	talent
tendencia (f)	tendency, trend
víctima (f)	victim

Now try this

Cover up the Spanish words in one of the columns. Write the English translations. Then challenge yourself to do it the other way round!

13 Travel and tourism

aeropuerto (m)	airport
alojamiento (m)	accommodation
arquitectura (f)	architecture
autobús (m)	bus
avión (m)	aeroplane
baño (m)	bathroom
barato/a	cheap
barco (m)	boat, ship
barrio (m)	district
bebida (f)	drink
bicicleta, bici (f)	bicycle, bike
bienvenido/a	welcome
billete (m)	ticket (transport)
bolsa (f)	bag
caliente	hot, warm
calor (m)	heat, hot
cámara (f)	camera
camping (m)	camp site
capital (f)	capital (city)
carretera (f)	road
castillo (m)	castle
coche (m)	car
coger	(to) take, catch
conducir	(to) drive
costa (f)	coast
dirección (f)	address, direction
directo/a	direct, straight
disfrutar	(to) enjoy
dormitorio (m)	bedroom
edificio (m)	building
espacio (m)	space, room
España (f)	Spain
estación (f)	station, season
este (m)	east
euro (m)	euro
europeo/a	European
excursión (f)	trip, excursion
extranjero (m)	abroad, foreigner
fresco/a	fresh, cool
frío/a	cold
geografía (f)	geography
grado (m)	degree (temp)
hotel (m)	hotel
idioma (m)	language
invierno (m)	winter
isla (f)	island
jardín (m)	garden
kilómetro (m)	kilometre
lengua (f)	tongue, language
limpio/a	clean
llover	(to) rain

lluvia (f)	rain
maleta (f)	suitcase
mar (m/f)	sea
mercado (m)	market
metro (m)	tube, metro, metre
montaña (f)	mountain
montar	(to) ride, set up
mundo (m)	world
norte (m)	north
oeste (m)	west
otoño	autumn
país (m)	country
paisaje (m)	landscape
perdido/a	lost
piscina (f)	swimming pool
piso (m)	apartment, floor
plano (m)	map
planta (f)	plant, floor
playa (f)	beach
precio (m)	price, cost, value
primavera (f)	spring
puerto (m)	port, harbour
recepción (f)	reception
recuerdo (m)	memory, souvenir
región (f)	region
reservar	(to) reserve
restaurante (m)	restaurant
río (m)	river
salida (f)	exit, departure
sol (m)	sun
soñar	(to) dream
Sudamérica (f)	South America
sur (m)	south
temperatura (f)	temperature
tienda (f)	shop, tent
tomar el sol	(to) sunbathe
tráfico (m)	traffic
tranquilo/a	calm, tranquil
transporte (m)	transport
tren (m)	train
turista (m/f)	tourist
vacaciones (fpl)	holidays
verano (m)	summer
viajar	(to) travel
viaje (m)	trip, journey
viento (m)	wind
visitar	(to) visit
vista (f)	view, sight
vuelo (m)	flight
vuelta (f)	return, trip, ride
zona (f)	area, zone

acuático/a	water, aquatic
alquilar	(to) hire, rent
arena (f)	sand
ascensor (m)	lift, elevator
atraer	(to) attract
aventura (f)	adventure
calefacción (f)	heating
ciudadano (m)	citizen
cobrar	(to) charge (money), earn
costo (m)	price, cost
cruzar	(to) cross
destino (m)	destination, destiny
distancia (f)	distance
divertir	(to) amuse, entertain
documento (m)	document
firmar	(to) sign
frontera (f)	border, frontier
gastos (mpl)	expenses, costs, spending
hispanohablante	Spanish-speaking
lago (m)	lake
llave (f)	key
llegada (f)	arrival
monte (m)	hill, hills, countryside
nación (f)	nation
nacionalidad (f)	nationality
natación (f)	swimming
quejarse	(to) complain
quemar; quemarse	(to) burn; (to) get sunburnt
representante (m/f)	representative
retraso (m)	delay
rincón (m)	corner
situado/a	situated, located
torre (f)	tower
traducción (f)	translation
turismo (m)	tourism
velocidad (f)	speed, velocity
visita (f)	visit, visitor

Now try this

Describe your last holiday using some of the words on this page.

14 Media and technology

Spanish	English
acción (f)	action, act
anuncio (m)	advert
apagar	(to) turn off
app (f)	app
artículo (m)	article, product
bajar	(to) download
buscar	(to) look for
cámara (f)	camera
caro/a	expensive
compartir	(to) share
compra(s) (f/fpl)	shopping
comunicar	(to) communicate
comunidad (f)	community
contacto (m)	contact
conversación (f)	conversation
correo (m) (electrónico)	mail, post (email)
cultura (f)	culture
débil	weak
delito (m)	crime
descubrir	(to) discover
eléctrico/a	electric
encender	(to) turn on
energía (f)	energy, power
enviar	(to) send
error (m)	error, mistake
fácil	easy
foto (f)	photo, picture
funcionar	(to) function, work
grabar	(to) record
gratis	free (of charge)
guardar	(to) keep, save
imagen (f)	image, picture
influencer (m/f)	influencer
informática (f)	ICT
Internet (m)	internet
jugar	(to) play (sport / a game)
mandar	(to) send, order
medios (mpl) de comunicación	media
mensaje (m)	message
moderno/a	modern
móvil (m)	mobile phone
música (f)	music
online	online
ordenador (m)	computer
página (f)	page
pantalla (f)	screen, monitor
película (f)	film, movie
peligro (m)	danger
peligroso/a	dangerous
popular	popular
programa (m)	programme
proteger	(to) protect
rápido/a	quick, fast
red (Red) (f)	network (Internet), net (fishing)
resultado (m)	result
riesgo (m)	risk
robar	(to) rob, steal
romper	(to) break
salud (f)	health
seguidor/a (m/f)	follower
seguro/a	safe, sure, secure
serie (f)	series
sitio (web) (m)	website
social	social
subir	(to) upload
tableta (f)	tablet
teclado (m)	keyboard
tecnología (f)	technology
tele, televisión (f)	TV, television
teléfono (m)	phone, telephone
vídeo (m)	video
videojuego (m)	computer game
apropiado/a	appropriate,
blog (m)	blog
canal (m)	channel
cargar	(to) charge (phone)
charlar	(to) chat
ciberacoso (m)	cyberbullying
colgar	(to) post (photo), hang (up)
comentar	(to) comment
comentario (m)	comment
cometer	(to) commit (a crime)
conectar	(to) connect
contenido (m)	content
contraseña (f)	password
desconocido/a	unknown
diálogo (m)	dialogue
diario (m)	newspaper, diary
digital	digital
diseño (m)	design
dispositivo (m)	device, gadget
documental (m)	documentary
emoticón (m)	emoji
experto/a (m/f)	expert
fabricar	(to) produce
generación (f)	generation
influencia (f)	influence
informe (m)	report
investigación (f)	research
memoria (f)	memory
navegar	(to) surf, browse
portátil (m)	laptop
prensa (f)	press
promover	(to) promote
protección (f)	protection
publicar	(to) publish, post
radio (f)	radio
seguridad (f)	security, safety
señal (f)	sign, signal
sistema (m)	system
sufrir	(to) suffer
tendencia (f)	tendency, trend
usuario/a (m/f)	user
velocidad (f)	speed, velocity
víctima (f)	victim
violento/a	violent
volumen (m)	volume

15 The environment and where people live

afueras (fpl)	suburbs	habitación (f)	room, bedroom
aire (m)	air	iglesia (f)	church
al aire libre	outdoors	industria (f)	industry
animal (m)	animal	isla (f)	island
apagar	(to) turn off	justo/a	fair, just
árbol (m)	tree	limpiar	(to) clean
arquitectura (f)	architecture	limpio/a	clean
aumentar	(to) increase	llover / lluvia	(to) rain / rain
banco (m)	bank, bench	medioambiente,	environment,
baño (m)	bathroom	medio	natural world
basura (f)	rubbish, junk	ambiente (m)	
biblioteca (f)	library	mezquita (f)	mosque
bosque (m)	forest, wood	montaña (f)	mountain
café (m)	coffee, café	morir	(to) die
caliente	hot, warm	muerto/a	dead
calle (f)	street	mundo (m)	world
calor (m)	heat, hot	museo (m)	museum
cama (f)	bed	naturaleza (f)	nature
cambio (m)	climate change	olor (m)	smell, odour
climático		pájaro (m)	bird
campo (m)	countryside,	papel (m)	paper
	field	pared (f)	(interior) wall
casa (f)	house	parque (m)	park
causa / causar	cause / (to)	peligro (m)	danger
	cause	piso (m)	flat, floor
centro (m)	shopping	práctico/a	practical, useful
comercial	centre	proteger	(to) protect
cielo (m)	sky, heaven	pueblo (m)	village
cine (m)	cinema	puente (m)	bridge
ciudad (f)	city, town	puerta (f)	door
clima (m)	climate	reciclar	(to) recycle
colegio (m)	school	recoger	(to) pick / tidy up
contaminación	pollution	reducir	(to) reduce
(f)		río (m)	river
contaminar	(to) pollute	ruido (m)	noise
costa (f)	coast	salón (m)	living room
daño (m)	harm, damage	salvar	(to) save
destruir	(to) destroy,	seco/a	dry
	ruin	separar	(to) separate
dueño (m)	owner, landlord	sinagoga (f)	synagogue
efecto (m)	effect	sucio/a	dirty
energía (f)	energy, power	supermercado	supermarket
escalera (f)	stairs, ladder	(m)	
especie (f)	species	temperatura (f)	temperature
esquina (f)	corner	tierra (f)	earth, land
fábrica (f)	factory	tirar	(to) throw
falta (f)	lack, mistake	vacío/a	empty
flor (f)	flower	viento (m)	wind
fresco/a	fresh, cool		
frío/a	cold		
fuego (m)	fire		

abajo	downstairs
advertir	(to) warn
alrededores (mpl)	surroundings
altura (f)	height, altitude
amenazar	(to) threaten
arena (f)	sand
arriba	upstairs, above
calefacción (f)	heating
camino (m)	way, path
cantidad (f)	quantity
conservar	(to) conserve
construcción (f)	construction
cortar	(to) cut (up)
cultivo (m)	crop
desastre (m)	disaster
descuento (m)	discount
devolver	(to) give back
emitir	(to) emit
entorno (m)	surroundings
fuente (f)	source,
	fountain
gas (m)	gas
hogar (m)	home
huele (a)	it smells (of)
humo (m)	smoke, fumes
incendio (m)	fire
libertad (f)	freedom
madera (f)	wood
manifestación (f)	protest
muerte (f)	death
natural	natural
nube (f)	cloud
obras (fpl)	roadworks,
	building works
paz (f)	peace
piedra (f)	stone, rock
planeta (m)	planet
población (f)	population
pobreza (f)	poverty
profundo/a	deep, profound
puro/a	pure, clean
químico/a	chemical
recurso (m)	resource
reflejar	(to) reflect
sobrevivir	(to) survive
sombra (f)	shade, shadow
sonido (m)	sound
suelo (m)	ground, floor
sufrir	(to) suffer
vidrio (m)	glass

Now try this

Write five sentences to say what you do to help the environment. See how many words on this page you can use.

Answers

The answers to the Speaking and Writing activities below are sample answers – there are many ways you could answer these questions.

1 Introducing yourself

1 B   2 A   3 A   4 B

2 Physical descriptions

A, D, F

3 Character descriptions

1 agradable, tranquilo
2 serio, aburrido
3 dicen, trabajador

4 Family

1 B   2 A   3 C

5 What makes a good friend

Mi mejor amiga es divertida y simpática. Tenemos muchos intereses en común y siempre está allí cuando la necesito. Me ayuda y me apoya cuando tengo un problema y sabe hacerme reír si estoy triste porque tenemos el mismo sentido del humor. Nos divertimos mucho juntas. (Answer around Grade 9)

6 Relationships

Listen to the recording

C = candidate, T = teacher
T: ¿Cómo te llevas con tus amigos?
C: Me llevo muy bien con mis amigos y nos divertimos mucho. En general son simpáticos y comprensivos.
T: ¿Por qué razones discutes con tus amigos?
C: No discutimos mucho, pero a veces hay problemas cuando no estamos de acuerdo sobre lo que queremos hacer.

7 Helping a friend

1 C   2 B   3 A

8 Food and drink

Listen to the recording

C = candidate, T = teacher
T: Buenas tardes.
C: Quisiera una mesa para cuatro personas por favor.
T: Muy bien. ¿Dónde quiere una mesa?
C: Prefiero una mesa cerca de la ventana.
T: De acuerdo. ¿Qué quiere tomar?
C: Quiero el pollo con patatas fritas.
T: Muy bien. ¿Y para beber?
C: Me gustaría un vaso de agua.
T: Claro. ¿Algo más?
C: ¿Cuánto es?

9 Healthy eating

1 B   2 C

10 Sport and exercise

Listen to the recording

C = candidate, T = teacher
T: ¿Qué ejercicio te gusta hacer?
C: Me gustan la natación y el fútbol.
T: ¿Cuándo haces ejercicio?
C: Voy al instituto en bicicleta todos los días, y suelo ir a la piscina los martes y los domingos.
T: ¿Te gusta ver el deporte en la televisión?
C: Sí, me gusta ver el fútbol en la tele. Es muy emocionante y hay unos jugadores excelentes como Rodri y Luis Díaz.
T: ¿Qué actividades físicas hiciste la semana pasada?
C: Hice una excursión al campo en bicicleta con un grupo de amigos. Hicimos unos diez kilómetros en total.
T: ¿Qué deporte o ejercicio vas a hacer la semana que viene?
C: El sábado voy al parque con mis amigos para jugar al baloncesto. Será muy divertido.
Cuando vas de vacaciones, ¿te gusta descansar o hacer actividades? … ¿Por qué?
Me gustan las dos cosas. Me gusta tomar el sol, pero es aburrido después de un tiempo. Entonces juego al fútbol con mi hermano o nado en el mar.
T: ¿Qué deporte te gustaría probar en el futuro?
C: Me gustaría probar el vóleibol. Posiblemente en el centro de deportes con mis amigos, o en la playa durante las vacaciones.
T ¿En general, piensas que los jóvenes hacen bastante ejercicio?
C: Depende. Algunos hacen mucho ejercicio, van al gimnasio y les encanta estar en forma. Otros, no. Se quedan en el dormitorio jugando a los videojuegos y comen comida basura.

11 Physical wellbeing

1 Es importante pasar tiempo al aire libre.
2 Hay que relajarse un rato cada día.
3 Vale la pena proteger la piel.
4 Tu salud física es muy importante.
5 El ambiente es calmado.

12 Mental wellbeing

Listen to the recording

C = candidate, T = teacher
T: Háblame de las actividades relajantes que haces.
C: Veo la televisión y escucho música. También me gusta pintar.
T: ¿Qué piensas del deporte para reducir el estrés?
C: Pienso que ayuda mucho, especialmente los deportes de equipo.
T: ¿Qué tipo de amiga eres?
C: Soy simpática y siempre apoyo a mis amigas cuando tienen problemas.
T: ¿Qué cosas te preocupan hoy?
C: Me preocupan varias cosas, sobre todo el instituto y los exámenes porque son difíciles.

13 Role models in sport

En la primera foto hay cinco jugadoras de fútbol con camisetas blancas.

Están muy contentas y una jugadora tiene una copa en la mano porque han ganado un concurso.

En la segunda foto hay un grupo de niños en el campo de fútbol. Los niños tienen ocho años, más o menos. Están escuchando a su profesor antes de entrenar. Creo que hace sol y calor.

14 Sporting events

C = candidate, T = teacher

T: ¿Qué deportes te gusta ver?

C: Me gusta ver el fútbol en la televisión cuando hay concursos internacionales. También me gusta ver el baloncesto porque creo que es fácil seguir un partido cuando lo ves en la tele.

T: ¿Prefieres ver el deporte en casa o en el estadio? … ¿Por qué?

C: Depende. Creo que es mejor ver algunos deportes en la tele, como el golf, porque las cámaras te muestran la acción más importante. Pero con el fútbol, es mejor estar en el estadio, especialmente si juega tu equipo.

T: Háblame de un evento deportivo que viste en el pasado.

C: Fui con mi primo a ver un partido de rugby muy importante. Mi primo es un gran aficionado del rugby y me explicó las reglas. Fue muy divertido y lo pasamos muy bien.

(Answer around Grade 8–9)

15 School subjects

1 Estudio matemáticas y ciencia(s).
2 Dejé (la) historia el año pasado.
3 Quiere continuar con (el) español y (el) inglés.
4 Espero estudiar dibujo en el futuro.
5 Tenemos una clase de educación física a las dos hoy.

16 School subjects – likes and dislikes

C = candidate, T = teacher

T: ¿Cuál es tu asignatura favorita?

C: Mi asignatura favorita es la historia. Es muy interesante estudiar los eventos del pasado y cómo era la vida hace muchos siglos. Me gusta más la historia antigua y creo que voy a estudiarla en la universidad.

T: Háblame de una asignatura que no te gusta.

C: No me gusta nada la educación física. No me interesa el deporte y no soy nada deportista. Por lo tanto, no disfruto de las clases.

(Answer around a Grade 9)

17 The school day

1 his sports kit / sports clothes / PE kit
2 (playing) basketball
3 for a lift to school / to take him to school in the car
4 it is raining (a lot)

18 School facilities

B, E, F

19 School uniform

1 A (shirt)
2 B (small)
3 A (long)

20 Activities in class

1 En nuestras clases los profesores explican las cosas.
2 Luego hacemos ejercicios o contestamos preguntas en el libro de texto.
3 Después trabajamos en grupos para resolver problemas.
4 Ayer vimos un vídeo en la clase de historia.
5 Fue muy divertido y aprendimos mucho.

21 School rules

C = candidate, T = teacher

T: ¿Qué piensas de las reglas en tu instituto?

C: Creo que las reglas son necesarias y, por lo general, son justas. Por ejemplo, algunos estudiantes quieren usar sus móviles en clase para buscar información en Internet, pero me molesta cuando suena el teléfono – y esto pasa con frecuencia. Muchas de las reglas son simplemente sentido común, como llegar a clase a tiempo y traer los materiales necesarios. Las reglas sobre el uniforme me parecen menos importantes.

(Answer around a Grade 9)

22 The good and the bad about school

1 A   2 C

23 School clubs and activities

En mi colegio hay varios clubs después de las clases, pero no hay nada durante la hora de comer porque es muy corta y no hay tiempo. Los miércoles hay actividades en el gimnasio como baloncesto y tenis, y los jueves hay un club de música para los estudiantes que quieren cantar o tocar un instrumento en una banda. Yo fui una vez al club, pero no tengo mucha confianza y no volví. Me gustaría tener un club de lectura para hablar de nuestras novelas favoritas; me encanta leer.

24 How to be a good student

1 leaving homework until the last minute
2 you don't get the chance to ask for help (to solve the problem)
3 a homework timetable

25 Options at 16

El año próximo puedo quedarme en este instituto para continuar con mis estudios o puedo ir a otro colegio. Me gusta este instituto, pero me interesan las asignaturas diferentes que hay en el otro colegio. Voy a visitar el colegio y después voy a decidir. Voy a trabajar en una cafetería los sábados.

26 Future study plans

1 A   2 C

27 Future plans

2 university, work

28 Part-time jobs and money

1 they work weekday afternoons (as well as at weekends)
2 supermarkets and fast food restaurants
3 their studies suffer / they can't give enough time to their homework

29 Opinions about jobs

Listen to the recording

C = candidate, T = teacher

T: ¿Qué tipo de trabajo te gustaría?
C: Me gustaría tener un trabajo con responsabilidad, posiblemente en el mundo del diseño o en los medios. No me importa trabajar solo o ser miembro de un equipo. Lo ideal sería tener un empleo cerca de la casa, porque no quiero pasar horas en el coche o en el tren cada día. También sería maravilloso ganar un buen salario.
(Answer around a Grade 9)

30 The pros and cons of different jobs

1 danger
2 work in a library
3 risk

31 Job adverts

1 C   2 A

32 Applying for jobs

B, D, F

33 Preparing for interviews

1 naturally
2 successes that she has had in her current job
3 the number of people that worked at the company / how many employees there are
4 They will phone her on Friday.

34 Working to help others

Llevo tres meses ayudando en el banco de alimentos y me gusta mucho. Mis compañeros son trabajadores y divertidos y me encanta saber que nuestro trabajo hace una diferencia. Recibimos comida de varios sitios, pero principalmente supermercados, y la organizamos en cajas para nuestros clientes.

35 Free-time activities

1 go for a walk, relaxing
2 play videogames, exciting

36 Music and dance

1 Me gusta bailar música rock.
2 Un día espero aprender a tocar el piano.
3 Tiene una voz bonita y canta bien.
4 Escribí la letra para la canción.
5 Escuchamos música online.

37 Music and dance events

B, D, E

38 Reading

C

39 Television

1 C   2 A

40 The cinema

C, D, E

41 What's the story?

Listen to the recording

Mis películas favoritas son Los Juegos del Hambre, una serie de tres películas sobre una chica que tiene que luchar por sobrevivir los juegos del título. Solo una persona puede sobrevivir y evitar la muerte para ganar. El personaje principal es una chica independiente y fuerte, pero también simpática y fiel a sus amigos.

42 Everyday life

1 at 7.50 / ten to eight   2 get dressed (and leave the house)
3 having breakfast   4 it was Saturday / the weekend

43 Meals at home

Tomo el desayuno a las ocho y la comida a la una. Ceno con la familia sobre las seis. Normalmente comemos en la mesa en la cocina. Generalmente mi padre prepara las comidas porque le gusta hacerlo. Tomamos carne o pescado con patatas fritas y verduras. No me gustan las ensaladas.

44 Celebrations

Listen to the recording

C = candidate, T = teacher

T: ¿Qué te gusta hacer para celebrar tu cumpleaños?
C: Me gusta tener una cena especial en casa con mi familia. Si es el fin de semana, me gusta salir con mis amigos y comer en un restaurante.
T: ¿Cómo celebraste el último día especial en tu familia?
C: El último día especial fue el cumpleaños de mi abuelo. Preparamos una comida muy rica y le compramos unos caramelos, porque le encantan. Le cantamos «Cumpleaños Feliz»
T: ¿Cuando sales a cenar, ¿dónde prefieres comer?
C: Me gusta comer en un restaurante italiano en el centro de la ciudad. La comida es muy buena y los camareros son muy simpáticos.
T: ¿El próximo año te gustaría más celebrar tu cumpleaños con tu familia o con amigos?
C: Me gustaría celebrar con mi familia y abrir mis regalos en casa. Después podría ir al cine o a una fiesta con mis amigos.
T: ¿Es mejor recibir dinero o regalos en tu cumpleaños? … ¿Por qué?
C: Eso es difícil. Me gusta recibir dinero, porque luego puedo ir de compras, pero me gusta recibir regalos porque me encantan las sorpresas.

45 Customs and festivals

Listen to the recording

Creo que las fiestas españolas son maravillosas. Tenemos muy pocas fiestas en mi país y me encantaría ir a España para ver las Fallas o la Tomatina. Creo que el ambiente es muy emocionante y alegre. También, me gustaría ver los desfiles y los trajes tradicionales y probar los platos de la región.

46 Spanish festivals

1 B   2 C   3 A   4 B

47 Latin American festivals

1 gave thanks to the sun
2 15 days / a fortnight / 2 weeks
3 24 June
4 60 thousand

48 My favourite celebrity

1 David is an Argentinian footballer / football player.
2 My favourite French singer writes all his (own) songs.
3 He is a good looking / handsome Mexican actor with lots of / many followers.
4 I like reading the lyrics when I watch (the) videos.
5 He is an influencer on Spanish social media.

49 Profile of a celebrity

1 1980
2 basketball
3 football
4 doctor
5 one year
6 2021
7 (younger) brother

50 Celebrities as role models

1 Many famous personalities are excellent role models for young people.
2 A Spanish football player helped his neighbours after a natural disaster.
3 I know a Colombian singer who helps poor children.
4 They are very good examples and they deserve our respect.
5 There are others who have a negative image in the media.

51 TV reality shows

1 successful, media
2 support, public

52 The good and the bad of being famous

1 B   2 A   3 C

53 Plans for the holidays

En las vacaciones de verano me gusta ir a la piscina al aire libre cerca de mi ciudad.
Me gusta mucho la piscina porque está muy limpia. Voy con mis amigos. A veces mi hermano menor va también. Vamos allí cuando hace calor. Después, vamos a un restaurante a comer.

54 Holiday preferences

1 B   2 C   3 B

55 Types of holidays

Un día me gustaría hacer camping en las montañas con mis amigos. Sería muy divertido preparar las comidas en un fuego. Me gusta la idea de dormir al aire libre, ¡pero solo si no llueve!

56 Where to stay

1 The facilities in the hotel are great.
2 Our room has views of the mountains / has mountain views.
3 We decided to stay in an apartment / a flat.
4 There was a (swimming) pool and a sports centre.
5 We are going to choose a three-star hotel.

57 Booking accommodation

1 what time the pool opens in the morning
2 swim before breakfast
3 help with her suitcase / luggage
4 where the lift is

58 Holiday activities

1 next Tuesday
2 today
3 yesterday

59 Trips and visits

1 El viaje a la isla es interesante.
2 El autobús llega en una hora.
3 Me encantan las vistas desde el castillo.
4 Tenemos entradas para visitar el estadio.
5 Ayer el barco salió a las dos.

60 Giving and asking for directions

1 B   2 C

61 Tourist information

1 It's 10 euros per day.
2 It's a few kilometres out of town; Paula doesn't have a car.
3 get the number 23 bus
4 a bus timetable

62 Tourist attractions

Listen to the recording

Acabo de pasar un fin de semana en Londres con mi familia y lo pasamos muy bien. Hicimos una excursión en barco en el río y aprendimos mucho sobre la historia de los edificios que vimos. Comimos en un restaurante excelente y por la tarde fuimos al teatro para ver un musical. Quería ver el Ojo de Londres también pero no tuvimos tiempo. Tendré que volver otro día.

63 Holiday problems

1 A   2 B

64 Accommodation problems

1 The apartment / flat that we rented on the coast was nice / pretty.
2 There was not much space and the bedrooms were very small.
3 On the patio / In the yard, the only table was dirty.
4 One of the chairs broke when I sat on / in it.
5 The area is lovely but there isn't much to do for tourists.

65 Eating out

Listen to the recording

C = candidate, T = teacher
T: ¿Qué te gusta comer?
C: Me gustan las hamburguesas, y me gusta también el pescado, pero prefiero las patatas fritas.
T: ¿Qué piensas de comer en restaurantes?
C: Me encanta. La comida siempre está muy buena.
T: Háblame de la comida en España.
C: La comida en España es muy rica. La paella es mi comida favorita.
T: ¿Cómo prefieres viajar cuando estás de vacaciones?
C: Prefiero ir en coche.

66 Opinions about food

1 B 2 C 3 A

67 The weather

1 grey skies (1 mark) and chance / risk of rain (1 mark)
2 cold (1 mark), temperatures going down (1 mark)
3 quite sunny (1 mark) and cool / fresh (1 mark)

68 Me and my mobile

B

69 Social media

1 Uso las redes sociales para bajar música y compartir fotos.
2 Entiendo / Comprendo que es importante proteger mi información personal.
3 Nunca subo cosas que son privadas.
4 Ayer mandé un mensaje a Ana.
5 Muchas veces me manda vídeos divertidos.

70 The internet

En mi casa usamos Internet todo el tiempo. Mi padre lo usa para leer los periódicos y ver las noticias. Mi hermano lo usa para jugar juegos y ver vídeos. Yo lo uso mucho para ayudarme con mis estudios. Mi sitio web favorito es 'WordReference' porque es ideal cuando necesito buscar palabras para mis deberes de español.
La semana pasada tuvimos que buscar información online en nuestra clase de historia. Fue muy interesante.
Este fin de semana veré una película de acción en Internet y bajaré nuevas canciones.
(90 words)

71 Computer games

1 I like playing my favourite computer game / videogame.
2 The action is very exciting and the characters seem very real.
3 I think some videogames can be very educational.
4 In some you have to take / make decisions and solve problems.
5 I think (that) they are relaxing as well.

72 The good and the bad of technology

1 C 2 A

73 Places in town

Listen to the recording

En la primera foto hay un hombre joven con el pelo marrón. Lleva gafas de sol y tiene una mochila. Lleva una camisa azul. Está mirando un plano porque es un turista en la ciudad. Está en una gran plaza. Hay otros turistas también. En la segunda foto veo una ciudad histórica. Es bonita y está cerca de un gran río. Hay un puente muy grande sobre el río y una gran iglesia. Hay unas pocas nubes y hace buen tiempo.

74 Things to do

1 B 2 A 3 C

75 Shopping for clothes

Listen to the recording

C = candidate, T = teacher
T: ¿Dónde te gusta ir de compras?
C: Me gusta ir de compras al gran centro comercial en la ciudad. Tiene muchas tiendas y mis amigos y yo comemos allí también.
T: ¿Qué piensas de ir de compras con tu familia?
C: No me gusta mucho – prefiero ir con mis amigos. Pero, me gusta cuando mi madre me compra ropa nueva, es genial.
T: Describe el pueblo o la ciudad donde vives.
C: Mi ciudad está en el este del país. Es moderna con mucha industria.
T: ¿Dónde quieres vivir en el futuro?
C: Quiero vivir en España.

76 Transport

1 car 2 train 3 bus 4 plane

77 Travelling on public transport

C

78 My region – the good and the bad

1 rice and oranges
2 paella

79 My region in the past

1 B 2 C 3 B

80 Town or country?

1 Me gusta vivir en el campo.
2 En cambio, mis padres prefieren la vida en una ciudad grande.
3 Vivían en Valencia donde había muchas instalaciones y transporte.
4 En el futuro viviré / voy a vivir en el campo.
5 Hay espacios abiertos, campos verdes, árboles altos y flores preciosas / hermosas.

81 The environment and me

Listen to the recording

82 Local environmental issues

1 B 2 A

83 Global environmental issues

Listen to the recording

Para mí, el cambio climático es el problema más serio que hay actualmente porque afecta a todo el planeta. No estamos haciendo bastante para bajar las temperaturas y por todas partes del mundo, la tierra y los animales están sufriendo los efectos.

84 Caring for the planet

1 It's a protected area / zone.
2 Someone stole some birds' eggs.
3 The bird is an endangered species.

85 A greener future

1 I am not going to use plastic bags.
2 Electric cars are better for the environment.
3 We have to protect the forests.
4 We are all responsible for caring for / looking after nature.
5 Yesterday I helped to pick up the rubbish / litter in the park.

94 Nouns and articles

1 (a) mercados
  (b) luces
  (c) tradiciones
  (d) cafés
  (e) actores
2 (a) la ciudad
  (b) el tema
  (c) el nivel
  (d) la educación
  (e) la imagen

95 Adjectives

Las Islas Baleares son un grupo de islas **pequeñas**. Tienen muchas playas **bonitas**. Hay muchos turistas **internacionales** en estas islas. La gente allí es muy **simpática / trabajadora** y **trabajadora / simpática**. Las islas tienen muchos museos **históricos** y muchas actividades **divertidas**. También, se puede visitar muchos pueblos **hermosos**.

English translation:

The Balearic Islands are a group of small islands. They have lots of lovely beaches. There are many international tourists on these islands. The people there are very nice / hard-working and hard-working / nice. The islands have many historical museums and lots of fun activities. You can also visit lots of beautiful villages.

96 Possessives and pronouns

Mi, Sus, Mi, que, Su, el mío, él, el suyo

English translation:

My stepfather's name is Omar. His daughters are very nice. My sister, whose name is Sara, has a boyfriend, Andrés. Her boyfriend is older than mine. I've been dating him for six years. Sara has been dating hers for a month.

97 Comparisons

1 el peor
2 los mejores
3 la más bonita
4 aburridísimo
5 la mejor
6 el más feo
7 más deportista
8 más divertida

98 Other adjectives

1 Ese chico es mi primo.
2 Esta manzana está dura.
3 Quiero comprar esos zapatos.
4 Aquella casa es muy grande / grandísima.
5 Esta película es aburrida.
6 No quiero este camisa. Prefiero esa camiseta.

99 Pronouns

1 Voy a dárlo a mi padre. / Lo voy a dar a mi padre.
2 Le mando muchos mensajes.
3 Voy a comprarlo. / Lo voy a comprar.
4 Ponlos en la bolsa.
5 Voy a decirle la verdad. / Le voy a decir la verdad.

100 The present tense

1 escucho – I don't listen to classical music.
2 hablan – My parents speak English.
3 juega – My friend plays basketball with me.
4 quieres – Do you want to go to the cinema with me tonight?

5 comemos – We always eat fruit to be healthy.
6 encuentran – They always find money in the street.
7 vivís – Do you live in the countryside?
8 duerme – My brother sleeps in his own room.

101 Reflexive verbs

1 me
2 se
3 nos
4 te
5 se
6 os

102 Irregular verbs

1 salgo – I leave at 7.30 to go to the concert.
2 tienen – My cousins have blue eyes and they are blond.
3 sé – I really like to go / going to the beach but I don't know how to swim.
4 cojo – I always take the bus when I go to school.
5 hacen, hago – My friends do their homework in the library but I do it at home.

103 *Ser* and *estar*

1 está
2 es
3 es
4 estoy
5 son
6 es
7 están
8 está

104 The gerund / present participle

1 estoy / estaba jugando
2 estoy / estaba escribiendo
3 está / estaba hablando
4 está / estaba durmiendo
5 estoy / estaba comiendo
6 estoy / estaba tomando
7 está / estaba navegando
8 estás / estabas cantando

105 The preterite tense

1 I go to Spain. (present)
2 I arrived at six. (preterite)
3 I surf the internet. (present)
4 He / She listened to music. (preterite)
5 He / She went to a party which was cool. (preterite)
6 It was cold and it rained a bit. (preterite)
7 We saw Pablo in the market. (preterite)
8 I played basketball on the beach. (preterite)

106 The imperfect tense

1 trabajaba
2 comí
3 iba
4 había
5 visité
6 lloraba

107 The future tense

1 (a) Nunca fumaré.
  (b) Ayudaré a otras personas.
  (c) Cambiaremos el mundo.
  (d) Trabajaré en un aeropuerto.
2 (a) Voy a salir a las seis.
  (b) Voy a ser médico.
  (c) Va a ir a Ecuador.
  (d) Mañana voy a jugar al tenis.

108 The conditional tense

bebería, haría, practicaría, tomaría, bebería, comería, me acostaría, dormiría, llevaría

109 The perfect tense

1 ha recomendado / he visto
2 han perdido / he podido
3 has probado / hemos hecho
4 han pedido / han dicho

110 Giving instructions

Foundation and Higher	Higher only
1 Write to your cousin.	1 Eat the vegetables, children.
2 Put the flowers on the table.	2 Talk to the director / head teacher.
3 Catch the number 10 bus.	3 Upload the photos to the internet.
4 Do your homework now.	
5 Prepare the meal for the family.	4 Come and play in the park.
6 Come here, Paula.	5 Wait for the bus on the street corner.
7 Read this novel. You will love it.	6 Catch the 8 o'clock train.
8 Dance with me. It's my favourite song.	7 Put the books on the table.
9 Buy me a magazine.	8 Send me some photos.
10 Wake up, Miguel!	9 Drink more water, children.
	10 Share the sweets.

111 The present subjunctive

1 When I go to university, I will study science.
2 I want you to have these tickets for the concert on Saturday.
3 Diego, I want you to be more responsible in the future.
4 I will ask Sofía to wait for us in the café.
5 It annoys me that my daughter does her homework at this time of night.
6 I'm going to help you so that you have time to go out with your friend.

112 Negatives

Suggested answers:
1 Nunca como verduras.
2 No tengo ningún libro.
3 No conozco a nadie.
4 Nadie juega al baloncesto.
5 Nunca hago mis deberes.
6 No me gusta ni navegar por Internet ni bajar música.
7 No tiene nada.
8 No tengo ningún amigo en Madrid.

Translation answers:
1 I always eat vegetables.
2 I have a book.
3 I know everyone.
4 Everyone plays basketball.
5 I always do my homework.
6 I like to surf the internet and download music.
7 It / He / She has everything.
8 I have lots of friends in Madrid.

113 Special verbs

1 Me duele
2 Le gusta
3 Te gustan
4 Le duelen
5 No me importa
6 Les interesan
7 Llevo
8 Les hacen falta

114 *Por* and *para*

1 (a) para, (b) para, (c) por, (d) para, (e) para, (f) por, (g) por
2 (a) para, (b) por, (c) para, (d) ✓, (e) ✓, (f) para, (g) ✓, (h) ✓

115 Asking questions

1 d	3 h	5 a	7 c
2 f	4 e	6 b	8 g

116 The passive

1 The novel was written in 2019.
2 The exercises are done online.
3 The results will be published on Friday.
4 Lots of people are invited to the party.
5 The facilities were improved before the visit.
6 The climate is affected by the actions that we take.
7 The consequences are not yet / still not known.
8 Toys are not sold on the market.
9 Some new flats will be built on the outskirts.
10 The money was found in the street.

117 Numbers

1 las nueve menos veinte
2 cuatrocientos sesenta y cinco
3 el doce de junio de dos mil catorce
4 quinientos cuarenta y tres
5 las once y media
6 setenta y seis
7 el primero / el uno de enero de mil novecientos noventa y siete
8 tercero

Credits

Published by Pearson Education Limited, 80 Strand, London, WC2R 0RL.

www.pearsonschoolsandfecolleges.co.uk

Copies of official specifications for all Pearson qualifications may be found on the website: qualifications.pearson.com

Text and original illustrations © Pearson Education Limited 2024
Edited by Pearson and Just Content
Designed and typeset by Integra
Cover design © Pearson Education Limited 2024
Cover illustration by Subrayan. R (Creative Artist)
Audio recorded at Tom, Dick and Debbie Productions
Written by Viv Halksworth

First published 2024

28 27 26 25 24
10 9 8 7 6 5 4 3 2 1

British Library Cataloguing in Publication Data
A catalogue record for this book is available from the British Library

ISBN 978 1 292 471693

Printed in the UK by Bell & Bain Ltd, Glasgow

Acknowledgements
The author and publisher would like to thank the following individuals and organizations for permission to reproduce photographs.

Non-Prominent Photo Credit(s) for this book:
123RF: William Perugini 2, Antonio Guillem 6, Milkos 7, Cathy Yeulet 15, 23, 24, 25, 89, 96, Auremar 17, Elnur Amikishiyev 39, Blueskyimage 41, Dolgachov 44, Taiga 45, Michalknitl 54, Antonio Guillem 60, Wavebreak Media Ltd 63, Fizkes 64, Wavebreakmediamicro 66, Sam Wordley 73, Viki2win 76, Pavel Devin 78, Yhelfman 80, Nickolay 82, Niserin 83, Photolight2 96, Goodluz 98, Deagreez 108, Daisydaisy 114; **Getty Images:** JackF/iStock/Getty Images Plus 98, Tadamasa Taniguchi/Stone 101, Nikada/iStock/Getty Images Plus 103, Julia Klueva/iStock/Getty Images Plus 114; **Pearson Education Ltd:** Gareth Boden 1, Jon Barlow 5, 19, Jules Selmes 40, 65, 77, Steve Shott 71, Miguel Dominguez Muñoz 73, sopotniccy 73, Studio 8 99; **Shutterstock:** YAKOBCHUK VIACHESLAV 2, Xavier Lorenzo 3, Fotoluminate LLC 4, Albina Glisic 9, Lucky Business 10, Nito 11, Marino Bocelli 13, Rawpixel.com 13, Shutterstock 13, 20, 26, 43, Pjcross 16, Molfar 18, Elnur 21, lzf 27, Robert Kneschke 28, Maridav 29, Elena Elisseeva 31, Zimmytws 32, Studio Romantic 33, Dragana Gordic 34, Nestor Rizhniak 35, RTimages 36, Andriy Solovyov 37, Wavebreakmedia 38, PV productions 38, photo_oles 40, Champ Natthanan 42, Hananeko_Studio 43, Iakov Filimonov 46, Moab Republic 47, Dragon Images 48, Dean Drobot 49, metamorworks 50, Billion Photos 51, Trzykropy 53, Oscar garces 55, Ramon Cliff 56, Africa Studio 57, 75, Tandem 58, Philip Lange 59, Rawpixel.com 61, Sergey Novikov 61, VGstockstudio 62, KYTan 67, Take Photo 68, Mimagephotography 69, McLittle Stock 70, BearFotos 74, Pierre-Yves Babelon 79, Aleksandra Suzi 81, Stephane Bidouze 84, Majeczka 85, Blackregis 89, VH-studio 89, Jacek Chabraszewski 91, XiXinXing 92, Lunamarina 97, Smile photo 101, LightField Studios 102, Tracy Whiteside 103, Diogoppr 104, upthebanner 105, Ground Picture 106, Phovoir 106, Aframeinmotion 107, Mlopez 108, Nerthuz 108, Elena Sherengovskaya 109, Grinny 109, ImageFlow 111, Pressmaster 111, Voyagerix 112, Leungchopan 113, Lanych 115, ESB Professional 116.

Non-Prominent Photo Credit(s) for the Quick Quizzes:
123RF.com: Elena Duvernay (Quick Quiz 3, Question 3); **Shutterstock:** SlipFloat (Quick Quiz 1, Question 1), Hvsht (Quick Quiz 1, Question 1) tjp55 (Quick Quiz 2, Question 1), Friendlyvector (Quick Quiz 2, Question 2), Belchonock (Quick Quiz 3, Question 3), Azizah's (Quick Quiz 4, Question 4), Ori Artiste (Quick Quiz 4, Question 4)